THINGS
WE WISH
WE'D
KNOWN

Compiled & Edited by
Bill & Diana Waring

Emerald
Books
P.O. BOX 635
Lynnwood, Washington 98046

Things We Wish We'd Known
Copyright © 1999 Bill and Diana Waring

10 09 08 07 06 05   10 9 8 7 6 5

Published by Emerald Books
P.O. Box 635
Lynnwood, WA 98046

ISBN 1-883002-42-7

Printed in the United States of America.

Contents

Introduction 7

Part 1: The Concepts

One Word of Advice: Balance! 10
Jessica Hulcy

Curriculum: Tool or Tyrant? 14
Holly Sheen

The Three R's: Relationships, Reasoning, and Resolve 18
David and Shirley Quine

For the Love of Books 24
Tommi Ryan

Keep It Fun! Keep It Simple! 28
Fred and Sarah Cooper

The Heart of Homeschooling: The Learning Lifestyle 32
Vicky Goodchild

Learn to Recognize Learning 36
Joan Veach

Running the Homeschooling Marathon 40
Steve and Jane Claire Lambert

What Are You Doing to My Grandchild!? 44
Stacy Mhyre

Part 2: The Basics

Great Books Produce Great Minds 50
Valerie Bendt

Hanging Haman: Exploring the Bible One Day a Week 54
Madelaine Smith

As Arrows in the Hand: Establishing Your Targets 58
Ranell Curl

Strengths + Weaknesses = Learning to Find Everything Intriguing 64
Beverly Miller

Teaching to a Child's Heart: Preparing Yourself for
Spontaneous Instruction 68
Katherine von Duyke

Getting the Fun Back 72
Carol Severson

Part 3: The Priorities

You Can't Do It All...and Don't Have To! 78
Sharon Grimes

Your Homeschool Mission Adventure 82
John Rush

A Journey of Faith 86
Miriam Heppner

The Gift of Resources 90
Lynnette Delacruz

Advice on Teaching: My First Year of Homeschooling 94
Sharon Jeffus

For This Season: Lavishing Your Children with Time 98
Jody Gutierrez

Planning to Be Spontaneous: Letting Love Spill into Every Task 102
Candy Summers

Accomplish What Is Important 106
Joy Schroeder

Reduce Your Rigorous Roster and Optimize Your Opportunities 110
Cindy Wiggers

Part 4: God's Involvement

Someone Has Been Here Before Me 116
Clay and Sally Clarkson

From Confusion to Confidence: Making Choices in Curriculum 120
Camilla Leedahl

His Burden Is Light 124
Margie Gray

Home Educating for Eternity 128
Ed and Kathy Green

The Compass 132
Janice Southerland

Moses Didn't Feel Qualified, Either!. 136
Nancy Robins

Becoming a Confident Homeschooler 140
Debbie Strayer

Fear Not, For I Am with You 144
Gail Schultz

Can I Homeschool without Commitment?. 148
Frank and Debbie Schaner

Part 5: Christian Character

The Heart of the Child: Homeschooling's Highest Objective. 154
Monte and Karey Swan

Curriculum and Character 158
Barbara West

What Is Education?. 162
Karen Andreola

Character Building Is Whose Job?. 166
Maxine and Ronnie Harris

Aiming for a Heart of Wisdom 170
Robin Scarlata

Plants, Pillars, and Palaces – Psalm 144:12 174
Bonnie Ferguson

Part 6: The Blessings

The Habit of Listening 180
Michael and Susan Card

The Blessings of Time. 184
Carol Singleton

The Importance of the Father's Leadership in the Homeschool 188
Wade Hulcy

Grandpa's Bus and Glowing Reports. 192
Jill Darling

A Lifetime of Learning: Have Books, Will Travel 198
Tina and Bob Farewell

Family Unity: A Letter from Beverly 202
Beverly Thomas

Achieving the Right Results, or The Cake Might Fall 206
Debbie Ward

Homeschooling Pieces Our Hearts Together 210
Theresa Osborne

The Family Culture 214
Diana McAlister

Learning to Adapt 218
Carol Munroe

Homeschooling with Principles, Not Formulas 222
Diana Waring

Index of Contributors 227

Introduction

Time tested. Tried and true. Words of wisdom. Nuggets from the mine of experience. We see these phrases used so often in reference to everything from dog collars to home mortgages, but they usually turn into nothing more than empty clichés. There is a distinct difference, though, when real people with a real interest in their topic write about issues that have been their total focus for years. If we agree that the proof is in the pudding, then, when reading an article on schooling or parenting, we are suspicious of theories espoused by experts once we learn that the expert has reared no children, or that his children are in jail. The chef whose pudding tastes good is the one we are likely to read for pudding recipes. Likewise, the author with a remarkable family led by insightful and creative parents living in vital relationships is the one we turn to for true help in homeschool concerns.

The parents contributing to this book have created some wonderful "puddings," most of which Diana and I have sampled. Though a few of the authors in this collection were invited because we had heard about their "puddings," most of the authors included here are friends whom we wholeheartedly recommend to you. We have enjoyed their hospitality, or sat under their ministry, or gabbed over dessert for long sessions until we tasted what their lives were really made of. The families in these authors' "puddings" come in all flavors—you will want to try some of each!

When you need encouragement in a hard time or instruction for something unfamiliar, you want it direct, with no added ingredients to sort through. Rhubarb pie is good, but when we sat in the back yard with a slender red stalk on a hot August morning, that was straight, twist-the-tongue-upside-down, scrunch-down-the-eyelids, direct, nothing added, rhubarb flavor. This book offers direct, honest, straight from their hearts to yours encouragement, instruction, and help. This is not green rhubarb—a sob story followed by some miraculous triumph, unusable and impractical to your experience—but ready and ripe rhubarb—real struggles with real solutions discovered over time—ready for immediate use. There is a depth of wisdom offered here gained over ten, fifteen, and twenty years of daily life with earnest care and heartfelt prayer. Enjoy it raw.

Diana and I asked our friends to explain what they had come across in their homeschooling that they wished they had known earlier, that "Aha!"

moment when their questions and frustrations were resolved. We wanted them to write, for your encouragement, the main message, from their perspective, of how homeschooling can be a place of victory, joy, and accomplishment. These authors, who come both from the famous conference podiums and from humble, quiet obscurity, have opened their homes and hearts wide to reveal to you their motivations, their insider tips, their most profound secrets. You will cry and laugh as you read some of these honest accounts, and you will have, perhaps for the first time in your homeschool life, that moment when you exclaim, "Aha! I get it now!"

If you are an experienced homeschooler, these insights will brighten your heart and remind you of lessons learned, and, I daresay, they will teach you new things, too. If you are considering whether to homeschool, you have come to the right place to learn how it is done and what it is all about—this is where the heavy hitters hang out! There is contact information in the back of the book for most of these contributors. Drop them a line, thank them for sharing, and get them to answer those other questions you have been pondering.

We want to thank Tom Bragg and Warren Walsh at Emerald Books, our publishers, for pitching to us this incredible idea and for trusting us to take care of it. You men of faith are remarkable professionals. We appreciate you greatly.

Bill and Diana Waring

—— *Part 1* ——

The Concepts

One Word of Advice: Balance!

——— *Jessica Hulcy* ———

Jessica Hulcy and her husband Wade are natives of Dallas, Texas. Jessica is a graduate of The University of Texas at Austin and has done post-graduate work at East Texas State University. She is the mother of four boys, ages 22, 18, 15, and 10. The Hulcy family lives on 125 newly acquired acres of Texas farmland forty miles north of Dallas.

Jessica taught for five years in the Dallas public schools in under-privileged areas where she learned the value of hands-on, discovery learning methods of teaching. She resigned her teaching post in 1975 when the Lord blessed the Hulcys with their first son, Jason. After six weeks of public school first grade, the Hulcys and Jessica's new friend, Carole Thaxton, decided to try a year of homeschooling.

Jessica and Carole wrote their own lesson plans, which they shared with other families. In 1984, they decided to publish their "lesson plans" to see if anyone would buy them. They named their new curriculum KONOS Character Curriculum. The Hulcys have depended on the Lord's provision through KONOS as the sole support of their family for the last ten years.

Those two little first graders are now 22 years old and in college. Jessica presently writes curriculum and marketing ads for KONOS, speaks nationally on a variety of public education and homeschool topics, is a contributing editor to several magazines, is in her sixteenth year of homeschooling, and occasionally sleeps!

Back in the eighties, I spoke at a homeschool conference in Amarillo, Texas, where I met a family with ten or twelve children who toured the U.S. on a Greyhound bus singing gospel music. The mother informed me that they were just returning from a singing engagement in the Dakotas. "Dakotas" meant Mount Rushmore to me, so I asked whether they had just loved seeing the incredible mountain. The mother hesitated, dropped her eyes, and said something I'll never forget: "We had to drive right past Mount Rushmore because some of the younger children had not completed all of their workbook pages." I am sure I did a poor job of concealing my true feelings, yet I did manage to check myself and not say, "You mean your family passed up the opportunity of a lifetime to view magnificent Mount Rushmore, because some of the children needed to fill out another page or two on commas and contractions?"

That incident crystallized in my mind the importance of balance. It was the impetus behind a seven-hour video series I did on having balance. It has been said that variety is the spice of life. I propose that balance is the meat and potatoes of life. The person who learns to balance the various aspects of his or her life early on is not only ahead of the game, but is also well positioned to defuse and eliminate potential problems.

Nowhere is balance more critical to success than in teaching at home. Without balance, moms burn out and children lose their love for learning. Many people think that my children are always dressed in costume, that we spend the entire day every day doing a myriad of hands-on activities, that we never use a textbook, and that we read only library books. Nothing could be further from the truth. The truth is, I have spent the last sixteen years attempting to maintain balance in my own homeschooling, and encouraging others to institute balance in their homeschooling for the sake of the mothers' sanity, as well as for the children's learning.

Balancing Workbooks vs. Hands-on Learning

We tend to equate education with filling in blanks. The Mount Rushmore example is a dramatic reminder that there is much more to education than simply sitting at a desk filling out umpteen pages of workbooks. Most would consider Thomas Jefferson an educated man, yet he never filled out workbooks. He simply applied the rules of grammar as he wrote. How much more interesting is it to write about Mount Rushmore than to fill in blanks? Which would any child remember? Workbooks are for mothers who want to feel that all their bases are covered, and, in that sense, they serve a very real purpose.

No doubt, hands-on learning is a much better way to learn. Compare reading about how to operate a computer to sitting down at the computer and beginning to operate it. On the other hand, activity for activity's sake is just as out of balance as no activities. The incoherent skipping from one activity to the next, with little or no regard for wrap-up or conclusion, is a waste of time and energy. Although I love hands-on learning activities, I have passed up many good field trips with my support group because my kids had workbook pages to complete. However, I never complete an entire workbook—only those pages that my kids need. Further, I do not use a language arts workbook every year since they tend to cover the same subjects over and over again each year. For high school, I might use a grammar workbook every other year. Writing alone will not teach what a gerund or a dangling participle is. This is where workbooks are very helpful.

I usually preach against workbooks because parents tend to get so out of balance using them. They seem to consider workbooks *core curriculum*, instead of supplements to the curriculum, as they should be. Young children understand nouns much better if they collect twenty-five in a bag. They understand verbs much better if they go outside and do twenty-five verbs, and then write them down. Workbooks are great for reinforcing concepts already taught by hands-on methods.

Balancing Textbooks vs. Classic Literature

Lately, I have seen a growing interest in emphasizing reading the classics—great literature, real books. When we wrote our curriculum, Carole Thaxton and I refused to teach from just textbooks. We had a real love for great literature and viewed the entire library as our textbooks.

When children read great literature, their vocabularies are expanded; their personal writing and composition is improved; their speed of reading and comprehension is enhanced; and their ability to trace plots, subplots, and complex story lines, as well as their ability to analyze characters, is heightened. However, reading a classic historical fiction book alone, such as *Johnny Tremain* or *Quo Vadis*, without an accompanying textbook, is merely getting a flavor for a particular period in history. It does not replace a history text. Knowing fictional characters is not the same as a complete knowledge of the battles, the government, the art and architecture, and the religion and philosophy of a historical period. To neglect fact books or textbooks is to be out of balance.

On the other hand, reading only one textbook on the Civil War will never give your children the perspective that a great literature book, like *Across Five Aprils*, or a biography on Lee, Lincoln, or Stonewall Jackson can give. Textbooks and fact books provide the bones of the historical period, while literature and biographies add flesh to the period. Activities make the period memorable.

Balancing Traditional Course Texts vs. Subject Books

There is a tremendous array of informative, clear, attractive subject books available which never fail to teach me some new and interesting fact. They cover various history and science subjects, and they are exceptionally interesting. Homeschoolers are kidding themselves, though, if they think these books constitute a full science course, or a full history course. These are excellent companion books, supplemental books, research books, or added information books. However, just as classic literature books do not give a complete picture of any historical period, so subject books do not make a full ancient history course, or a full biology course, etc. Upper level courses should use a textbook as their core, but should not limit themselves to textbooks exclusively. Just as history courses are rounded out with literature of the period, so science classes should be accompanied by a full lab curriculum. Chemistry sets from a novelty shop do not constitute a full-fledged chemistry lab curriculum!

When we entered the homeschooling arena sixteen years ago, the bulk of homeschoolers were using traditional workbook and textbook curriculum. We felt we had to jump very hard on the other end of the seesaw, emphasizing character training, unit studies, classic library books, hands-on activities, and discovery learning just to get people to slide to the middle of the seesaw where there was an actual *balance* of teaching methods. Sixteen years later, we do not want homeschoolers to slide off the other end of the seesaw. Maintain the balance!

⟦▯▯▯▯▯▯▯⟧ *This essay is based on the article "One Word of Advice: Balance" from the March/April 1998 issue of* Practical Home Schooling. *Used by permission.*

Curriculum: Tool or Tyrant?

————— *Holly Sheen* —————

Holly is a veteran homeschooling mother who has served the homeschooling community in many ways for the past fifteen years. She has been a local support group leader; newsletter editor for both her local support group and for a statewide homeschooling organization; convention coordinator for Connecticut's homeschooling conventions; board member on both Connecticut's and Iowa's statewide Christian homeschooling organizations; and legislative liaison to her state government for homeschooling. In addition, she and her husband have been homeschooling their two daughters for the past fifteen years. During that time, Holly and her family have homeschooled in four different states: California, Connecticut, Iowa, and Pennsylvania.

Holly and her husband, Ray, have been married for twenty years. Between her husband's military service and business career, they have moved often. Everywhere they have lived she has also been involved with her local church in some ministry capacity such as librarian, choir member, or deaconess.

Currently Holly is a member of the Board of Directors for The Education Association of Christian Homeschoolers (TEACH), Connecticut's statewide organization for Christian homeschoolers. She is also the newsletter editor, convention coordinator, and heads the statewide legislative alert network for TEACH.

✎▷ Ahhhhhhhhhhhhhhh. The end of another perfect homeschool day. This morning—like all mornings—all of the children jumped joyfully out of bed at the crack of dawn to meet the day. The hour of family worship set the tone for all—and it was so satisfying to hear the children reciting the Pentateuch. All of the chores were cheerfully accomplished, making the house a spotless and inviting center of learning. Each child applied himself to his assignments with alacrity and intensity of purpose. Now, dinner is simmering aromatically, awaiting the arrival of a happy Daddy from work.

What do you mean this doesn't describe your homeschool? Oh. I see. Instead, you are thinking: The end of another long homeschooling day has arrived. You are brain-dead. Your children are cranky. The house is a wreck. What in the world will you fix for dinner? Your long-suffering husband is getting tired of coming home to leftovers. In fact, you haven't spent much time with your husband for weeks—you have been too busy homeschooling the children!

Wasn't homeschooling supposed to be fun...or at least satisfying? Didn't people tell you that your children would enjoy learning? What could be wrong?

You stack up all of the school books. Look at all of those books! Why, you have diligently made sure that your children have read all of the chapters in the book, and have answered all of the questions at the end of those chapters. They have completed a good stack of worksheets every day. You have given them every quiz in the test booklet. You had them write book reports for all of the books they have been reading. According to your record book, you are right on schedule—your almighty schedule!

Still, nothing else is going right. Maybe you are giving them too much school work...but...on the other hand, those books were written by education experts. If they didn't expect you to teach everything in the book, they would not have put those lessons in there. Right? If you could only get your children to understand that! They keep complaining that they are bored and already know the material, but lots of repetition is a good thing, after all...isn't it? If the children weren't so grouchy and uncooperative, you could finish all of those books!

Maybe...maybe you just were not cut out to homeschool. (Sniff.)

Guess what has happened to you! (Sinister music builds in the background.) You have been ensnared by...The Curriculum Tyrant! (Dum da dump dum daaaa!)

Yes. The Curriculum Tyrant! The Curriculum Tyrant sneaks into your home under the guise of "Good Books." He begins to whisper to you that these books are the answer to all of your children's needs. He then quietly, but persistently, begins to insist that you must not waste any of these Good Books, but must do all contained therein. He virtuously points out, just for good measure, that you spent a fortune on these Good Books, too. Certainly, you would not want to waste hard-earned money by not getting the most out of these Good Books. Before long, you are feeling guilty and anxious for not having your children spend more and more of their time slaving away in the Good Books. It's for their own good, after all!

You might be in the grip of The Curriculum Tyrant, but, hark! There is hope! To rescue you from the domain of The Curriculum Tyrant, we must step back to the beginning. First, you must take the following pop quiz:

1. Who owns your children?
2. Who has God deputized to raise His children?
3. Does anyone on this earth know your children better than you?

Answers:
1. God does. Of course, He does. The magnificent Creator of the universe owns all things, including your precious children. You knew that, remember?
2. You. Yes, God has graciously allowed you, as a parent, to be steward over the dear blessings He has given you. Imagine the influence God is allowing you to wield—influence with eternal consequences. Wow!
3. No! God has placed you in the unique position of having special knowledge about your children that no one else can ever completely have. No one will ever know them the way you do.

Now, an essay question. What is an "expert"? Dictionary definition: "a person who has special skill or knowledge in some particular field." So, in the "particular field" of your children, the "expert" is you! Not The Curriculum Tyrant. You! Do the authors of Good Books really know more about your children than you do? Does Scripture exhort authors of Good Books concerning how to raise children, or does it exhort parents? God has given the job of "resident expert" to you, and not to a stack of Good Books.

Now that we have established who the real experts are, let's take another look at the ways of The Curriculum Tyrant. The Curriculum Tyrant is unbalanced and relentless. He wants to take over your entire family life. Should your children slog through school work just because it's in the book? If your daughter readily knows her multiplication tables, why are you wasting time with endless drills? If your son excitedly rushes in to give you a blow-by-blow description of the book he is reading, why are you saddling him with a laborious book report? If Mary is bored with a textbook-dictated writing assignment, why not let her write about something she likes? If the chemistry text is covering the same math as the math textbook, does Johnny really need to do the same material again? Anxiety and chaos are the price you pay for obeying The Curriculum Tyrant. God is always balanced, and He is the God of order. Obeying Him brings peace and orderliness as we allow Him to tame The Curriculum Tyrant.

So, you have reviewed all of the symptoms and have decided that, indeed, you have been seduced by The Curriculum Tyrant. Now what? Stop what you are doing. Put the Good Books back on the shelf. Pray for wisdom. James 1:5 says: "If any of you lacks wisdom, he should ask God, who gives generously to all without finding fault, and it will be given to him" (NIV). Take some time and look at the skills each of your children has been demonstrating. Pay attention to what they are truly able to do, not just what the Good Books have been dictating. After you have taken an in-depth look at your children's abilities, and have prayed for God's leading, then you can pull the Good Books back off the shelf.

You are now ready for...(happy music builds in the background) Curriculum Tools! (Tee de TEEE!) That's right: Curriculum Tools. Curriculum Tools are gifts God has given us to help raise our children properly. Good Books are wonderful Tools to be used, at your discretion, in teaching your children, but they need to be used wisely. Tools are used by the expert to create, build, and fix. The expert masters his tools, and is not intimidated by them. We need to see how an expert handles curriculum.

You do not necessarily need to throw out your curriculum and begin something new. I like the statement, "Any curriculum will work if the teacher does." In other words, if you—and remember, you are the real expert!—take charge of what you have on hand, and regularly assess your children's schoolwork and attitudes, you might not need to spend more money on new material. After evaluating what you have on the bookshelf, decide where your children should "plug in" to a book or a plan of study. What can they skip— yes, skip!—either because it is twaddle, or because they have already mastered it? What areas need more practice? Your answers will vary from subject to subject. New curriculum might be necessary, but be certain you make an informed decision and not a snap decision based on frustration.

You have made the transition! You are now using Curriculum Tools to meet the needs of your children, rather than following the demands of the despotic Curriculum Tyrant. Such freedom! Life returns to normal as you fit curriculum into its proper place along with housekeeping, family time, devotions, and other important responsibilities. The frazzled, brain-dead mother disappears, replaced by a calm, smiling mother. The neglected daddy and perpetually cranky children disappear, too. Is life perfect? Well, no, but home should now be a more pleasant place, and the daily routine should flow more smoothly. Learning can now be interesting instead of the draining drudgery it once was. Hurrah for homeschooling!

Just a word of caution, though. The Curriculum Tyrant is never defeated. He will try to return, and he is very sneaky. But you will know when he returns if you pay attention. Recall the anxiety? The chaos? You will know. Trust me. I'm an expert!

The Three R's:
Relationships, Reasoning, and Resolve

——— *David and Shirley Quine* ———

David and Shirley have been married twenty-six wonderful years. They have been abundantly blessed by God with Bryce (22), Ben (20), Blaine (18), Betsy (18), Blessing (14), Byron (11), Bethany (9), Bonney (7), and Brett (6). All have been home educated since birth.

Shirley studied early childhood education in college. Homeschooling has given her the opportunity to explore great literature with her children. She loves sewing, cross-stitch, growing African violets and roses, and teaching her children. David holds a masters degree in curriculum and instruction design. He taught junior high science for five years and was the science director for grades K–12 in the fourth largest school district in Texas. In 1984 David left public education to help other parents, through his writing and speaking, to teach their own children.

In 1984 David and Shirley began The Cornerstone Curriculum Project. David's love for the works of Dr. Francis Schaeffer, and a desire to equip children for the challenges to Christianity presented by the secular culture, motivated him to create curricula such as Adventures in Art, and World Views of the Western World, a new interdisciplinary study for grades 8–12. He is also author of Making Math Meaningful and Science: The Search, and has written Understanding the Arts for Homeschooling Today for seven years. Together, David and Shirley have coauthored Let Us Highly Resolve. Their book is an encouragement for Christian families to enter the twenty-first century equipped and prepared to meet the new battles they will face.

In 1980, as David and I began to homeschool our oldest son, Bryce, we were intent upon teaching the "Three R's: Reading, Writing and Arithmetic." Since we thought homeschooling meant school at home, we followed the traditional school approach. Thus began several years of guilt and frustration. I was trying to cover five to six subject areas every day with several children. Because I was unable to finish all the expected work, I felt very discouraged. Like running on an ever increasing treadmill, the pressure to succeed intensified. Our parents, friends at church, neighbors, and business associates watched us—just waiting for failure so that they could congratulate themselves that this homeschooling idea was as crazy as they thought.

Now, almost twenty years later, with five of our nine children godly young adults, three of whom are in college, we have a different perspective. We consider three different R's—relationships, reasoning, and resolve—to be just as essential.

Relationships

To other people, it seemed like such a strange idea: choosing to keep our children at home with us all day long. However, God was calling us (and He is probably calling you)—calling us back to be families. We wanted to spend our entire day learning together, working together, playing together. We wanted to be our children's role models for how to live successfully in families. We were choosing to keep our children at home with us to build closer, deeper relationships with them.

After several years, I realized that true learning and deeper relationships were simply not happening. Now, I know the reason—I was trying to reproduce my own school experience in our home. Using traditional textbooks did not facilitate learning or positive relationships. How could they? Textbooks were written for group instruction. I wanted to spend one-on-one time with our children. When our children were spending all their time with a workbook or textbook, they were neither relating to me, nor understanding their lessons. In fact, I found that we were actually being isolated from each other. This was exactly the opposite of what I had hoped would happen. Maybe, homeschooling wasn't for me.

I began to ask David every night, "How do I do this?" In response, he began to write one-on-one conversations for me to use. Our children responded wonderfully to our new times of learning together. Our relationships grew stronger as we enjoyed natural conversations about math and science. Our relationships flourished as I taught them in this new, natural way. We began to view homeschooling as discipleship. I was rebuilding our family, and, at the same time, equipping our children to have successful families of their own.

First Peter 5:2–4 is excellent for helping us establish a proper attitude regarding teaching our children: "Tend—nurture, guard, guide and fold—the flock of God that is [your responsibility], not by coercion or constraint but willingly...eagerly and cheerfully. Not (as arrogant, dictatorial and overbearing persons) domineering over those in your charge, but being examples—patterns and models of Christian living—to the flock...And [then] when the Chief Shepherd is revealed you will win the conqueror's crown of glory" (AMP). Our "flock," as parents, is our children. Once your unconditional love is firmly established, then your children will want to follow your leadership and to embrace your teaching and beliefs. When children grow up in a home where their mother and father demonstrate love to each other, where they receive unconditional love as expressed through eye contact, physical closeness, and focused attention, they will want to have a relationship with their parents, and will hold dearly the Christian world view.

Reasoning

As a child, David used to love going to the Oklahoma State Fair with his family. He was fascinated by the chicken which had been trained, through behavior modification, to play the "Star Spangled Banner." Later, he was to learn that this teaching/training model was used extensively in education to "teach" school children across the nation. However, these were not just any school children. They were us! We were taught simply to *parrot back* information without understanding. In other words, many math facts, dates, and names of people and events were memorized for the test and quickly forgotten. They held no meaning for us, thus adding to the meaninglessness of our own lives. This kind of education was certainly not what David and I desired for our children!

Paul encourages us to grow to maturity in Christ. "When I was a child, I used to speak as a child, think as a child, reason as a child, but when I became a man, I did away with childish things...," "...We are no longer to be children, tossed here and there by waves, and carried about by every wind of doctrine, by the trickery of men, by craftiness in deceitful scheming: but, speaking the truth in love" (1 Cor. 13:11; Eph. 4:14, 15).

In today's culture there is a constant battle for the hearts and minds of our children. The picture Paul paints is of children in a boat being hopelessly tossed to and fro between gusts of teaching from opposing philosophies: cleverly disguised lies made to sound like the truth. It is true that children reason differently than adults. A person reasoning at the childish level is not able to understand the philosophical presuppositions behind the ideas being presented. If a nation were made up predominately of adults who reasoned at the childish level, that nation would be vulnerable to great deception and manipulation by those dispensing information to the people of that society.

Neither the chicken nor the child, who has been taught through behavioral modification, is being taught to reason. When we examined materials for teaching subject matter to our children, we found logical reasoning to be missing. Teaching our children to evaluate ideas by critically examining what is being presented is one of our primary resolves. As our children mature, we want them to reason as adults, on the highest level of reasoning, so that they will be able to combat these cleverly disguised lies, to stand independent of the secular thoughts and ideas of this culture, and to give an adequate defense for the hope that is within them.

Resolve

After a few years of homeschooling, we discovered that it was absolutely necessary that we have a very determined purpose before us. Simply maintaining a home and family were so challenging that, without a clear set of goals, we could easily become lost in the sea of details. There were so many balls to juggle: lesson plans, schedules, curriculum, sports, and other extracurricular activities. So many good programs and activities were available to crowd out the very best which we wanted to impart to our children. We had often heard the saying, "If you aim at nothing, you will hit it every time." We were seeing the truth of this in our own family.

Dr. Francis Schaeffer has said, "We must be consciously preparing the next generation for the new battles they will face." This was our desire: to prepare and equip our children for these new battles. We realized we needed to resolve (determine once for all) the goals that would give direction to our homeschool.

The thoughts and ideas at the end of the twentieth century, which are being delivered in the most entertaining and powerful ways, are challenging the Christian world view. We resolved to set a course of action for our children that would give them the ability to stand ready to meet these challenges to their faith. Like Paul, we have determined not to rely upon own strength, our own knowledge, or our own abilities (1 Cor. 2:2), but, by God's strength, we have resolved:

> To build our family upon the biblical world view;
> To establish our children's lives upon truth and absolutes;
> To equip our children to reason;
> To enter into true spirituality;
> To be "by faith" families;
> To prepare our children as a "Letter of Christ" to the culture;
> To challenge our culture with the truth of Christianity and the life of Christ.

We wish we would have clearly settled our resolves from the very beginning of our homeschooling. Definite goals would have given us greater strength and courage on the difficult days. When our purposes are clearly established, when we know *why* we are doing *what* we are doing, the *how* comes naturally.

Now we encourage families to teach reading, writing, and arithmetic within the framework of strong relationships, reasoning from the biblical world view, and clearly established resolves. Then your children will be fully equipped to enter the twenty-first century.

[━━━━━] *"The Three R's: Relationships, Reasoning, and Resolve"* is adapted *from* Let Us Highly Resolve, *written by David and Shirley Quine. Used by permission.*

For the Love of Books

―――― *Tommi Ryan* ――――

Grades were extremely important in Tommi's family, and she always achieved them, but she remembered only a small portion of what she learned. In 1978 she married John Ryan, who, by the grace of God and one of his teachers, barely managed to graduate from high school. However, he has a tremendous reservoir of knowledge. One of his favorite comments to Tommi is, "Where did you go to school?," after he's asked her a question that she should know, and which, of course, he does know.

John and Tommi are the parents of four beautiful and brilliant (in their humble opinion) children. Danielle (18) and Marie (17) are attending College of the Ozarks in Branson, Missouri. They enjoy all the varied activities of college life and are both on the President's list. Johanna, at age 14, tolerates school, but her real love is horses and goats. Jonathan (11) loves to play with Legos and read books and longs for Mom to make school more fun. The Ryans have lived on a farm in the Ozarks for fifteen years. They have cattle, horses, goats (there were six new-born kids in the house this spring), chickens, ducks, and, of course, plenty of dogs and cats. Sometimes, it's a bit overwhelming, but seldom dull, and Tommi would not trade it for anything—well, maybe sometimes!

Looking back thirteen years ago to our first year of homeschooling, it seems almost idyllic. At that time there was only one little 5-year-old girl eager to learn and her 3-year-old sister who thought she could do anything her big sister did. My first step was to order a complete kindergarten curriculum. How exciting to open the box and see all the things we would be learning. However, as we got started and found the supplier had enclosed three different methods for teaching phonics, and I had never had phonics, it got a little bit confusing, to say the least. We tried one method and then another. In the end I settled for just one small book and decided we didn't need workbooks. All we needed was paper, pencils, (a chalkboard was helpful) and that tiny book. Before long the children were saying Ba, Be, Bi, Bo, Bu, and then they were reading, so we skipped the rest of the book. Believe me, I know it's not always that easy. My third child did not read at all until she was 8, so do not get discouraged. Each child is on a different timetable, and I firmly believe that almost all children will learn to read easily if they are read to a lot and not rushed. Which leads me to what I believe was the secret to our homeschooling.

Shortly after beginning homeschooling, I read a book by Raymond and Dorothy Moore, who believe that many education problems arise from beginning formal schooling too early. So, we basically dispensed with the rest of the kindergarten curriculum and began reading lots of good books together. My criteria for a book was that it had to be something we could all enjoy, including me. It was so much fun reading all the books I had either forgotten or missed during childhood: *Anne of Green Gables, The Chronicles of Narnia, The Prince and the Pauper, Swiss Family Robinson.* Our tradition was to sit down after lunch and read, sometimes for hours. The children would beg for one more chapter, and how easy it was to give in. Those hours remain some of my most treasured memories: all the children seated as close to me as they could get, one or two in my lap. Now that they are older, and prefer reading by themselves, I really miss those times of closeness. For you moms who say you don't have time, those are the times you will remember—not how clean your house was, or how many subjects you crammed into your children's school day.

This remained the backbone of our "curriculum" throughout the grade school years. When my two oldest girls reached high school age, they took the educational ball in their own hands and did their studies (basic high school curriculum) on their own, the younger graduating shortly after the older. Today they are both in college and have retained their love of learning. They do not understand when they see other students who do not study, and who complain about working. Even though they did traditional studies during their high school years, I believe the freedom they experienced in the earlier years cultivated their natural curiosity for knowledge, understanding, and (we pray) wisdom. They also had time to develop their innate talents.

For example, my oldest loved playing the piano, and when she was between the ages of 10 and 13 she would often play for three hours during the day. Meanwhile, her sibling developed an interest in animals. Our local library ordered dozens of animal science/veterinary books for her, which she practically memorized. She trained several foals born on our farm and now has her own small herd of cattle. If we had filled up the school day with hours of seat work, our children might have become bored and decided they hated school. They might never have had the opportunity to discover the things they truly love to do.

Through the years I have had plenty of doubts and worries. Am I requiring enough of my children? Will they be able to make it through college if they choose to go? Believe me, I breathed a big sigh of relief when my girls both made it through College Comp. successfully because I knew how slack I had been in teaching grammar and writing. I might add that I plan to be more diligent in that area with my next two. I asked our two oldest children what they thought homeschooling should be for the early years. Their answer was, "No TV or videos; lots of reading and playing."

Another area we consider extremely important is to have on hand as many reference books as we can afford. It is exciting to watch your children bring in toads, snakes, whatever, and, with creature in one hand and reference book in the other, figure out exactly what the thing is. That's what learning is all about. Think back over your education. How many of the facts you memorized do you remember? Education is not cramming facts into one's head. We believe that education is guiding a child's natural curiosity and equipping them with godly ways with which to satisfy that curiosity. An old proverb says that you can give a person a fish and feed him for a day, or you can give him a fishing pole and teach him how to use it, and feed him for a lifetime.

I could end this article right now, but I know from my own experience that for many it would be a discouragement instead of an encouragement. It sounds too easy. However, I firmly believe that homeschooling during the early years should consist mainly of reading aloud together. If your child is ready to read, teach him to read, teach him some basic math, but don't get bogged down in "seat" work. So many things can be learned by reading a variety of books and, of course, through talking with your child and involving him in your daily activities. Children learn about their world as naturally as they learn to walk and talk, and learning together through books is easy and fun. For those of you who are now homeschooling young children, I urge you to relax, gather them close to you, and open up a good book.

Keep It Fun! Keep It Simple!

———— *Fred and Sarah Cooper* ————

Fred and Sarah Cooper met in Sunday school at the First Baptist Church of Dallas and married in 1978. After their first son was born in 1981, they began thinking about education. They attended their first homeschool seminar fifteen years ago when their first child was 2 years old, fell in love with the concept, and have been "dyed-in-the-wool" home-schoolers ever since.

Fred was born and raised in San Antonio, Texas, and earned degrees in chemistry and hospital administration from Trinity University in San Antonio. He spent twelve years in hospital administration in Ft. Worth and Dallas, leaving the field in 1979 to start his own company in executive search.

Sarah was born and raised in Baytown, Texas. She enjoyed studying music from her earliest years and was playing piano and organ for churches by the time she was 13. She graduated from Baylor University in music education in 1969, and taught public school music in Dallas for four years. She then served as secretary to the president and registrar of Criswell College.

When their children were very young, Sarah found that putting Bible verses to music made the memorizing process fun and very, very fast. She then discovered other teaching programs using music. The Coopers' business, Sing 'n Learn, was born when Sarah's friends began asking for the programs, also. Since 1992, Sing 'n Learn has been selling programs that use the power of music and audio learning to make learning fun and easy.

Twelve years ago, we began to undertake the most exciting adventure of our lives: homeschooling our oldest son. In those days, it was a really strange thing to do. When people asked where we were sending our son to school, and we told them we were schooling him at home, they gave us all sorts of strange looks and grimaces. Almost no one had heard of such a thing in those days, and they asked all the usual questions: "Is it legal?" "What about socialization?" "How will he be able to relate to other people?"

My sister taught her kids at home and we had a few other friends from whom we could glean some advice, and there were a few books written on the subject, but in many respects, we were flying in the dark. By the time we had completed six months of homeschooling, we were considered experts, veterans!

Since that time, we have tried just about every approach you can name— some successful and some not. We helped start two support groups and did our stint in leading those groups. We started a homeschool related business which gives us continuing exposure to both new and long-time homeschoolers. Now that we are completing the job with our oldest son, here are some things we have learned along the way.

One of the most important things we could suggest is to determine your child's learning style and learning modality. Every child learns differently. For instance, our oldest son loves to read. He soaks up information from the pages of books. Our younger son is not that way; he is an auditory learner. He remembers just about everything he hears and really does not care to do any more reading than he absolutely must. In his case, we found that using an audio book along with the printed version helps him to gain proficiency in reading and to develop an appreciation for great literature. In the past, almost all learning in schools was based on reading books. Those who did not fit into that mode of learning were often left on the side of the road because visual learning was the only real choice available in traditional education. That is one of the greatest advantages of homeschooling: we do not have to fit into the standard mold of a public or private school. We can teach our children according to their natural bent for learning. There are many good books available on learning styles and learning modalities. Such a book should be one of your first purchases as you approach homeschooling.

Our second piece of advice is to keep it simple! Do not try to do too much. For first graders, in particular, concentrate on two major subjects: language arts (phonics, reading, writing, and spelling) and basic arithmetic. As people visit homeschool book fairs, their eyes are bombarded with thousands of colorful, beautifully designed programs which all call out, "Buy me!" "Buy me!" Everything looks so attractive, it is tempting to load up on five times more material than you could possibly use. Resist that temptation. For first graders, there are only two objectives: (1) teach them to read and write, and (2) teach them to count, add, and subtract. If parents or teachers can accomplish those two things, the whole world of information, knowledge, and discovery will be open to their students. Oh, it is OK to do a few little extra studies on the side, but beginners really are not ready for full blown science and history curricula. Much can be learned from audio cassette programs because young children can often learn much more through their ears than through their eyes.

The next thing we suggest is that you select curriculum that is fun for your child. Earlier this year, a mother told us she had been praying for some time about curriculum choices to make for her children. She was a veteran homeschooler with several children spanning a number of years in age. She was drawn toward materials which use multisensory methods, like music cassettes, audio cassettes, and videos. She said she had decided to use programs that were fun and simple, and to de-emphasize those things which required laborious reading and drilling. As she looked back on her experience with her older children, she realized the only things they truly remembered were the fun things they had done.

That principle also holds true with older children. Two years ago, we were trying to teach our boys American history. They were reading aloud from a standard history textbook chock full of facts, dates, and names of people, laws, places, and battles. The boys seemed bored, and Sarah's voice carried a tediousness that could not produce much enthusiasm. Thinking myself to be the great example of a vivacious teacher, I marched into the living room, scolded my charges, and told them to move over and listen to a pro read this material and make it interesting with great expression and enthusiasm. After about the second paragraph, I became overwhelmed with all those facts, too. They were things neither I, nor anyone I knew, could remember, even from our college courses in American history. If we could not retain those facts from higher education, how could we expect our children to appreciate them in their early years? We have found that, on any subject, regardless of a child's learning style, they are far more likely to remember things like songs, videos, and stories than an endless recitation of facts.

Our fourth suggestion is to be consistent with your curriculum in those subjects, like math, which continue sequentially from one year to the next. Unless it is clearly ineffective or uninteresting, it is better to follow the consistent pattern of one approach to teaching than to switch to a different program every year. Every curriculum has its good and bad points. If you have chosen a program that seems basically sound, stay with it. If you try to change in midstream, chances are you will not like the new program any better, and you will lose ground in the transition. An example of this was our Spanish curriculum. Although there were things I disliked about our first year curriculum, we stuck with it because we found that we would lose ground by switching to a different program for the second year. It sort of follows the spiritual principle of being content with what you have.

Another thing we learned over time was the value of finding partners in certain subjects for our children. This was especially true in high school math. Through the years, we have homeschooled several children along with our own. It was very helpful for our older son to have a partner with whom he could work in tandem on algebra. Our younger son did not have this advantage, and it proved harder for him as he had to do it all by himself. Of course, he had old Dad to help him, but it is often more fun when there is a friend with whom he can struggle to conquer a common goal. Perhaps you could join or generate a learning co-op or club to create this opportunity in your area.

In just three years, both of our sons will be in college. We will have completed the job of giving them a basic education. It's been fun and rewarding. We then hope and pray that they will find wives who are also geared toward the idea of homeschooling. Then, maybe, we can start helping with our grandchildren, and can put this advice to work in our extended family.

The Heart of Homeschooling: The Learning Lifestyle

♪

————— *Vicky Goodchild* —————

Vicky, born in 1956 and raised in Miami, Florida, married Jack Goodchild in 1977 and moved to Fort Lauderdale, Florida where they reside with their five children: Tim (17), Kimberly (12), Stephen (9), Laura (7), and Michelle (5). They have homeschooled their children since 1983 when Tim was a preschooler.

Vicky graduated from college in 1978 with a bachelor's degree in secondary education and is a Florida certified teacher. She taught for a couple of years before having their first child. In 1983 they learned about homeschooling, and, within a short time, began their county's first support group, becoming administrators for a private school for homeschoolers. They worked with others to organize their state homeschool association and lobbied in their state capital for the Florida homeschool law. Vicky is a frequent convention speaker at support groups and state conferences. In 1990 she wrote a book entitled, An Orientation to Home Schooling in Florida— Answers to the Most Commonly Asked Questions. *Due to the many requests outside of Florida to turn the above title into a "generic" book for all fifty states, in 1997 she wrote* The Simplicity of Homeschooling. *It features the Learning Lifestyle as the route to streamlining and ultimately simplifying home education. An accompanying cassette, developed by her husband, Jack, provides practical tips on how a man can support and help his wife during the homeschool years. Their home-based homeschool business, HIS Publishing Company, was established in 1990.*

✏▷ "God, help! I don't want to quit homeschooling, but there just has to be a better way." This was my heart cry as I lay across my bed in tears, overwhelmed with all the expectations placed upon me by myself and others. God was faithful—He answered with just one word, "WAIT." I was not sure what I was waiting for, but felt so paralyzed by discouragement I could do little else. During the following year we learned two important lessons which revolutionized our homeschool. The wonderful result has been a liberation of learning in our family.

Simplify Life

Up to that point, Jack and I, for several years, had homeschooled our children, led a homeschool support group, operated our own home-based business selling and developing homeschool materials, and I had often spoken on issues pertaining to homeschooling. We had enjoyed many years of prosperous learning experiences, yet had allowed too many outside responsibilities to gradually crowd our lives and cause us to resort to dull, lifeless, rote work which strangled the very heart of our homeschool. So, the first revolutionary lesson we learned in walking toward recovery was to simplify our lives. Even though the things we were doing were "good," we found many got in the way of the "best." It became essential for us to control the areas which were sapping our family's joy for living and learning. Much more than Jack, it was clear that I needed to cut back, as the mother and primary teacher, in order to provide time for mothering, teaching, and creativity.

While we were in the "waiting mode," we put away all the textbooks and workbooks. That might sound drastic and irresponsible, but, as you will see, it became the act which revealed the truth regarding real learning.

So what did we do? Everyone, from oldest to youngest, began to do work on our home. It, too, had suffered from neglect. An analogy between the condition of our house and of our lives became apparent when we faced the hole in the wall which we had hidden behind a quilt. The hole in our homeschool/family wall needed more than a patch-up job—it needed a skilled craftsman. You can only cover up a problem for so long before you must deal with it. Jesus, the best carpenter we know, took the job seriously.

During our home improvement project, we learned many skills. Most importantly, I learned how to relax and enjoy my family again. I noticed that when the home projects began to wind down, the children found their own projects in which to become involved. Here is where we discovered real learning and what we now refer to as the Learning Lifestyle.

For example, our oldest son, Tim, and his cousin started a project in a field adjacent to our home. They built forts, a solar water still, and rappelling platforms among other things. They read books and magazines on survival skills. They identified edible plants and insects (only daring to eat the plants). Many nights, they hauled out the halogen lamp to work after sundown. They taught both our families what they were learning, and before long their enthusiasm was infectious. For all of us, testing our skills at self-sufficiency became a fever. For the other children, it translated into more forts and books, and more plant and insect identification. For my sister and me, along with our oldest girls, it became herb gardening. From that start, we went on to full-scale gardens. We knew little about gardening, so we ended up in the library checking out books, eventually building our own libraries on the topic. We are still avid gardeners to this day.

By the way, Tim and his cousin, now 17, have extended their survival skills interests to helping others survive extreme circumstances. They are both involved in a Fire/Rescue apprenticeship program in our county, and plan to go to the Fire Academy and college for a paramedics course when they turn 18.

Just about every subject imaginable was covered during that time of intensive study, yet each child applied the learning to his own frame of reference, which gave it meaning and purpose. Little did we realize that by simply allowing them to pursue subjects in which they were interested, they could be so motivated to learn. We have often heard it said that a child's play is his work. We would add that it is also his education. Since the survival skills experience, we have pursued many other interest-based projects. Some incorporate the whole family, but most are individualized according to the interests and maturity of each child.

Another very interesting thing happened that year. Eventually the children began asking me to help them with their math, spelling, reading, and composition skills. They began to see, on their own, that these tools would be necessary in order to pursue the topics they were interested in. We reinstated a morning schedule of the basics, pulling out many of the dusty books, but we saved the rest of the day for their own self-directed, interest-based units. They now beg for library visits, since they know they will be searching for books on their own topics.

As their parents, we are aware of the basic skills of reading, writing, and arithmetic which our children will need for their future success. We teach those basics, but we have become firm believers in equipping our children with the tools to learn, and then allowing them to learn, both from a need-to-know basis and according to their interests. Textbooks, workbooks, and "real" books have become our resources rather than our masters. We agree with the British educator, Dorothy Sayers, who said, "The sole end of education is simply this: to teach men how to learn for themselves; whatever instruction fails to do this is effort spent in vain."

The Learning Lifestyle

The second revolutionary lesson we learned was that rather than relegating homeschooling to a particular room in the house, on particular days of the week, during particular hours of the day, instead, we approach learning as a lifestyle. Within this concept of the Learning Lifestyle, we allow our children to learn through living while they self-educate through units of their own choosing. At the same time we are careful to provide the necessary structure and academics. One great realization was that I could also pursue my own interests (such as gardening) and be a model of learning. We believe it is important for children to see their parents as learners, and not just as educators. Modeling a passion for learning inspires children and helps them internalize the notion that learning is valuable and worthy of pursuit, even after they leave the homeschool.

While counseling both new and veteran homeschool parents, we most often find ourselves telling them about the benefits of simplifying their lives, and simplifying education, through the Learning Lifestyle. We are not talking about becoming simplistic. That is a false simplicity which ignores complicating factors. Simplicity, however, seeks to reduce (not ignore) the unnecessary complexities, and leads to clarity of purpose. A simplified education will allow your children to spend less time at the desk and more time on the living application which provides that clarity of purpose. Motivated by their own curiosity, they will generally spend more time at a task than you thought possible. It encourages the integration of all facets of life, rather than fragmenting and compartmentalizing learning. It promotes relationships within the family because your children will spend more time enthusiastically conversing about their latest discoveries, rather than silently filling out endless workbook pages. Soon your family will be celebrating life, rather than the achievement of a completed workbook, even as praiseworthy as that might be.

At the point you and your children discover the freedom in learning through living, then you will have realized the simplicity of homeschooling: reducing education to its basic essentials to provide clarity of purpose in learning. Perhaps, the greatest benefit you will experience is the freedom to enjoy the development of your own family's unique learning lifestyle—the very heart of your homeschool.

Learn to Recognize Learning

——— *Joan Veach* ———

Joan M. Veach was born and raised in Idaho Falls, Idaho. When she was 17, she moved to Washington state to attend the University of Washington and has lived in Washington ever since. She is married to Don Veach and has two (wonderful, of course) children: Luke (17) and Christy (15).

Originally, Joan earned her teaching certificate so that she would have a skill that she could use on the mission field, because Don thought that he might be able to use his flying skills in mission aviation. The course of their lives did not go that way (yet), so Joan worked in two different Christian schools. When Luke was 2 years old, she heard Dr. Raymond Moore on the Focus on the Family radio program. She listened with fascination as he described homeschooling, and was immediately hooked!

Along the way, Joan has taught workshops and classes for homeschooling parents, both locally and at the state homeschool convention. To help homeschoolers satisfy the law requiring annual testing, she founded Lewis River Educational Services, which offered the necessary testing. In addition, for eight years, she taught a class that equipped parents to fulfill the legal requirements for educating their children at home.

Glimpses: two children playing with a tree frog they found in the wood pile (while I work in our home office); family vacations to interesting places (plus, every museum and visitor's center along the way); driving from Seattle to Boise (reviewing math facts out loud, pretending it is a game); forts in the living room made out of couch cushions, (drama, don't you know!)...

We started homeschooling when the children were born. With Luke at 17 and Christy at 15, we are on the downhill side now. When I think back to the "early days," there are several ideas, or ways of thinking about education, that stand out as pivotal to our homeschooling philosophy. First, since I had worked as a classroom teacher, I had to reevaluate many of the strategies I used in the classroom. Instead of focusing on paper products that "prove" that the children learned something, I found that I could easily evaluate most of their learning by asking questions and saying, "Explain that to me," or "Show me." My friend and mentor, Diana McAlister, from Arlington, Washington, taught me to study my children and learn to recognize when learning was taking place. She told me, "Learning does not require a book. Learn to recognize learning and encourage it." For example, when Luke was playing with Legos he was using his analytical ability and creativity. When we discussed an article in a magazine or a news account, we were discussing principles of science, or politics, or geography. When the two children were building forts in the living room, they were participating in creative dramatics at a level that would make a classroom teacher green with envy. Money management skills were learned while budgeting their allowance. The list goes on.

Second, reading Mary Pride helped me clarify a concept that I knew, but had never consciously put into words. She referred to "closed" and "open" subjects. A closed subject is finite—when you have learned it, you do not have to learn it over again, but you will be applying it for the rest of your life. Basic skills, such as learning the times tables and other math facts, or the rules for grammar, capitalization, and punctuation are examples of closed subjects. Once the children have learned them, you do not have to keep teaching them, but you do need to review them, and more importantly, apply them. An open subject is something like history, science, music, or literature. You could study these the rest of your life and never master them. I tried to budget enough time to teach the basic skills, but, once they learned them, I shifted to spending as much time as possible on the open subjects.

Another foundational principle that carried me through those years, and that paved the way for junior high and high school studies, was to ask, "What is really important?" Being able to recognize, "This is good learning," gave me the confidence to let them play all afternoon with the tree frog. After they found the frog and put him in a safe container, we talked about where he lived, what he ate, etc. Then they spent an hour building a popsicle stick "raft" that would fit in my largest mixing bowl. They were so disappointed when that frog kept jumping off the raft. Of course, that led into another discussion. As far as I was concerned, they had spent the afternoon studying biology, applied physics, and psychology!

Many homeschool parents I talk to say that they want their children to learn to think, not just regurgitate information. I felt the same way. Let me share with you something I learned in school that was really helpful on this issue. A professor named Bloom devised a system to help understand the level of difficulty of students' thinking. Called Bloom's Taxonomy, it is a scale of thinking skills. Dr. Bloom identified six levels of student mental activity—

Recall, Comprehension, Application, Analysis, Synthesis, Evaluation—and arranged them from simplest to most complex. Bloom's Taxonomy helped me to recognize when my children were "really thinking," not just "regurgitating." It helped me answer my questions about, "What is really important?" and "Are they learning anything?"

According to this scale, the simplest level of thinking is recall, or remembering facts and details. It is assessed using questions like, "What color was the truck?" or, "What is 2 x 2?" The next level is comprehension. "Do you understand what I said?" or "Do you understand what you read?" In textbooks, most questions at the end of the chapter are written at these two levels because they allow the classroom teacher to assess whether the children actually read the piece. However, there is much more to "really thinking." After your students understand something, can they apply that knowledge to something else? If you have ever asked your child to draw a picture of what happened, or to act something out, you were leading them to the application level. This would also include applying a story from the Bible to daily life, or a topic from history to a current situation.

The levels that follow are hard work, and we need to recognize them as such and reward the effort they take! The analysis level causes the student to ask questions of the materials or concepts he is studying. Your children are working at this level when they scrutinize a piece of writing to distinguish the author's bias, or to identify his purpose for writing. If they are able to debate both sides of an issue, or to design an experiment to test an hypothesis, they are working at the analysis level.

Interestingly, I found that the easiest way to prompt my children to function at this level was to discuss things with them. I think that we, as homeschool moms, sometimes fall into the trap of believing, "If it is not on paper, it does not count." Remember the question, "Are they learning anything?" Discussion is often the best way to find out.

The fifth level is synthesis, or creating. At this level the student is composing, or drawing, or writing, or building, or planning, or designing, etc.—doing something that is new to him or her. As I mentioned, these levels are hard work, and yet, children get here by themselves when they build something new with Legos (not copying the picture), or when they sing a song that is all their own, or use color in a new way. Understanding the synthesis level is what gave me the confidence to let my children play with the frog, or build forts out of couch cushions. Not that this is what they did every day—we had our share of basic skill practice and read aloud time—but, if they were doing something really creative, my motto was: get out of their way!

The highest level, according to Dr. Bloom, is evaluation. Activities that lead to this level include assessing, selecting, or judging material based on specific standards and criteria. We are at this level when we ask our children not only to apply a Bible story to a situation, but also to determine the underlying principle and to make good choices based on biblical standards.

Your librarian can help find a copy of Bloom's Taxonomy you can read. Some versions are very wordy explanations, some are more in outline form. Possibly, you will need a little of both to really make it your own.

Homeschooling, for my family and me, has been a journey with some slow, rough spots and some easy, level spots, just as it is for many of you. Each year, as we began planning for the next, we looked to the future, considering our long-range goals for our children. We also looked to the past to see what had been successful and whether I had dropped the ball anywhere. With those two views in mind, we made course corrections and forged ahead. Of course, the uniqueness and individuality of our children threw in regular surprises. Who would have guessed that Christy's love of water would lead to scuba diving lessons with her father, or that her skill in sewing would lead to a source of income for summer missions trips? I never imagined, as I sat with Luke grinding out piano practice for all those years, that the music the Lord had put in his soul would come out in original composition and worship leading in church. My advice to all of you, whether just getting started, or several years along the journey: keep on keeping on! It is not always easy, but it is worth every bit of effort you pour into it!

Running the Homeschooling Marathon

——— *Steve and Jane Claire Lambert* ———

Steve and Jane are the classic high school sweethearts. Married at 21, they recently celebrated their twenty-seventh anniversary. Together, they have been homeschooling since 1982. With a grandmother who owned a private preschool and a mother who taught first grade for more than thirty years, perhaps it was inevitable that Jane would end up as an educator, too.

The Lamberts' sixteen years of teaching experience and their lifelong love of children's literature, have combined to give birth to Before Five in a Row *for children ages 2 to 4 and* Five in a Row *for children ages 4 to 8. Jane's articles have appeared in various homeschooling magazines including* Homeschooling Today. *Each year Steve speaks to thousands of homeschoolers at numerous state homeschool conventions from coast to coast. He also manages the day-to-day operations of* Five in a Row Publishing. *The Lamberts maintain a very active Web site and message boards at: www.fiveinarow.com.*

Their older daughter, Becky, is the author and creator of Beyond Five in a Row *for ages 8 to 12. Their younger daughter, Carrie, is finishing her last year of homeschooling while taking several college classes, before attending college full-time next year. She, too, plans to continue working in the family homeschool business.*

After sixteen years of homeschooling, the two most important concepts we wish we had known at the beginning are that homeschool is not "school at home" and that real education is a marathon—not a sprint.

As we began the homeschooling experience, we were so easily overwhelmed by the pressure to produce academic achievement that we often lost perspective, focusing on the daily ups and downs instead of enjoying the journey. It became all too tempting to conclude we were failing after a particularly bad day, instead of focusing on long-term goals. The criticism of our culture and the concern of well-intentioned friends and family only fed the flames of our own anxieties. The result was too often a headlong rush toward academic accomplishment which left us tired and frustrated, and our children disheartened.

We somehow believed that "homeschool" was "school at home" and, understandably, attempted to adopt classroom methodology and schedules into our homeschool. We wrongly assumed that textbooks and workbooks and tests were the only way to teach a child. Likewise, we assumed that school must begin at 8:00 in the morning and move relentlessly toward that 3:30 bell. And, perhaps worst of all, we assumed that because we lacked professional training as educators we were going to have to work twice as hard to achieve the same results as classroom teachers.

All of these assumptions were understandable since we, like nearly all adults today, had only one educational paradigm upon which to model our teaching style—our own childhood experience in school. It was nearly impossible in that first year or two to think "outside the box" and to look for educational solutions which were beyond our very limited experience. In hindsight, our experience was not unlike that of many homeschoolers.

The result of our limited experience and our anxieties was too often predictable. More days than not we found ourselves locked in a battle of wills with children who did not want to fill out yet another workbook page, or take yet another test. What had promised to be a joyous experience together was quickly becoming a difficult struggle to climb an increasingly steep uphill grade. Ironically, the very anxiety we felt to produce academic achievement was working against us—our children were increasingly disinterested in learning. The entire experience threatened to implode if we couldn't find a more workable model on which to base our homeschool structure.

After a year or two of failing in our attempt to bring "school" home, we decided, out of desperation, it was time to try something else. While we continued to use traditional classroom methodology for core subjects such as arithmetic, phonics, and spelling, at the same time we began exploring different approaches to teaching in areas such as history, geography, science, art, and creative writing. We stopped staring so intently at the clock and filling out endless workbook pages, and began to simply enjoy what we were reading and discussing together. "School" became a daily adventure filled with outdoor rambles, trips to the library, pleasant rainy afternoon discussions, experiments, cooking, singing, and games. Out of desperation, we had stumbled upon what we now think of as "homeschooling."

The whole atmosphere was much more relaxed, less intense. Suddenly, it did not even feel like "school" anymore. Instead, for the first time, we began to experience the joy of learning. Any fleeting feelings of guilt we may have encountered in this new, more relaxed atmosphere quickly disappeared as we began to see the results. Almost immediately, our children stopped resisting school and became willing participants. We suddenly found ourselves having intelligent, meaningful discussions with them about important ideas and concepts. It became apparent that our children were not only grasping important truths, but retaining that information. Even more amazing was their ability to apply this new information to life and to relate it to other new concepts. They were actually beginning to learn!

A friend used to say, "If a little is good then more is better and way too much is just right!" Never was that *less* true than in homeschooling. We soon discovered that our anxiety-driven rush to push so much upon our children academically was actually self defeating. Suddenly, a new view of education emerged, and we discovered that, sometimes, less is more. We found ourselves spending less time having "school" and more time learning; less time filling out workbook pages, and more time discovering the world around us. Slowly, day by day, a new model began to emerge of what real learning was all about. Our old paradigm of "school at home" began to dissolve as we focused on learning instead of on having school.

We also found ourselves taking more time for recreation and relationships. We began taking more field trips and spending less time in the classroom each week. Our children needed time to run and breathe and play and discover God's amazing world around them. What would begin as a picnic over the noon hour, would often turn into an entire afternoon of science as we explored ant colonies, flowers, clouds and more. These impromptu field trips led us to the library again and again where, suddenly, the children were taking the initiative in finding books about ants or flowers or weather. They were becoming active participants in their own education. Learning became something that they did instead of something that was done to them.

Over the next few years, independent standardized testing confirmed what we already knew in our hearts: our children were learning much more than their peers. We spent hours reading aloud with our children. In one year alone, we calculated we read more than forty thousand pages aloud with our children, exploring the wonderful world of children's literature, including Laura Ingalls Wilder, Lois Lenski, Arleta Richardson, C.S. Lewis, and dozens of others. Our children developed a lifelong love of reading, and their test scores improved dramatically in many areas, including reading comprehension, vocabulary, and creative writing. After a year or two of confining ourselves to desks, textbooks, workbooks, and examinations, the entire world suddenly became our classroom, and each day was a learning adventure rather than "going to school."

We made another important discovery at the same time. It became increasingly apparent that the tutorial system of education was much more efficient than a classroom. We discovered that one parent working with one or two children could accomplish in twenty minutes what might take several hours to achieve with twenty-eight students in a classroom. The constant feedback as we looked into our children's eyes instantly confirmed whether or not they were grasping important concepts. Our daily dialogues with them were a sort of continuing test, demonstrating clearly whether there were any gaps in their understanding.

After several years of seeing textbooks as goals to be completed and tests as targets to be hit, these became more of a baseline upon which to build. We were delighted to discover that our children were learning concepts and information literally years before they would have covered it via textbooks. Standardized testing confirmed that they were often many years ahead of the norms created from classroom data. Most amazing of all was that these achievements were taking place in a relaxed environment without the pressure and frustration we had formerly experienced.

As we near the end of our homeschooling career, it is obvious that the more relaxed, marathon approach to homeschooling was successful. What began as a frenzied sprint to do "school at home" became a long, pleasant journey to help our children enjoy the world around them and to discover their place within that world. Along the way, they became well-rounded, socially adept adults, able to speak articulately, interact with others, play musical instruments, pursue team sports, and more.

It was when we abandoned trying to do "school at home," and began truly "homeschooling," that real learning began to take place at last. It was only through the long, paced marathon of homeschooling, rather than the frenzied sprint of daily classroom activity, that our homeschooling experience became the rich, rewarding family activity that we had dreamed of in the beginning.

What Are You Doing to My Grandchild!?

—— *Stacy Mhyre* ——

Stacy was born and raised in Washington state and attended Western Washington University, majoring in elementary education, minoring in English. She married Stewart Mhyre in 1984. They have four children: Brendan (12), Philip (11), Callison (7 ½), and Caleb (4). The Mhyre family lives on a small farm in Ferndale, where they are raising their children and a menagerie of animals (horses, pygmy goats, sheep, chickens, rabbits, cats, and a faithful farm dog!).

As a certified teacher who is now homeschooling, Stacy has been especially interested in providing professional educational assistance for the homeschool community in her area. Her tutoring and educational assessment service for homeschoolers, T.E.A.C.H. (Tutoring & Educational Assessments for Children at Home), offers, along with tutoring, a non-test educational assessment for homeschooling parents who prefer their children not be tested utilizing standardized tests. Stacy also provides private piano lessons.

Being a mom continues to be her most noteworthy accomplishment. Being able to teach her own children at home is one of her greatest delights! Stacy has enjoyed the opportunity to speak at her local homeschooling support group about curriculum. She also enjoys working with families whose children have been in the school system and who are being taken out of school for the first time. She provides mentoring about curriculum and learning styles, as well as encouragement through the transitions from school to homeschool.

You have done it. For whatever reason, you have had it with the "system," and you are taking your child out of school in order to homeschool.

Congratulations!! You have mastered perhaps the hardest part of homeschooling: making the decision to do it! Every homeschooling parent has had to make that very same decision. At various times during your homeschooling experience, you will come back to some of those same questions: "Can I really homeschool?" or "Do I want to keep homeschooling?" or "If it's not done by this Friday, I'm calling your old school and reenrolling you! Do we have an understanding!?"

There are many issues and decisions relating to homeschooling you will face, but having resolved the most difficult decision, whether or not to do it, you can now consider four of the most common areas of frustration new homeschoolers face: socialization, learning styles and curriculum, time management, and reading.

The "S" Question: "What about Socialization?"

It only takes one well-meaning "friend" to plant seeds of doubt as to whether or not you have made the right decision. And those seeds can quickly grow! Usually, those skeptics are primarily concerned with your child's socialization, not with your child's academic achievement. Our answer to these well-meaning friends has always been, "Who would you prefer to have socialize your 6-year-old child: a close-knit, loving family, or thirty other 6-year-olds? Who will best model and mold your child's behavior and etiquette in those formative years?" (Use this answer whenever you are faced with the "S" question and insert whatever age your child happens to be—it works just as well for teenagers!)

This issue came to us shortly after our first child was born. We decided to homeschool when he was not quite 2 years old. And, as the title of this article declares, my parents' reaction was: "What are you doing to my grandchild!?" It was a very emotional situation for me. ("You just graduated with a teaching degree and now you are not going to even use it?") For the life of me, though, I could not imagine putting my own child into school, so that I could go out and teach other people's kids! With time, my family has moved from somewhat hostile skepticism to acceptance and support. Hopefully, your skeptical friends and relatives will, too!

Perhaps, your child is the one giving you grief about being taken out of school and away from friends. If "negative socialization" was one of the reasons you pulled your child out of school, it will take more work on your part to provide the opportunities to meet new friends. Local homeschool associations, 4-H clubs, church youth groups, and a network of relationships you will build with other homeschool families can provide opportunities for new friendships.

Learning Styles and Curriculum: Sorting through Volumes of Information

If you are not already overloaded with books on homeschooling, my advice for early reading would be to find a book about learning styles. I wish I had read this information before I started homeschooling! As a teacher, I had lots of ideas about curriculum, but I never knew much about different learning styles, or about choosing curriculum to match your child's learning style. Then, when I realized we were battling over school work more than we were accomplishing school work, I read a book about learning styles. I found out that my child's style of learning and the use of workbooks did *not* fit together! I had loved workbooks when I was in school! When I read about learning styles, though, I realized that I had the freedom to choose curriculum that would be responsive to my child's learning strengths and weaknesses.

When you are selecting curriculum, you do not always have to select materials to meet your child's strengths—we cannot always go through life learning things the easy way! However, if your child has struggled academically, it is very likely that his learning style was not compatible with the "read, review, regurgitate" method most common in the school systems! Discover your child's learning style preferences, and you will be on the road to reawakening your child's joy of learning!

Time Management and Homeschooling

Some may tell you that time management and homeschooling create an oxymoron—a combination of contradictory terms. My advice to new homeschoolers about setting up a schedule: be flexible! This is one of the beautiful things I have learned about homeschooling.

Like a good teacher, I had my first two (ages 5 and 6) in class 9:30–3:30, Monday through Friday. I even bought lunch boxes for them! I planned "this much time" for reading (Don't they always do reading first thing in the morning at school!); "this much time" for social studies (Have you ever asked a teacher to define "social studies"?); "this much time" for language arts; don't forget, math, music, science, art, P.E. (P.E. class with two students!?). My poor children!

A change hit me one day during lunch recess, when my 5-year-old came in from the backyard with a beetle in his hand. "Mom, I found a deaf beetle."

"How do you know it's deaf, dear?"

"I've shouted at it and banged big rocks next to it, and it doesn't move or wiggle. Do beetles even have ears?"

Picture the light bulb coming on over my head! For the first time in my homeschooling efforts, I saw what we call a "teachable moment." We put his beetle in a box and began looking through some of our science books. Finding nothing about beetles in our own collection of books, we headed for the public library to find some insect books. We found out *lots* about beetles, but nothing about their hearing and senses. So, we headed up to the science section at the university library! Even they could not help us answer our question! We never did find out the answer to that question, but that day was a turning point in our homeschooling. We had gone looking for answers to a question together, and had a great time discovering.

The lesson I learned that day was to listen to my children's questions and to help them discover the answers. It required a great deal of "letting go" on my part, what we call flexibility—but the joy of discovery was born in our homeschool that day!

Another comparison about time management: Do you remember potty-training? Was your child agreeable to giving up diapers and using the bathroom? (M&M's, jelly beans, stickers, potty trucks, you name it, we tried it! They didn't work!) Your first efforts at homeschooling, just like your first efforts at potty-training, may need to be revised—several times! Flexibility is just one of the many blessings of homeschooling. Do not be afraid to try things differently, or try them again at a later date!

Reading: When Do You Teach It?

I do not know! The time frame varies from child to child. If there were one tried and true, proven method for teaching reading to every child, wouldn't all the schools be using it? We have yet to buy a reading curriculum—it was the one thing I did not purchase in those earlier years of our homeschooling. Yet our third child has just begun reading. We read together often, and always have. We model reading; we answer their questions; we haul as many books out of the library as we can manage.

If you have a child who does not like to read, for whatever reason, that will be the first obstacle to overcome. Many of the schools will have taught your child using the "whole language approach," or the sight word/word recognition approach. Your child may have heard someone say, "Sound it out," but will have never learned how to actually say the sounds. If your child has had problems in school with reading (which means there have also been problems in other subject areas because reading is so integral to all of learning), I would recommend a phonics review. Whatever interests that child (we have one who loves reading nutritional labels, and another discovered mysteries), find some reading material about it, or ask the librarian for recommendations.

Through all the obstacles you have faced in your decision to homeschool, the most difficult decision has now been made. You are a homeschooling parent! Yes, it's a large responsibility, and there are many decisions you will have to make along the way. The great news is that you are not alone! Many have already "been there and done that," and we are here to tell you it's exciting, fulfilling, challenging, and extremely rewarding, in spite of any obstacles life may send your way!

— Part 2 —

The Basics

Great Books Produce Great Minds

—————— *Valerie Bendt* ——————

Valerie and her husband Bruce have been married since 1978. They have home educated their six children since birth. As of summer 1998, their children are: Michelle (19), Melissa (17), Robert (15), Raymond (13), Mandy (9), and Randall (3). The Bendt family resides in Tampa, Florida, where they have lived for the last thirteen years. Valerie's credentials: she is a full-time, professional mom.

I am a Professional

I am a professional,
And I hold a high degree,
My clients are but children,
And they're very dear to me.

I work extended hours,
And the pay is not too fair,
But the benefits are great!
No other job compares.

So as I look around me,
And see women at their jobs,
I gladly claim the title,
"Full-time, Professional Mom."

by Valerie Bendt

Valerie has written the following books pertaining to home education: How to Create your Own Unit Study, The Unit Study Idea Book, Success With Unit Studies, For the Love of Reading, The Frances Study Guide, and Creating Books With Children. *Valerie has also produced audio cassette workshop tapes:* "How to Create Your Own Unit Study Workshop" *(ninety minutes) and* "Teaching Tips" *(three forty-five-minute tapes). She currently has two new books in production. Valerie is a frequent seminar speaker at homeschool conventions.*

People often say to me, "Well, it's fine to read all those books with your children, but how do you find the time?" Reading great books must be our first educational priority. Let the textbooks and workbooks take second, or even third, place. I believe that the education of homeschool children would be enhanced if an entire school year were taken off to focus on reading excellent literature.

When I was pregnant with my fifth child, I had an opportunity to test this theory. It was not by choice, but by necessity, that we implemented this mode of learning. I was sick almost the entire pregnancy and spent much of the time in bed. (One of my teenage sons relates now that all of his memories of me during that period are horizontal.) The children gathered in my bed and listened to me read aloud for hours, though, I admit, I worried that they might suffer academically. The opposite proved to be true as I observed that their vocabulary, thinking, and composition skills soared. When it was time for annual testing, their reading, spelling, and math scores had actually improved. This was enough proof for me: exposure to great literature stimulates the mind. Since that time, literature has held a high position in our home.

It is whether we, as parents, value reading that determines whether our children will be attracted to reading. Parental involvement and absorption in reading relates directly to the child's ability and desire to learn to read. In other words, the more involved the parent is, the more interested the child will be.

My strong belief in the value of sharing great literature with my children is confirmed again and again as I study the works of educators such as Ruth Beechick, Charlotte Mason, and Susan Schaeffer MacCaulay. Reading widely not only helps to stimulate our children's academic abilities, but it stimulates their creative abilities as well. Sharing great books with our children—books teaming with life—provides an avenue for creative activity. Reading these books together allows us to spend precious time with our children while strengthening their academic and creative skills.

A good book will transport us to another place and time and help us to become intimately acquainted with great individuals—real heroes and heroines. A biography offers us an opportunity to tread in another person's footsteps, enabling us to share in their triumph, defeat, anguish, and jubilation. Even a well-crafted fictional character may offer us a glimpse of true heroism. I treasure memories of my children acting out characters from classics such as *Pilgrim's Progress, Heidi, Swiss Family Robinson,* and *The Secret Garden.* The majority of children today spend more time watching TV and videos than they do absorbing good literature. They are generally held hostage by cookie cutter heroes (pressed out of an inferior mold) formed by the latest TV or movie craze. One cannot walk down the aisles of a store without being bombarded by this mediocrity. I think that over-stimulation from the media has squelched our children's natural inquisitiveness so that they settle for the mundane and the mediocre. I will grant that some videos and TV programs have good things to offer and are not to be discounted entirely. However, we should not allow the good things to crowd out the best things.

Follow a plan of reading aloud that introduces new levels of difficulty as the child develops. Begin with picture books for young children. Bright pictures focus the child's attention while still leaving much to the imagination—more so than videos, which bombard them with fast moving pictures and sounds. Picture books also help young children develop an appreciation for art while building a familiarity with the rhythm and flow of our language. As children mature they will enjoy other types of books: fantasy, fiction, non-fiction, poetry, biographies, and more.

My children have learned to enjoy literature from an early age. It is exciting for me to see that literature continues to hold a place of high importance for my teenagers. Recently, my 17 year old daughter, Melissa, said to me, "One of my goals in life is to read all of the classics. I think I have a pretty good start so far." We then discussed our favorite authors and books, and she commented, "I'm interested in reading books that were written at least a hundred years ago. Most of the books that are being written today can't compare with these, so why waste my time?"

Years of learning alongside my children have taught me the value of reading great books with them. By "great books," I mean books that stimulate the mind and arouse the heart. Great books help us to grow intellectually and spiritually. They allow us to experience loyalty, courage, honesty, truth, wisdom, and other enduring qualities through the creative expression of the author. Great books are of outstanding literary quality.

I wish that I had realized the importance of reading literature with my children earlier in my homeschooling experience. It is so easy to be caught up in completing this textbook or that workbook to the point that meaningful education is pushed aside. Reading great books with our children has provided us with many wonderful educational experiences, and reading from an early age has prepared them to begin formal reading instruction.

As my children play I am reminded of the positive influence of literature in their lives. Last year when my youngest daughter, Mandy, was 7 years old, she began taking piano lessons. This sparked an interest in the lives of the great composers, so we read more than twenty biographies. Some were the easy-reader type, which she could read to me, while others were more lengthy books which I read to her. I was amazed at how she kept the events of the different composer's lives so neatly sorted.

This enthusiasm flowed over into her playtime where she centered her activities around a composer's era. She managed to draw her 3-year-old brother, Randall, into her pretend world. I recall one day in particular when they were totally absorbed in their play. I rushed into the bedroom because we were hurrying to leave for an appointment, and there they stood—coats on (in the heat of summer) and suitcases in hand. I abruptly commanded, "Hurry up! We are going to be late for the orthodontist. Take off these things, and get into the van."

Mandy and Randall took no notice of me. I repeated my orders. Then Mandy said, in an emphatic tone, "He's Mozart and I'm Nannerl. Mozart's performing at a concert tonight in Vienna. We must be off to Vienna at once!" "I'm sorry," I said, "Mozart can have his concert when we come back home. We must go to the orthodontist *now*."

My teenage son, Robert, was listening from the hallway. He burst into the bedroom, exclaiming, "Nannerl, Mozart, we must hurry! The last coach leaves for Vienna in five minutes!"

Without a word, the two little waifs, with coats on and suitcases in hand, ran outside and jumped into the van. I stood silently in the bedroom for a few moments, until my son put his hand on my shoulder and said, "Mom, you just have to meet them in their world."

I encourage you to begin producing great minds as you assist your children in creating worlds of their own. A great book is a gateway into such golden worlds.

Hanging Haman:
Exploring the Bible One Day a Week

———— *Madelaine Smith* ————

Madelaine was raised in the public schools of Dallas, Texas, and completed high school in the Seattle area. She met her husband, Greg, at Western Washington University, marrying in 1978 during her senior year. Greg finished his M.Div. at Regent College nearby, and they remained at WWU as campus ministers for the next eight years. The Smiths then moved to The Evergreen State College in Olympia where Greg has been the campus minister for almost eleven years.

Homeschooling began for the Smith family in 1985 when Alyssa was age 4. She has now been accepted and will attend Pomona College, beginning the fall of 1998. Michelle began one year later at the same age and has two more years of high school to complete at home.

Madelaine has encouraged numerous parents as they decided to homeschool. She has loved her thirteen years of homeschooling and, as she's seen the girls mature and accomplish goals so successfully, she enthusiastically continues to assist others in teaching their children at home.

The girls woke up excited. Today would be the culmination of their homeschool Bible class on Esther. Stuffed bears, dogs, kitties, and bunnies had already been selected for the personality types that most resembled the characters in Esther. The collection of stuffed animals had been fitted into lace skirts, red ties, dresses, and strings chosen from baskets of small clothes. Now, the girls needed only to collaborate on the final details before their stuffed animal rendition of the entire book of Esther could be presented.

We had studied one chapter of Esther from the Bible each Friday for the past few months. One of the main advantages of homeschooling for us was the chance to take time to explore subjects. We did not have to be rushed through a forty-minute class, review yesterday's homework, remember where we left off from the previous assignments, or discuss a brief new section and then do a little work. At home, we could do one subject a day, and that's what we did for the first eight years. Math was our exception since the girls, 8 and 9 years old, felt their brains might explode if they did several math lessons a day. Since they were usually only required to do every third math problem anyway, math did not take much time, so we still had about two hours to do our one big subject and finish by lunchtime, a goal we maintained until high school.

After perusing numerous Bible curricula, I decided I did not want them to get sermons or publishers' opinions; I wanted them to know the Bible. So, beginning in second grade, we read through one chapter a week and casually discussed it as we went along. Then, my two students, Alyssa and Michelle, helped think of creative ways to show they understood what we had read.

To begin their study of Esther, they read the entire book, ten short chapters, to themselves, and then together they gave me a brief, ten-minute oral summary of the highlights.

For week two, after we read the first chapter of Esther aloud and discussed King Xerxes' banquet, they each wrote a page long summary. Next week, for the episode about Queen Vashti's refusal to be flaunted for her beauty, and of King Xerxes' subsequent fear that women would be disrespectful of their husbands throughout the land, they wrote a modern, parallel story which followed a similar plot and theme.

On week four, they made a list of all the characteristics they could find which described the main people: Mordecai's being kind, brave, and loyal; Xerxes as demanding, unfair, selfish, and sociable; Esther as submissive, understanding, trustworthy, and dependent; and, Vashti being stubborn and independent yet hospitable. This helped us look beyond the facts so we could grasp the interpretation of the Scripture, making the assignment more difficult.

The following week the girls each outlined the chapter about Haman's plot to destroy the Jews, selecting the main points, subheadings, and details. These assignments provided different writing experiences, a chance for them to have input in their assignments, and variety in their daily school routines. For about ten years, they studied an excellent language arts program by Alpha Omega. It is inexpensive and very easy to teach. It includes reading assignments, grammar, punctuation, handwriting, poetry, critical thinking, creative writing, letter writing, and all the other skills needed to become a master of the English language. Their English curriculum gave them a solid foundation, while our Bible discussions enabled me to guide their thinking and view of life. The workbooks taught them needed skills and knowledge; Bible class gave them an opportunity to apply that knowledge of the language, be creative, and have fun.

When we got to chapter four of Esther, they wanted to do a play on Mordecai's exhortation and Esther's courage. First, they wrote a brief sketch of the play which we discussed and revised. Then they went to their rooms to practice their parts. After a few minutes, they called the teacher and principal (mom and dad), and performed their humorous skit. They sketched a cartoon sequence for chapter five about Esther's carrying out her conviction to the king, with Haman's subsequent anger and plot against Mordecai. Though not good artists, drawing gave them an opportunity for expression outside their normal thinking process. It was a challenge to get them to do that which was not natural, though they liked getting out newspapers and reading cartoons to get ideas. Not every new approach would work as well, but often it would open new doors inside them, and they would want to repeat the assignment over and over again.

For Esther six, I wrote out questions about Haman, King Xerxes, and Haman's wife, Zeresh. These were to help the girls think about the characters, and about what was revealed by their actions. Haman was arrogant and wanted to be exalted; but it resulted in his humiliation, and the exaltation of his enemy, Mordecai. In Esther seven, Haman was hanged, and the girls were tired. They just wanted to do a simple, no-brainer assignment, and, since my patience was short, I said that would be fine. They wrote a summary by listing what had happened. As usual with a written assignment, we read them aloud, discussed them, and made any necessary corrections. Their writings varied between factual, funny, insightful, boring, and fascinating, depending on their moods and personalities.

In chapter eight, the king issued the second edict in the book. The first was to annihilate the Jews, and the second was to warn them, so they could avenge themselves. The girls drew pictures of both edicts, including the signet with which the documents were sealed. These pictures helped them remember details of the Scripture. Esther nine was the battle of the Jews striking down their enemies and Purim. Of course, it needed to be acted out in a play. We called a Jewish friend and discussed how Purim is still celebrated among the Jews to remember the day when Queen Esther, Mordecai, and King Xerxes saved their people.

We came down to two weeks before spring break, when it was time to summarize the book of Esther. Being a book of history, it seemed easy to retell the story as a play. They wrote an outline of the entire book of Esther, going through their Bible page by page to be sure they remembered it all. They chatted and discussed various dialogue possibilities, and concluded with a general idea for their play, which would be presented on one exciting day the next week.

Their final school day arrived. The girls had decided to let their stuffed animals do the acting. They chose from among their stuffed animals the ones they felt best represented each central character of Esther. Their big panda bear was Mordecai; their beautiful, pink, musical bear was chosen for Queen Esther;

Tigger represented King Xerxes; and their cute, pink bunny was cast as the proud Queen Vashti. The cast of characters was filled out with many stuffed animals dressed in appropriate doll clothes, ropes were secured for the hanging of Haman, and the entry hall was prepared as a stage. The parents were summoned to attend, and were treated to a half hour we will all remember.

Bears were confronting Tigger, pink bears were getting beauty treatments, bunnies were disrespectful to the haughty Tigger, papers were unrolled as decrees were read, and battles were won by throwing animals to and fro. It was fabulous! They had remembered, with no script in front of them, the entire book of Esther and its importance in God's history.

We all had a wonderful time studying the Bible without tests, fill-in-the blank workbooks, or lectures. They will remember the sequence of events which transpired in the book of Esther the rest of their lives, and will think of Queen Esther as a woman to be respected, imitated, and followed.

As we continued to study many other narrative books, including Luke, Ruth, Acts, Joshua, and Genesis, they practiced many of these same study methods. As the girls got older, we studied the more didactic books including Proverbs, Romans, Ecclesiastes, Revelations, Ephesians, and John's Epistles. These were studied more in-depth, with more sophisticated methods; but all taught them God's Word, gave them a chance to think about life, to see God's character, to understand Jesus' salvation, and to be creative. Various assignments—including outlines; summaries; comparing similar scriptures; character studies; geography studies; cartoon sketches; poetry writing; memorization; studying the customs, social groups, or metaphors in the passage; and plays and puppet shows—gave them different methods to learn observation, interpretation, and application of the Scriptures we studied.

I am glad that we took one day each week of homeschooling to study the Bible, and that we took time for it to be understood and become part of their lives for eternity.

As Arrows in the Hand:
Establishing Your Targets

———— *Ranell Curl* ————

David and Ranell have been romantically married for thirty years, living in rural Oregon for twenty-five of those years. Their two children graduated from their family's high school. Their daughter, Starr (29), holds degrees from Eugene Bible College and Northwest Christian College. She currently teaches pre-kindergarten and after-school club. Their son, Sky (25), earned degrees from Western States' College of Commerce. He is a project manager for a Portland trade show exhibit company.

Ranell has actively participated in her local home-school group, organizing a weekly co-op for forty children. She also has served on the board of Lane County's Inter-Christian Guild of Home Teachers (LIGHT), a support system of three hundred families, holding the position of president for three years. Ranell continues to minister as LIGHT's events coordinator and special projects coordinator for HIS Net (Homeschool Information and Service Network) of Oregon, a statewide organization.

The Curls own Custom Curriculum Company, which markets five thousand items for integrated studies and creative learning. Along with Starr, Ranell authored three manuals for historical unit studies: The Ancient World, The Middle Era, *and* United States History. *In the last eight years, hundreds of families have scheduled appointments to have her organize their own tailor-made unit studies. Ranell has presented workshops on various topics including "A Hands-on Walk through History," "An Introduction to Learning Styles and Temperaments," and "Options for Homeschooling Older Students." For fun, Ranell teaches swimming, coaches synchronized swimming, reads voraciously, and daydreams about the joys of grandchildren.*

Nine A.M. and my two children are sitting at the table ready to begin our adventure of homeschooling. I supervise as they labor through their workbooks and textbooks until 10:30, when we take a ten minute recess/break.

At noon, my husband, David, joins us for lunch, and then we complete our school day.

David and I had finally succumbed to our children's pleas to be taught at home. We all had great expectations of how uncomplicated and effective it would be. After all, we had embarked on this odyssey with all the "proper" equipment: appropriate texts for each school subject, lots of paper, pencils, and erasers, and a teacher's lesson plan book. What could possibly be missing?

What was missing was *real* education! After two years, we found we were just as frustrated with our attempts to do "school" as we had been with previous learning situations our children had been in. Like most parent/teachers, the only learning model we possessed was our own school experience where teachers taught subjects in compartmentalized and timed segments, fortified with textbooks full of dull facts, and where grading corresponded to the number of those facts a student recalled on test day. Did we really want our son to spend time memorizing dates related to the Assyrian Empire, or would we prefer he invest that time hiding God's Word in his heart? I found I was merely facilitating someone else's learning objectives for my children.

We chose to home instruct with the hope that our children would be better prepared for life, yet, we realized, we were merely getting through the books! What benefit was it to finish a particular textbook if the children had little recollection of the information? Or, even if the facts presented were retained past the test, were they valuable enough to apply in the future? During the second summer, our school went back to the drawing board—we needed to build a new foundation based on our own definition of "being educated."

Determining that definition was the first step toward becoming our school's administrators, rather than merely the curriculum selection committee. How would we be able to determine whether we had successfully aimed the arrows God gave us (Psalms 127:4), if we could not clearly see the target? We began with these fundamental questions: "As graduates of our home-school, what will our children need to know?" and "How will we prepare them to be able to appropriate needed information in the future?" We began prayerfully setting goals, somewhat haltingly at first, then, as we realized we truly did know what was most important for our children, with more confidence. We formulated a list of broad objectives on important topics and courses, then separated those into the segments to cover during each school year. This was the turning point of our home education experience.

Our goals covered each area of life for our children: spiritual, academic, physical, life skills, and employment. Examples of long-term objectives are: "ability to research a topic biblically," "know the flow of history and apply its lessons to current events," "maintain physical fitness," "learn to properly keep house," and "possess admirable work ethics." Some of the respective annual goals under those long-term objectives are: "become familiar with purpose of each section of Strong's Exhaustive Concordance of the Bible," "study achievements of ancient Romans," "calculate target heart rate and implement, three times a week, applicable exercise program," "learn to clean the kitchen (defrost and clean refrigerator, clean oven, etc.)," and "faithfully perform duties as neighborhood paper boy." These objectives and goals became our scope and sequence.

We had a clearly defined target, now we needed to determine the best method for taking aim and shooting our arrows. We read several books, especially from Mary Pride and Cathy Duffy, and talked with many other parent/teachers, culminating in the discovery that there are many different and inspiring methods for imparting knowledge to youngsters. When one removes the needs for controlling twenty-five students, using material created to be teacher-friendly (despite how tedious it might be for most students), and fitting it all into tidy little time frames agreed upon by school administrators and teachers' unions, there were profuse options!

In deciding what would be most effective for our family, David and I contemplated our own frustrating school experiences. In public school, one of us had succeeded while the other had struggled, yet even the "A-student" parent lacked academic confidence. Although the familiar public school model seemed easiest to administer, neither of us felt it resulted in the type of thinking, reasoning individual that we yearned for our offspring to become. We also considered several other factors: my strengths and weaknesses as a teacher (since I was to handle all subjects except devotions), our children's individual learning styles and needs, and previously acquired resources we enjoyed.

We decided to learn together as a family through the "unit study method." Unit studies take a central theme and link as many other subjects as possible to it. In doing a unit study on Ancient Egypt, for example, a family might employ some of the following:

Bible: Read portions extending from the time of Joseph's becoming an Egyptian slave to the Hebrews crossing the Jordan River. Study the significance of Passover (first instituted while Hebrews were Egyptian slaves.)

Memory Verses: Genesis 50:20 or the Ten Commandments.

History: Check out a well-illustrated library book on Egypt; read encyclopedia articles; do internet searches.

Geography: Do a survey of Egyptian terrain, emphasizing deserts and Nile River; research plant and animal life (crocodiles and hippopotami are favorites); read "Journey Up the Nile," *National Geographic*, May 1985.

Art Appreciation: Study pyramids, profile painting, and Egyptian sculpting style; build a sugar cube pyramid or clay Sphinx.

Music Appreciation: Study Egyptian instruments; listen to Verdi's Opera, *Aida*, set in ancient Egypt.

Crafts/Field Trips: Make paper; embalm chicken; make up eyes (besides beauty, this gave protection from sun's glare); bake barley/date cakes; visit zoo (Pharaoh Hatsheput created the first zoo).

Science: Study the Egyptian invention of the 365-day calendar; study the simple machinery used in constructing pyramids and treasure cities.

Literature: Read aloud as a family *The Golden Goblet*, by McGraw; locate appropriate individual reading: *Croconile*, by Gerrard; *Bill and Pete Go Down the Nile*, by de Paolo; *Mummies Made in Egypt*, by Aliki; *The Everyday Life of an Egyptian Craftsman*, by Caselli; *Queen Cat*, by Turnbull; *Tirzah*, by Travis; *Moses, Born to Slavery* or *Joseph*, by Traylor; *Tales from Ancient Egypt*, by Green; *His Majesty, Queen Hatsheput*, by Carter; *The Egyptian*, by Waltari.

Penmanship: Write memory verse in perfect handwriting; younger children copy only one letter or one word of verse.

Composition: Younger children: draw pyramid and caption with one word or sentence; intermediate: write descriptive paragraph about Sphinx and narrative paragraph or short stories set in Ancient Egypt; advanced: research and write biography of a particular pharaoh; write a play set in Egypt with parts for the entire family; present a speech on the evils of slavery; or write a eulogy for Jochebed.

Vocabulary/Spelling: Use words from your studies: asp, calendar, cataract, delta, embalm, hippopotamus, irrigation, lotus, papyrus, etc.

We employed world history units, focusing on our Judeo-Christian heritage, as the framework for the above-mentioned subjects. Our own experiences with social studies in public school had consigned us to total bewilderment as to how it all fit together. We knew we did not favor the same scattered approach for our children. We opted to trace "His-story" to modern time, allowing us to analyze such causes and effects as how Alexander the Great's conquests were a cornerstone to the Early Church's spread of the Gospel, and how the Crusades contributed to the advent of the Renaissance.

Our evaluation method was discussion, supplemented with occasional written compositions and semester essay tests featuring such questions as: "How is Constantine's choice of Byzantium for his capital city of Constantinople similar to George Washington's choice for our nation's capital?" and, "Do you think there are similarities between the Medieval feudal system and today's gap between rich and poor?" Our questions were designed to stimulate thoughtfulness and application, rather than rote learning and regurgitation. We continued to use textbooks for math. In the first year of implementation, not only did we see a marked change in our children's level of knowledge and demonstrated ability to apply that knowledge, but we saw our school week shrink from twenty-five hours to about twelve. This gave us time to pursue individual interests and activities.

The most important lesson of our first years was to stop trying to "do school"! We, as parents, needed to take the responsibility to set educational goals for our children, and then to decide the methodology best adapted to reach those goals. We must clearly see our target, and then we must take aim and shoot our arrows in our own unique style.

The author recommends these titles which she found helpful in setting goals: World Book Scope & Sequence K–12; *Teaching Children*, by Lopez; *What Your Child Needs to Know When*, by Scarlatta; *401 Ways to Get Your Kids to Work at Home*, by McCullough and Monson; *The Dictionary of Cultural Literacy*, by Hirsch; and *The HISNet Older Homeschooler Information Booklet* (at http://www.efn.org/~hisnet).

Strengths + Weaknesses =
Learning to Find Everything Intriguing

——— *Beverly Miller* ———

Beverly is the mother of two wonderful boys and a mother-in-law with the addition of Angela. She celebrated her twenty-fifth wedding anniversary the summer of 1998. Beverly grew up in the small town of Fox River Grove, Illinois, and has many wonderful memories of enjoying cousins and grandparents all around. When she was 11, her parents moved the family to Fairbanks, Alaska, as missionaries. There she really did walk a mile and a half to school each way in the −20° to −60° weather in complete darkness (although it was uphill only one way!).

It was in Fairbanks that Beverly met her husband, Tim, and married him right out of high school. (Remember, it was the last frontier!) This is also where she developed her creative skills running an Awana program for thirteen years, along with operating the local Christian bookstore for ten years. In 1987, the Lord moved the family to Auburn, Washington, where she began to homeschool their sons and, later, became a representative for Lifetime Books & Gifts.

Since the boys graduated from the Art Institute of Seattle, Beverly has helped set up a bookstore ministry with her church, Grace Community Church, in Auburn. She continues to encourage others who are wondering what it is like to homeschool, or are getting discouraged.

Astronomy! How can you teach a subject you barely remember covering twenty years ago, and which definitely held no interest for you—then or now? It needed to be done sooner or later, and, since I was in one of my more disciplined modes at the time, fortunately, I chose sooner.

Astronomy! The boys, at ages 11 and 13, were definitely not excited. Having only my high school education, a few used science textbooks of varying grade levels, a couple of old notebooks needing recovering, a love for making things fun, and a desire to give the boys the best education any teacher could ever give, I started our astronomy unit.

First, we took a trip to the largest library around, and checked out as many books on the subject as we could find. Being a firm believer that there are no grade levels to really great books, we chose anything from picture books to the encyclopedic type, throwing in a few biographies of famous astronomers for good measure. Then, as I scrambled to read ahead to become a little familiar with this dreaded subject, I had the boys draw their ideas for great astronomy book covers to use on their notebooks. They could take as long as they needed on the covers—I knew the process would get their creativity aroused. Of course, the longer they took, the more time I had for developing the science unit so I could stay a little ahead of the them.

The local library also had a list of 16mm films we could check out for our old, twenty-five-dollar projector. We still remember a catchy little song from one of the films to help students memorize the order of the planets. Part of it went like this, "My very educated mother just served us nine pizza pies." We laughed! Looking back, it would have been very effective to have also pre-pared nine pizza pies!

Following a week of talking together, reading books together, and discov-ering all sorts of exciting pieces of information, the boys came bounding into our bedroom one morning, straight from their early morning paper route. My husband and I could feel their excitement as each of them announced he wanted to become an astronomer. They really gave us a sense of their enthu-siasm as they described how much longer it took to get the paper route done, since it was so much fun to stop and just look at the stars. We were stunned to hear such a report after such a start.

The realization that I could pass on that kind of excitement to my boys on a subject, even one where I was weakest and least interested, was a real eye opener. This was the beauty of homeschooling, that we could take any subject and spark the sense of imagination and curiosity, learning to find everything intriguing. I had to be willing to learn new things and stretch myself. More importantly, I had to find ways to present each subject to them so they would continue to awaken that natural sense of curiosity and love for learning, and, consequently, become the unique men they were designed to be.

My high school education left me without much background knowledge, and with a dread for each new subject we started. With this new understand-ing of what homeschooling was all about, though, I continued to tackle each subject as it came along. Science was particularly tough—I couldn't even remember taking any science classes. With this in mind, I always put art into each science unit as much as possible. Mixing their strengths into my weakest areas greatly helped us to succeed.

It didn't take too long, through their art work and our "dig in and learn" philosophy of studying, before the boys had developed a science book series designed for kids. They decided that students should be exposed to the sciences early and with a captivating presentation. If we had a particularly difficult time grasping a topic, we would all read and study hard to master that topic so we could write another book. They produced an exciting detective book series that led students to crack the mysteries of science.

Obviously, the boys were demonstrating a strong talent in art. They also were showing great ability in developing and communicating through their own animated characters. For the next Christmas, my husband and I took the "old bathroom turned storage room" and transformed it into a real animation studio for their growing artistic interests. Unbeknownst to the boys, we cleaned it out and bought a surplus eight-foot drafting table, a pair of stools, a supply of paper, posters for the walls, and all kinds of supplies. We even ordered a brass plaque for the door that read "Miller Family Entertainment."

The excitement on Christmas Day, as they unwrapped the door to the new "Animation Studio," was wonderful. Countless hours were spent in that little room quietly drawing, relentlessly creating, and steadily becoming the confident, talented, hard-working men they are today.

Within the next couple of years, the boys were overflowing with creative work. They produced a video missionary story about two brothers, written and partially animated, which was later used in some of their portfolios. One piece of work that still amazes us all is the start of "The Clock Cleaners." This animated piece not only showed their ability to develop great characters, but to create an entire video production with musical background included. They could remember many of the classical music pieces we had listened to, and could pick just the right portions that would give the needed dynamics to their animation.

Allan hurried to finish high school early so he could join Chris as they both attended the Art Institute of Seattle. They studied on the latest art and computer equipment, graduating together with honors and degrees in computer animation. Currently, they keep so busy with freelance jobs that they hardly have time to finish their own creations.

Homeschooling was laughter, fun, and excitement. I would never have dreamed that a mother who had no interest in astronomy, and couldn't draw a stick figure properly, could ever produce two successful artists who love to learn. The key was being willing to find their strengths, being willing to tackle my weaknesses, and mixing it all together with a new love for learning.

Teaching to a Child's Heart: Preparing Yourself for Spontaneous Instruction

——— *Katherine von Duyke* ———

Tim and Kathy von Duyke have been home-schooling for thirteen years, and have gradually built a family orchestra, which consists of five violins, two cellos, one viola, a folk harp, two noise makers, and a conducting baton (Dad). The best musicians are the children: Brian, Christie, James, Scott, Bonnie, Peter, Timmy, Isaac, Benjamin, and baby Heidi. Besides music, the family enjoys doing unit studies together, bringing both challenges and joy to each school year.

Tim has an M.Div. from Westminster Theological Seminary. Kathy has a B.S. in nutritional sciences. Kathy's "postgraduate studies" were engaged at home with her children, where she earned her "educational credentials" through digesting all she could about teaching, from the perspective of a parent rather than a college student.

KONOS Helps! is the von Duyke home business. They have, for nine years, produced newsletters designed to compliment the KONOS curriculum. Kathy also wrote The Month by Month Spelling Guide *(a companion dialogue to* The Writing Road to Reading*),* The Home Education Copybook *(a source of inspiration and reproducible forms to those who use unit studies), and a column for* Practical Homeschooling *magazine.*

I was certain I would never be able to teach my first child, Brian, how to cut with scissors, let alone to read, so I believed the phonics program when it told me that my child must finish every phonics page, complete each hurdle of the carrot track, and be programmed on a daily basis with correct spellings and rules. I wish I had known that this behavior modification type of approach not only disregarded some basic truths about the flexibility of the human mind, but could even be a detriment to his reading. Something kept telling Tim and me to respect God's plan for each child as He unfolded their unique characteristics to us. After all, we as their parents, are the people on earth who love them most.

After struggling and wavering over the question of whether to follow a curriculum or teach to my child's heart, I began to make my own intensive study of phonics instruction. I believed that if I really understood phonics as a whole, I could make learning more suitable to Brian's timetable, and not just a grind through workbooks. Later, I found I wanted that same advantage in many other areas, such as writing, math, and music theory. I have become a teaching "Jane of all trades," learning all subjects at all grade levels by burning the rubber on my prairie booties as I've skidded from seminar, to library, to practical experience, and back again. The benefit? Being able to teach each child with sensitivity and to catch those "teachable moments."

Please do not think I spend hours teaching my children. I don't! I want them to be independent learners, but by previewing their subjects each year I've gained the ability to freelance teach, drop tutor, evaluate subjects, and use academics to build relationships in our family.

Freelance Teach

Freelance teaching is a bit like freelance cooking. When I first married, I was enslaved to all the prepackaged foods at the grocery store because of my poor cooking skills. As I grew in skill, I began to notice that recipes I had memorized did not seem half as difficult to prepare as those I had to look up. For instance, with the knowledge of a basic white sauce, anyone can whip up a great dish from foods and spices on hand, adding just that personal touch that causes others to ask for your recipe.

It is like that with teaching. I marvel at the way many phonics programs present themselves as scientifically designed, perfectly sequential programs. As soon as the child closes his book, he is confronted by a world of print that is neither. Any child worth his intrinsic motivational salt will wonder at the words on his cereal box, attempt to write "Dade" a note, and try to read books far afield of his categorized word list. With a basic knowledge of phonics you can make use of materials on hand and teachable moments, and add that personal inspiration that sparks your child's interest. This is why tutoring is the most effective way to teach.

What basic skills should you work on to be a freelance teacher? Know the basic phonetic sounds that make up our language. Know the handful of truly useful spelling rules. Know the components of a paragraph and develop a set of questions to talk your child through a written assignment. Know the eight parts of speech and a short list of basic writing mechanics. Know how to teach the basic math operations and fractions using manipulatives. Know the major periods of history, and know the major divisions of science (i.e., biology, earth science, chemistry, physics). Initially, you might keep your own set of teaching notes, but as these basics become a part of you, your head will be all you need to carry around!

Drop Tutor

Children ask questions at the most inconvenient times. In the world of guerrilla homeschooling this means answering algebra problems near the changing table, remembering the order of the planets while cooking, and discussing an essay introduction with a frustrated young writer while solving a squabble over toys amongst nearby toddlers. At times like these, you need to be able to tutor without dropping everything to find the teacher's manual. It is the old adage that being prepared takes time, but ultimately saves time. Simply stated, read the teacher's manual ahead of time. If you don't have the teacher's manual, read your child's textbook ahead of time. If high school writing or chemistry is not something you will ever hope to learn, then decide ahead of time who your child will turn to for help, and delegate the subject to a class, tutor, or correspondence course.

Evaluate Subjects

To master the content of a subject, learn its vocabulary, framework, and skills (such as addition/subtraction, or map reading, or writing a paragraph) in order to impart these to your children. For single topics, such as information on the planets or animals, a simple children's picture book on the subject provides great basic vocabulary and information. In fact, I have learned more from little children's books than perhaps any other source! A little harder to find, sometimes, is an overview of a subject that would be taught over a period of years. Search to find the gem of a book that explains phonics, or grammar, or the art of teaching writing. Find a book that condenses all of elementary math instruction, or science, into a single book. You can sometimes get this same sense of overview by reading an expanded scope and sequence of what children need to know by each grade level.

Get to know the organizing framework used in each subject. These include things like: a phonetic chart, a timeline, classification charts, math tables, maps, or the periodic table. After you learn a subject's basic vocabulary, the framework shows the relationship between the parts, forming a mental net to hold all the bits of information. Teach your child the organizing framework for a subject as simply as possible. Why shouldn't children be given the broad overview first? Fill in the details of the subject with lively books; don't let textbooks blow your child's curiosity. Help your child "own" a subject by using the information or skill in fun or meaningful ways. Build the plant classification system on a basement wall using plants from your own backyard; act out the major events in the timeline of American History and photograph or film the production; let your child use the map to navigate your next trip to the store. In whatever way you can, make the framework alive. Wait until your child is in upper elementary grades before beginning subjects that require analysis, such as grammar or spelling.

Build Relationships

I remember my twelfth grade English teacher, Mrs. Foreman. Not only did she have high standards for English, but I now realize, because of the questions she asked us to consider from the books we read in her class, that she was a Christian. By the end of that year, I had received Christ. Though I prayed with someone else, it was because Mrs. Foreman had me asking the right questions about life.

When my daughter, Christie (age 15), reads a great classic, I can draw out her understanding by referring to my mental notes on literary analysis. Was the protagonist a static character? What principles did the character follow that led to his behavior? Was a scriptural principle violated? How did his character effect his relationships? Is there a subplot? What is the theme of the book?

Discussions like these turn academic lessons into important questions about life. Lessons become tools to mentor a child in godly character. I am not one of those to belittle academics for the loftier goal of godly character. I do not believe they are at odds with one another. Character is the person, academics a tool. I want to develop the character that will wield the tool. If my only focus is on the tool, the character is too weak to properly wield it; if only on the character, I have not equipped him with tools. The Scripture clearly teaches that both character and equipping are best developed within relationships, the first being with parents. Displaying an interest in your child's answers to your questions builds a strong bond with them.

The older children have thanked me for this teaching framework that we have used over the course of their education. I could not have asked for a better reward. Seven of our ten children are now reading, though none has ever needed to complete a phonics course. Not only does Brian, now 18, cut just fine with scissors—though I never taught him—he is also a fine human being, deeply committed to the Lord. Do not be afraid to minimize textbooks, to learn with your children, or to give your heart full play in their education. When parent's hearts are turned towards their children, God promises His blessing.

Getting the Fun Back

——— *Carol Severson* ———

Carol married David Severson right after high school. They have four children: Jeremy (18), Michelle (15), Joshua (13), and Matthew (11). They have lived out in the country near Malden, Illinois, for eleven years. The Seversons' children have been exclusively homeschooled. Their oldest son is presently working toward his degree in computer programming. David and Carol are support group leaders and work with "CHEC," Illinois' homeschool lobbying organization, as legislative liaisons. When Carol is not homeschooling, the family travels across the country giving workshops on computers, the Internet, picking software, and homeschooling. Carol has been helping parents by doing curriculum counseling for the past eight years. She also enjoys writing articles on homeschooling, when time allows.

The Seversons operate a family business building custom computers and selling quality educational software. They are involved with Jill and Alan Bond, founders of The Bonding Place, in their ministry (PREACH) to help parents with autistic and special needs children. After medical bills, most parents of autistic children can't afford the one thing that would help their child the most: a computer. Computers seem to be the one thing that autistic kids respond to. To help families, the Severson family asks people to donate their old parts when they upgrade their computer. When the Seversons have a system ready, they contact Jill and she donates it to a family. If you would like to find out how you can help, or how to get in touch with The Bonding Place, please contact the Seversons.

What would I do differently if I had it to do over again? This is a really difficult question. When we started this adventure fifteen years ago, there were no curriculum fairs. One, basically, had the choice of textbooks, or textbooks. The only example of education that we had to follow was our own school experience. There were no all-day workshops on unit studies, teaching science, using a computer, homeschooling high school, or how to issue a diploma. We had to just do the best we could and not worry about high school until we got there.

I started out like all the others at that time—workbooks and textbooks. I picked up discarded textbooks at library sales and garage sales. I basically lived at the teacher's supply stores. I bought flash cards, charts, reproducible workbooks, and of course, all kinds of stickers. At that time I must have thought that the workbooks didn't have enough pages to fill in, because I bought all the workbooks I could find. I even got one of the publishers to sell me the teacher's manuals, too. Not an easy thing to do in the days before homeschooling became popular. I followed the teacher's manuals page for page, exercise by exercise. We did every question on every page. I thought I was giving my child the best education available.

I did not realize at first that my son and I were miserable. Not to mention that my complaining was making my husband miserable. I spent late nights planning the next day's events. My son cried whenever I mentioned school. I cried when I thought about all I had to do. I did not know any other way to teach my child. I was also pregnant, tired, and confused.

What really made us miserable was that we were not having any fun. Before we began this school stuff, we had lots of fun. We went out all day and enjoyed nature. Our whole family loved long hikes and bird watching. We would actually spend hours and hours reading a really good book together. My son spent whole afternoons talking to his grandpa about World War II, and what he had done. But, I told myself, you can't do those things during school time.

Because I was pushing academics, my son began to resent school. He made comments about how we did not have any fun anymore, and he hated this. I could see this would be a long twelve years. The worst one was when he asked me what had he done that he was being punished. He actually thought I was punishing him!

At the same time, a lot of negative character traits began to surface. You see, I had so much to do planning these wonderful days of school, and so much to do preparing for a new baby, that I sort of let things slide in the behavior area. I was just too busy. After all, God does not create a special thirty-six-hour day for homeschooling moms. I was actually fostering a lot of negative character traits by ignoring them. They were nothing major, like lying or stealing, just attitudes I did not care for. When it finally dawned on me what I was doing, I had numerous character flaws to correct. We decided to take the rest of the year to just work on character, and to read all we could. It turned out to be a wonderful year.

After our little experiment, I was feeling much better. I had my relationship with my son back, and we were having fun. Best of all, we corrected those character traits, and developed a few more that I felt were essential. The only problem was that my husband and family members had doubts about our experiment. My husband agreed that some things were much better, but were we learning anything?

Just when I was ready to go back to the textbooks, I gave my son a review science test. Six months earlier, he had received a perfect score on this test, but I was in shock to find out that he really did not know the material we had covered. He had memorized it for the test to please his mom, but it had not interested him and it was boring; therefore, it was short-term memory and easily forgotten. Now we were in trouble. We couldn't continue "play time," but I knew the textbooks were not working. I could not go back to the way things had been because now I had a baby and a toddler to take care of.

At that point my husband and I called a staff meeting. We discussed all that had transpired and tried to come up with a solution. At about the same time, some magazines began to publish articles on unit studies, relaxed learning, delayed learning, and Charlotte Mason. More people were beginning to do this homeschooling thing, so, more people were expressing their ideas of what home education could and should be. As homeschoolers discovered that the typical textbook route was not working for them, a wonderful event took place: homeschoolers began developing and publishing homeschooling materials. These materials were more suited to homeschooling, and less suited to groups of thirty. They were written with the whole family in mind, so kids of all levels could study a topic together.

We decided that we would take the summer and talk to all the people we could. When an article in a homeschooling magazine interested us, we called directory assistance for the author's phone number. We made phone call after phone call. I talked to many different people and collected notebooks full of ideas. All these people had experienced the same struggles as my family. They were so eager to share their ideas and experiences with us. It felt so much better knowing that I was not the only one dealing with this. It was wonderful! They had been doing what I had wanted to do for so many years, and it was working for them.

What transpired next is the approach we have used for over ten years. We do not use textbooks, except for math. We have a few textbooks on hand as reference material since they are helpful to use for checking dates and facts against the living books we are reading. We use real books, computer programs, and games. Our curriculum budget is not equivalent to the national debt anymore. I do not stay up all night planning for the next day. All I need is a good math program and a library card. If I had those first years to do over again, I would make sure school was always fun with lots of hands-on learning and unit studies. I would never become a slave to all those workbooks.

We now do history chronologically, so we go to the library to get all the books we can on the time period we are studying. The history materials we use are a combination of the Greenleaf *Famous Men* series and Diana Waring's *Ancient Civilizations and the Bible*. The kids read real, living books on history and science topics. If you make the subjects interesting by showing your children how events in history are connected to other events, you will keep their attention, and they will then retain more information. Let them see that when things were going on in Europe, things were also going on in China—they did not happen at separate times.

For English we do a lot of writing about the topics they are reading. The kids are required to narrate, either orally or in written form, what they have read. This is not difficult to do—kids love to tell anyone who will listen about all the neat facts they have discovered.

We require the kids to keep a science journal, which is simply a notebook with a blank space at the top and lines at the bottom. They draw a scientific drawing, and then label or explain it. As an example, they might do the human hand, labeling all the bones, and then write a paragraph about the hand.

Before you decide how you want to go about this important adventure, read all that you can and attend as many workshops as possible. This research in preparation can save you more money, time, and frustration than I can ever begin to explain.

Keep it simple and go with your child's interests. Don't sacrifice character or relationships for what we think education needs to be. It is not a great education if your end result is an educated fool. Many before me have found that it is much easier to teach a child, if you first take the time to train the child.

Part 3

The Priorities

You Can't Do It All...and Don't Have To!

—————— *Sharon Grimes* ——————

Sharon says, "Homeschooling six blessings on loan to us from the Lord has been a real heir-raising challenge! I thank the Lord for my wonderful life partner and very best friend, my husband, Dennis. He pastors a small, family-friendly country church (Sempronius Baptist Church) in a community so rural our zip code is E-I-E-I-O. We have been married for twenty years and homeschooling since 1983. We love to serve the Lord as a family through the local church ministry God has given to us."
Dennis and Sharon are both graduates of Maranatha Baptist Bible College, where Sharon received a degree in elementary education. Her real qualification to be her children's teacher, however, is her double M.A.—"MaMa"! The Grimes were privileged to be used by God to start the homeschool organization in their state, New York State LEAH, and have been part of The Teaching Home *magazine's staff since 1989 (part-time out of their home).*

In addition to Sharon's work for The Teaching Home *magazine, the Grimes have been speaking at state and national conventions since 1990 on a wide range of practical topics, sharing their "Heir-Raising Tales." Dennis and Sharon have a great burden from the Lord to be a blessing and encouragement to homeschooling parents and their leaders, and also promote family involvement with Bible-preaching local churches.*

With the mindset of a classroom teacher, I thought we had to "do it all" to really be successful with our school at home. As a pastor's wife, emulating the Proverbs 31 role model seemed mandatory! I assumed her level of activities was normal. Why, in order to really be successful at this, we needed to go on field trips, have educational fairs, sponsor seminars, etc. Obviously, someone needed to organize them all, and since I saw these events as beneficial to my own family, I plunged into homeschool leadership with gusto, causing me to lose sight of my family priorities.

Looking back fifteen years later, how I wish someone had said, "Sharon, you *do not* have to do it all!" I am not alone here—homeschoolers are the busiest people I know! There was nothing wrong with any of the activities I was involved in, but my priorities were not right. Busyness is one of Satan's greatest tools to keep me from God's *best* choices for me. Was Martha wrong in choosing to prepare a good meal for her Savior? No, but Mary chose the *best* activity: sitting at Jesus' feet. I kept so busy serving God through our local church ministry and "the homeschool movement" that, like Martha, I believe I was often busy *for* God and yet was missing that close communion *with* God.

It became so frustrating trying to emulate my biblical role model that, eventually, I was compelled to really study that thirty-first chapter of Proverbs. I reached some startling conclusions that really changed my "I have to be busy all the time or I won't be a success" attitude.

First, I learned that the woman in Proverbs 31 was not a young mother with young children. I believe that she was in the next season of her life, with grown children. See the verse that says "her children rise up and call her blessed." Now, when was the last time your children got up in the morning and told you how wonderful you are? (Mother's Day doesn't count!) Can you remember when you first realized how hard your mother had worked and all of the sacrifices she had made for you? If you are like me, it was not until you became a parent and saw how much work it took to run a household. It is grown children who "rise up and call her blessed."

Now, some of you may still insist on emulating all of the Proverbs 31 woman's activities. All right, here is point two to convince you that the Proverbs 31 woman did *not* "do it all." What is the first thing that she did every day after she rose? (I rarely can find anyone who knows the answer. All that we remember is her multitude of activities.) Give up? Verse fifteen explains that she fed her maids. How many of you have a houseful of maids to feed in the morning? No, none of us has the multitude of household assistants taking care of our every whim that a woman of royalty would have had! I was starting to get a different picture.

I became convinced that these accomplishments were completed, not concurrently, but spread out over the course of this woman's lifetime. I had failed miserably in my efforts to "do it all." People always say, "prioritize your schedule," but my priorities were wrong! All of those urgent needs outside our home continued to pull me away from the most important jobs I had: wife and mother. And, for the first time in my life, I clearly understood that my attempts to please the Lord had been performance-based rather than a simple walk of obedience (1 Sam. 15:22–23).

A little book finally helped me understand the right priorities. It explained that Jesus did not feel like He had to do it all—He only did the will of His Father. I am to follow His example. Charles Hummel's *Freedom from Tyranny of the Urgent* helped me see the difference between my true priorities and all of those urgent tasks that kept stealing my time. This released me from the guilt I felt when saying "no" to others. Now saying, "Yes!" to God and focusing on His will for my life brings great joy and peace into my heart. I asked God to cause his priorities for me to be the desire of my heart.

Hummel challenged me to make a list of my top ten priorities. This "simple" exercise clearly showed me how far I had wandered from God's agenda—it took me three weeks! The next assignment was to list the ten most urgent tasks waiting for me to complete. In five minutes I listed twenty-six! Less than five were related to my priority list. I was really getting the picture now!

In order to say, "yes" to God's priorities, I needed a new schedule, so I decided to use a very visual means of scheduling. I ruled off a standard sheet of poster board into seven days and half hour segments, from 6 A.M. to 11 P.M. I found that the mini-size yellow Post-It Notes were about the same size as my time blocks. As I moved down my top ten list, one priority at a time, I covered time blocks with yellow notes.

Number one: God. How well I know that my day would be disastrous if I attempted to get through it in my own strength! So, I blocked off the daily time I needed for personal Bible study and prayer time, family Bible time, and our local church services/Bible studies.

Number two: my husband. My husband and I have been challenged recently to spend more time building our marriage relationship, not just taking for granted that God would bless it because we were raising His children! I do not want my children to "date to marry," but I do believe we "marry to date!" So, my husband and I have scheduled more "dates" together (one of our favorites: walking together under the stars!). More yellow notes on my board.

Number three: my children. I blocked off time for the various levels of child training I need to accomplish weekly: the physical, spiritual, educational, and emotional needs of our six children. Needless to say, the board really started getting yellow now! I had not realized until I looked at "the big picture" how much time my children really required from me.

Number four: my household. Well, you can imagine that by the time I scheduled laundry, meal preparation and cleanup, grocery shopping, cleaning chores, and so on, my board was getting full. (Here's a tip: you can free up some "white space" by transferring many of your yellow chore notes to your children!)

I continued to work my way through the list, having to make careful choices with the remaining time blocks. My remaining items included our extended family, my personal time, evangelism and discipleship, etc. (There are seasonal changes!) By the end of the list, the poster board showed me my time would now be spent on priorities *if* I would be obedient to God daily! Have I been one hundred percent successful? No, I am still not what I should be, but—praise the Lord!—He has brought me a long way from where I used to be. I know He will continue to perform a good work in me! (Phil. 1:6)

To stay on track, I needed to learn how to say "No!" Here's my secret: when someone calls and asks for my assistance, my husband helps me look over my schedule to see if there is something I want to remove from my schedule board. (You see, double layering is not allowed!) If there is nothing I can remove, because they are still priority items, and I do not have any free time to give, then my husband gently points out to me that I cannot do it. And, you know, it's amazing! I have not had anyone argue with me yet when I call them back and tell them, "Thank you for asking me to help, but, I'm sorry, my husband has told me 'no.'" My dear husband is my umbrella of protection, and as long as I stay under his authority, I will not get "soaked": overburdened once again by the tyranny of the urgent! I want my husband's heart to safely trust in me (Prov. 31:11).

I did not have to do it all...and my pride kept me, for many years, from admitting that I *could not* do it all. These changes have not happened overnight. We have learned it takes as much hard work and discipline to overcome "time debt" as it did to become financially debt-free, but the rewards are worth it! Find God's will for your life, walk confidently in it, and remember—you do not have to do it all!

Your Homeschool Mission Adventure

—————— *John Rush* ——————

John Rush is the founder of New Song, a New Zealand charitable trust that assists South Pacific church and school planting. He has been a leader in pastoral, missions, Christian education, and mercy ministry since his conversion from outspoken atheism over two decades ago. John speaks and teaches in a variety of settings including radio and television, conferences, and leadership schools and seminars. He has a warm humor and down-to-earth style that is widely appreciated.

The Rushes' homeschool environment is vital to their survival in a life filled with missionary transitions, and has made it possible for them to reach a Pacific cargo cult for Christ, a story John tells in his book The Man with the Bird on His Head. *John shares how homeschooling and the work of missions are natural allies. He encourages homeschool families to reap lifelong benefits by using their strength and Christian maturity to serve the mission field. John holds a B.Sc. from Bethany College, and an M.A. from Fuller Seminary. The Rush family can be found homeschooling either in New Zealand or the USA.*

✏️➤ In the May 1974 *National Geographic*, an article entitled "A Pacific Island awaits its Messiah" opens with the bold words "Tanna Awaits the Coming of John Frum." Islanders are pictured marching in formation with bamboo rifles, and seated at the rim of the active volcano with "USA" painted in red across their bodies. They are worshiping a bright red cross. During WWII, when military forces had filled their island, they could get food, clothing, and powerful medicine at the sign of the red cross. When the war ended, the abandoned islanders had sought to prove their devotion to "America" by taking on these military customs and symbols as their own religion. Ancient prophecies predicted that one day John "Frum" America would return on a white ship bringing free medical help and other cargoes, and would reward their faithful waiting. Soon after my arrival on the island, a local pastor exclaimed, "Pastor John, because of the way you have come and what you are doing here, these people believe that you are John 'Frum' America, the one that they have been waiting for."

When our family left America in 1992 to serve with a medical mission ship, we had no idea that the circumstances of our ship's brief visit to this remote island would fulfill these predictions and open the way for the Gospel. Later, on a subsequent trip to Tanna, I accompanied the chief to the John Frum chapel. I pointed to the red medic's cross at the front of the room and asked, "What does this cross mean to you now?" The chief responded, "John Frum gave us this cross, but it is the cross that Jesus died on for us, and that is what I want my people to know." I rejoiced to see that the lovely "John Frum people" were becoming "Jesus people."

Family Benefits

When we left our pastorate in California to spend a season in missionary service, we did not know that our homeschool lifestyle would become the foundation of a new ministry to the islands of the Pacific. As this life adventure continues to unfold, we have been amazed to see how mission service and homeschooling have been strong, natural allies.

We knew that our missionary training and service would require a number of transitions and relocations. As our mission work began, our oldest child was reaching school age. Homeschooling became the natural choice for us as it gave us the opportunity to make the changes without disrupting our children's educational routine and environment. This stability, in a sometimes very mobile life, is the single greatest benefit of homeschooling to missionary families. While I was at sea, the homeschool routine helped to alleviate the pain of homesickness and separation by keeping our family ties fervent.

Other obvious benefits have to do with the wealth of opportunities we have in exploring the history, culture, and geography of our mission territory. After a family homeschools in the same place for a few years, exciting new field trips can get harder to find. On the other hand, our mission adventure has given us the opportunity to climb the side of a volcano and see the exotic green parrot, chase the kangaroos and cuddle the koalas, explore the reefs and tramp through the rain forests, join in native feasts and talk into the night with the chief. We have visited fascinating foreign museums, galleries, and historic sites, learning to appreciate the richness of other cultures. Talk about a field trip!

Our children have met great Christian pioneers, missionary leaders, sports stars, and stunt women. They have playmates and friends from every walk of life, and have practiced their own Christian compassion in the poorest of places. Johnny, our oldest, has served as a radar operator aboard ship, and has tramped with me through glaciers and deserts. He has stood before large congregations and shared his joy in being a missionary and in learning that even though people are outwardly very diverse, inwardly, they all need the same thing: Jesus. The children have learned how to leave their treasured friends and amusements behind—to ride secondhand bicycles. They have learned the joys of sacrifice and received a more grateful perspective.

When we see families take time out for Christian service, we observe transformations of character. Parents who feared their children would suffer have seen them grow and improve because of the impact of Christian service. Children have seen Mom and Dad step out in faith, take new challenges, and break with the routine to serve God and others. Paul makes it clear in 1 Timothy 1:5 that the goal of instruction is to be "charity out of a pure heart, and of a good conscience, and of faith unfeigned" (KJV). A family mission experience can help to develop this focus.

Our mission experience, made possible by the homeschool environment, has given our children greater dignity and pride in their family and Christian heritage, and they have developed important friends and contacts for their future. This world is becoming a global, multicultural community, and our children have acquired confidence and important tools that will serve the Kingdom well in the coming century. It is no wonder that *Who's Who* has a disproportionately high number of missionary children among its young achievers.

Kingdom Benefits

Even as your family benefits from the mission adventure, you will find that you make a real difference out there! The mission field is always short of workers. There is a vital need for dedicated, mature Christian families who can work together and who are ready to serve. The example of your family can be a great blessing to new Christians on the field.

When your time of service ends, you can continue to bless the mission field by becoming a loving representative of the missionaries and their fields, helping them to communicate their needs, arranging for special "care packages," encouraging visitors, or arranging work parties. Your continuing support and prayers might be the reason a mission family is able to stay on the field. Don't be surprised to find that you will have the ongoing joy of being called upon to host overseas families or ministers as you continue to be a vital part of the mission network. If you work at it, your mission adventure can continue to influence your family for years. You might like it so much that you plan a regular family outreach, or even become full-time missionaries yourselves!

Planning Your Adventure

There are many opportunities to serve God as a short-term mission family. If you are already praying for and/or supporting a family on the field, consider contacting them to inquire how you might visit and help them. Your church might be very involved with specific missionaries. See your pastor or mission department leader to discuss how you might be a blessing to these missionaries.

In addition, there are hundreds of mission organizations involved in everything from Christian radio and drama teams to refugee camps and hospital ships. There are directories filled with thousands of opportunities around the world. (Youth With A Mission's GO *Manual* is just one such directory.) Our own organization, New Song, welcomes the help of homeschool families.

Lessons Learned

We would offer the following advice to homeschoolers contemplating a missions adventure:

1. It is important to plan ahead. Take plenty of time to communicate with your intended mission destination and hosts. Pray for their specific needs. Study the history and culture of the field, and ask your hosts how you can best prepare.

2. Make sure you have more than enough financial resources to cover your family's expenses, and plenty to contribute to the needs of those you meet on the field. Be a financial blessing and not a drain to the mission you seek to serve.

3. The electronic age and our many curriculum options make it easier to educate overseas. We would recommend that you travel light, with a simple core curriculum and emphasize special projects, outings, service, and journals to supplement the experience. Plan your curriculum around the experience, and you will enjoy it more.

4. Start off with a short-term experience in more hospitable field, and work your family up to more challenging assignments.

Conclusion

A family mission experience can give you a new faith adventure, allow you to make a difference for the Kingdom, and send you home knowing that your family has benefited the most. Homeschooling gave us the opportunity to leave our comfort zone, be stretched in our faith, and strengthened in our family. The miraculous way in which God used our mission adventure to bring the Gospel to a Pacific people group has shown us how important our family service is to God.

Because of homeschooling, I was able to be "John Frum America." The truth is that all of us are "John" or "Jane" from somewhere, and you never know how God will use you and your family. So start planing your family mission adventure!

A Journey of Faith

———— *Miriam Heppner* ————

DuWayne and Miriam Heppner reside in Warroad, Minnesota, with their thirteen children: Jemima (19), Benjamin (17), Samuel (15), Josiah (14), Joseph (12), Abraham (11), Micah (9), Moses (8), Solomon (7), Joanna (5), Susanna (4), Abigael (2), and Elizabeth (1). Their children have been solely home educated with the exception of a few supplementary courses.

When DuWayne and Miriam began homeschooling some thirteen years ago, friends and others questioned them on the whys and hows of this strange phenomenon. As they began sharing information and resources, God opened doors for additional family oriented ministry opportunities, which included servicing conventions and running Heppner & Heppner Construction, a homeschool supply mail-order business, from their home. Six years ago they opened a storefront for their business, quickly outgrew it, and one year ago moved to their present location. They carry both core curriculum and supplementary materials.

The Heppners are homeschool support group leaders, have served as speakers for regional, state, and provincial conventions, and have taught child training seminars. The family has been involved in select presentations, and they enjoy using music and memory work as part of their ministry. They believe their greatest ministry is that of passing on a spiritual heritage to their children; that the "outside" ministries are simply an overflow and extension of what God has been teaching them in the context of their family. They are grateful for the grace of God at work in their lives, and desire to pass this hope on to others.

✐══▷ "What? You're not going to send your child to kindergarten? What are you going to do with her all day? How is she going to fit in when you put her in school?"

This is just a sampling of the incredulous comments we received when we decided not to send Jemima to school. Initially, we based this decision on the issue of socialization. I had heard numerous moms bemoan that they had sent their sweet little girls off to kindergarten, only to have them return as "haughty little snots." A break had occurred in the beautiful bond they had once enjoyed. Mom no longer knew anything, the teacher knew everything, and friends were mini-gods. I felt I could provide the kindergarten skills necessary for Jemima's entrance into first grade without the negative socialization aspects. Thus, we began our venture.

We enjoyed reading, playing learning games, and just being together doing real-life activities. We spent only a small amount of time each day on actual academics; however, at the end of that school year, Jemima was academically ahead of those completing first grade.

We did not feel positive about placing her in school ahead of her age-mates, nor could we see placing her in the first grade, as it would be a boring waste of her time. Besides, I had enjoyed giving her the gift of reading (via phonics), and I treasured my time with her. Meanwhile, she delighted in getting her schoolwork done in the mornings, having time to play in the afternoons (while her peers had to sit in school), and still managing to be academically ahead of her age-mates. But, what to do?

At this time we were invited to a seminar by Dr. Raymond and Dorothy Moore. They presented the concept of home education in a sensible way. We then began to access information on home education via books and conventions. Because of the Moore's ministry, we never fell into the traditional workbook/textbook method. Rather, we went with "free to learn" and "make learning fun" themes. We found this method highly effective.

When her age-mates went off to first grade and Jemima stayed home, our school district contacted us and asked to view our teaching materials. When the elementary principal arrived, he started asking questions, and Jemima began bringing out materials she was using. By the time she finished with her "show and tell," the table was a mound of books and resources, and the principal was obviously taken by it all.

Suddenly realizing how much time had passed, he asked Jemima to read for him before he had to leave. She read so fluently he wondered whether this were memorized material. When he had her read parts he chose randomly, his eyes grew large as she easily decoded such words as "nocturnal" and "carnivorous." He expressed amazement over what we were accomplishing with Jemima, and declared that he wished more parents would do the same. This initial interaction paved the way for positive relations with our school district which still benefit us today.

As the years passed, we continued to be blessed with children, and I began to feel very overwhelmed with all my responsibilities. I wondered why God kept giving us more children when I felt I could not properly take care of the ones I had. (No, we did not set out to have thirteen children!) God used a book by Mary Pride to expose how we had set up our culture as a god, basing our ideas and decisions on what society says, rather than on what God says. We had viewed more children as a hindrance to our ministry. We were convicted of our arrogance for thinking we could best plan what we should do for God, instead of trusting Him and accepting His plan. With the understanding that children are truly blessings, a very special heritage from God, came also the realization that they are the greatest ministry a couple could ever have. From this new vantage point, we began a process of being transformed by the renewing of our minds.

With each of my first six pregnancies, I became very sick and experienced extended times when I accomplished virtually nothing (besides sleeping). Through this, I was forced to delegate responsibilities. I learned that children benefit from, and even enjoy being, a contributing factor in the home. I recognized the importance of having them learn real-life skills. We determined which chores needed to be performed to maintain order and cleanliness, categorizing them by how often they needed to be accomplished (daily, weekly, biweekly, monthly, etc.). We then assigned the chores according to each child's capabilities, and developed a chart system that listed all the daily duties in the general order they should be done (school responsibilities included).

Before we established this system, Saturday had been our assigned cleaning day. Of course, you can guess how much we looked forward to Saturdays! We all woke up dragging our feet. By noon, we would have barely begun. I usually worked late into the night, yet seldom felt we had accomplished even half of what I had hoped. Naturally, when would unexpected company drop in? Certainly not on Sunday when our house was in order! Now, with the chore system, each child does one household chore per day to maintain order. This is much more feasible, much less stressful, and much more visitor-friendly.

We have scheduled our school days to begin at 6:30, with all who can read independently having personal devotions. The content of our personal devotions and family devotions typically correlates with the biblical time-period we are studying in history. We have family devotions at breakfast (after the younger children are up). Before leaving the breakfast table, we recite the Scripture passage we are memorizing: first doing some review, and then learning a new verse each day. The meaning of Scripture unfolds in amazing ways when memorized in context. We believe that, as we put God first, what should be done, will be done (Matt. 6:33–34.)

Since math requires more mental energy than other academics, the older children do math before breakfast, when their minds are especially alert and there are fewer distractions. With good math resources, we are able to use the principles set forth in Isaiah 28:10, teaching one concept at a time and building concept on concept with constant review.

After breakfast, the older students study independently as I work with the younger ones on math and phonics. I have found tutoring is the best method for teaching the "Three R's" to young children. This time investment has a long-term payoff because they acquire an advanced, solid foundation on which to build the rest of their education. As the children grow older, their studies require less of our time, since they assume more control over their education. We provide accountability, instructing and advising when appropriate. Usually, we are able to complete our academics in the morning, with the older children sometimes finishing in the afternoon. In order for our system to flow, I am constantly juggling to provide individual instruction child by child and/or group by group in order to implement independent work.

We use a timeline unit-study approach. History, English, and art are integrated, and our science studies are generated as we read in history about the development and/or usage of a field of science. As we travel through time, we learn what was happening in politics, religion, philosophy and learning, literature, art, music, science, technology, and daily life; we see how a society's belief system affects every area of their culture. We hear the caution of ruined, sin-filled societies and the encouragement of blessed, God-centered societies. We see there is truly "nothing new under the sun," and we can learn from the mistakes of the past. We find history extremely interesting and very relevant to our lives.

An integral part of our children's education is learning life skills. Beyond household chores, life skills includes preparing meals, teaching younger siblings, working in our store, gardening, and helping their dad with construction work. Sometimes, these activities become more urgent than our unit study schedule, so we tend to move in and out of our school schedule as the life skills study takes more or less precedence.

We have learned to depend on God for wisdom and sustenance each step of the way. Looking back, we can see how God led us into home education, and is enabling us to complete the assignment He has given us. We can see how He has used even the difficult times to benefit us (Rom. 8:28).

You may feel like Abraham did when God directed him to leave that which was familiar and go to a strange land. Even if assuming the God-given responsibility for educating your children seems frightening, or if the path ahead looks foggy, rest assured. If you will take each step as God directs, He will show you the next. It is simply a journey of faith.

The Gift of Resources

———— *Lynnette Delacruz* ————

A native of Maine, Lynnette is a woman of faith. She lives life to its fullest. Listening to her tell about her latest adventure, you can be assured next week's news will be different from today's. The Delacruz home is a center of hospitality, wherever home may be.

Presently, Lynnette and Romeo, her husband of twenty-two years, live with their three teenagers in Washington, Maine. They have homeschooled since 1987. Leilani (19), a gifted communicator just back from her first missions trip, is an outgoing, petite, bundle of energy. Nadia (15) is a deep thinking theologian. A severe skin ailment has served to draw her closer to God and refine her into a lovely, insightful young lady. Alex (14) dreams of piloting. He studies flight manuals, diagrams airplanes, and builds and flies remote controlled airplanes.

Lynnette and her family are avid travelers and, although they have little monetary means, have not been prevented from having a wide variety of traveling experiences. From directing a children's home in the Philippine Islands to pruning olive trees in Israel, you will find her delighting to know and work alongside the indigenous people of the places she visits.

One of her joys is researching the Hebraic roots of Scripture and creatively presenting the Jewish festivals and Holy days. To keep track of all her memories, she weaves the joy of storytelling, art, and photography into the Creative Memories albums she creates.

The night before I started to homeschool, I wrote the following entry in my journal: "I seem to be filled with anxiety. Lord, I lift the homeschool before you: a venture You ordained."

90

It seemed a monumental task. I wish that, at that moment, someone had set me down, pointed a finger at me, and said, "You are not the sole resource in your homeschool, nor are you disqualified from teaching by the limitations of your present knowledge!" Those in opposition to my new endeavor never failed to remind me of my inadequacy. To have understood that God was with me, and that time was on my side, would have helped so much to quiet that looming fear.

Which of us would presume to begin such a task relying solely upon our own bank of resources? Not one of us excels in every subject, nor is that required. All around us are those whose passion may be history, or science, or mathematics, literature, art, music, geography, mechanics, or languages. Let us teach with passion the subjects we hold dear and bring in others who delight in subjects with which we are less familiar.

The communities around us hold these treasures—precious people—who have deep knowledge of events, issues, and historical facts. Don't experts love to share their expertise? I once read that Benjamin Franklin made a practice of inviting sea captains over for dinner. He would instruct his children to ask the man about his travels so they could learn geography. What were they doing?—homeschooling around the dinner table!

Learning is not confined to, nor limited by, our meager resources. Since we are as much facilitators as teachers, we can bring instructors and tutors into our home, or we can travel to them. Where there are no people to ask, there are books to read, films to see, events in which to participate, and places to visit.

When finances are strained we can barter our surpluses or talents in exchange for lessons. We had a piano and the local piano teacher was in need of a place to hold lessons for her students. We hosted the teacher and her pupils in our home once a week, and my children received lessons in return. Better still was the inspiration they gained listening to the others play their pieces of music.

Are you studying the Civil War? By all means invite a reenactor over for dinner. There are many reenactors in this country who take every opportunity to portray this major event from our history. They are a well-spring of information, and eager to share their enthusiasm. Ask them to come prepared to answer a multitude of questions. Perhaps, they will share visual aids, sing a song, or come dressed in costume! Usually, whole families reenact together—invite them all over! Imagine the excitement of your young ones at seeing others of their age dressed in period attire. Ask them for their favorite book titles, visit an encampment, or, better yet, join a reenactment group and experience living history for yourselves!

We did just that! It fostered not only knowledge of the subject, but, also, a love for history. We learned so much about life in this time period: the etiquette, dress, music, food, important personalities, and the thinking on issues of the day. We visited pertinent sites. We constantly read aloud together—about the child soldier, the religious pacifist, the females at home and on the battlefield. We watched films and interviewed reenactors. Did I know all about the Civil War when I first began? No! I learned right along with my children: I lived it, breathed it, and danced it together with them.

When we studied early American history, the girls and I volunteered at a museum as members of the Ladies Aid Society. We sat in our colonial attire and sewed costumes by hand as we sipped our tea at the fireside and listened to a different lecture each week. Through winter's cold and summer's heat, we gathered together and learned. We joined the colonial singing group and sang old fugues in four-part harmony. My daughters now can bake an apple pie in a Dutch oven and prepare a meal over an open hearth while keeping their long skirts clean and their conversation genteel. They can weave, play colonial games, and churn butter. A wealth of knowledge was bestowed upon us for the exchange of our time in volunteering. Do you think my young students enjoy history? Of course!

Be hospitable, barter, hire a tutor, volunteer, and ask. Let your home and life be a seat of learning. You are free to excel where you excel, and you are free to learn with your students, and you are free to hire someone else to lift a burdensome subject.

A friend of mine teaches math and science. What a joy to drop my children off at her home for weekly lessons in subjects that are her forte, but are definitely not mine. They have great fun making simple machines and models of muscles in the body. She can explain mathematical concepts well, and loves doing it.

It is well worth scrimping in some areas so that I can afford this kind of extra expense. Benjamin Franklin ate cornmeal mush often so he would have more money to spend on books. It is a matter of choices. There are lots of ways to economize in one area so that a special field trip can accompany a subject which the children are studying. This is where resourcefulness and creativity come in.

Once, while studying ancient Hebrew culture, we spent a month in the land of Israel. We learned desert life and archeology, as well as geographical and cultural studies—on location. In order to finance a month there, we all worked a few hours each day landscaping on a *moshav* (an isolated desert village where everyone relies on a common livelihood, though each family owns its own house and has its own identity) in exchange for room and board at a greatly reduced rate. One really gets to know the desert flora and fauna when pulling thorns out of the soil! Such opportunities cement the lessons and cause learning to be a joy.

We do not have to teach everything to our children. We must equip them with a love of learning and we must give them the tools to discover how they can quench their thirst for knowledge. From there, they will go way beyond our hopes and dreams.

Advice on Teaching: My First Year of Homeschooling

———— *Sharon Jeffus* ————

Sharon Jeffus has a B.S.S.E. in art education from John Brown University and her certification to teach English from the University of Arkansas. While teaching in the public schools for ten years, she developed an Indian Arts and Crafts Program for the Cherokee Indians in Oklahoma that got an outstanding rating from the Bureau of Indian Affairs. Sharon also taught Intensive English at the University of Missouri at Rolla. She has researched and developed curriculum that uses art to reinforce core curriculum subjects. She has presented workshops on teaching art and using art to reinforce core subjects at homeschool curriculum fairs, national Christian School Conventions, and public school teacher workshops throughout the country. Sharon studied sculpturing at Southern Illinois University and painting at Metropolitan College in Denver. She is in her seventh year of homeschooling her two sons.

Richard Jeffus, a licensed minister, got his degree from John Brown University, and has spent the last nine years counseling for the Salem Treatment Center. Before that he directed a home for delinquent and abused boys for the state of Kansas. He has a series of striking and compelling Christian paintings that teach biblical concepts visually. He has taken his art to various college campuses and shows throughout the country and has won awards in several Christian art shows in Kansas City.

Richard and Sharon wish to be an encouragement to the Christian community in teaching and using art to influence the world visually for Jesus Christ.

When a young child shows you, with happiness and joy, his own individual art project, you are experiencing one of the great moments in education. Because my area of expertise is art, I want to share a very important idea that will encourage parent/teachers concerning a way to let your children become creative individuals.

The most important thing that art education can do is to teach children to think independently. I believe it is far more important to expose young children to great works of art, including some art vocabulary, and then turn them loose to do a hands-on project to express themselves and enhance fine motor skills, than to do a structured, carefully managed program of learning how to draw.

Most areas of the school day are very structured—children do not have the freedom to put together materials and ideas and to come up with something original. However, in art things are very different. God created all the snowflakes different, and He did the same thing with children and the art that they create. Older children should have a more structured program in techniques and appreciation, but the primary goal should be for all children to understand that every artist has his own individual style. When children understand the individuality and the personalized approach of the various artists, it allows them to briefly break away from the conforming pressure of performing to certain standards. If you can show children a picture in the Impressionistic style, for instance, and then allow them to do sponge paintings to experience the technique of Impressionism, they will certainly remember that style, and, more importantly, they will not have to be told, "No, that is not good enough."

Creativity is such a fragile flower. It is easily crushed. Perhaps you have had that happen to you. Even Renoir, who created some of his beautiful paintings with paintbrushes tied to his hands because of arthritis, wanted to paint beautiful things because there was already so much ugliness in the world. As long as you are encouraging your children in the arts and making art a joyful experience, you will find that art will be the activity that refreshes you and your children the most during the school day! It is my prayer that the following story might be an encouragement to some of you who are in a position similar to the one I was in when I began homeschooling.

When my husband and I were married in 1979, I was a very dedicated public school teacher. I remember having a conversation with my husband and his cousin, in which my husband put forth the idea of teaching our children (not yet born) at home. His cousin (along with many other members of his family) was a public school teacher, and she was vehemently against even the thought of doing such a "crazy" thing. She got very upset and angry at us—how could we dare to think about teaching our children at home?

Her strong response managed to manipulate us into starting our children in the public school when the time came. Besides, my husband and I were both employed full-time—how could we live on only one income? I felt as though God had called me to love and minister to the children in my classes. I never really considered the condition of my own children—I was thinking about everyone's children except my own. Homeschooling was something I knew nothing about. Never in my wildest imagination did I believe I would end up homeschooling. God started working on my heart and doing things, ever so lightly, to get my attention. I began to believe I needed to put my own children first.

About two years before I did start homeschooling, I met a wonderful homeschool mom who found out I was an art teacher. She said that I should write an art curriculum for homeschoolers. That planted a seed. I had always written my own curriculum with projects I had saved, so it seemed like a great idea to add that opportunity. My teaching career was breezing along with lots of my students winning competitions and good things happening in school...and then it happened. Because of budget constraints, my teaching job was deleted from the curriculum, since art was the first thing to be cut.

I remember, right about then, listening to a program about homeschooling on the radio. All of a sudden, much to my surprise, I felt an overwhelming desire to homeschool my boys. I felt like God was giving me this direction, and over several weeks, I gave this idea much prayer. No one where I lived home-schooled. There was no one I could talk to about it. My parents and brother thought I was making a terrible mistake. I had some Christian friends who were supportive of, and even admired, what I wanted to do. They gave me the courage to write a letter to the superintendent saying that I would homeschool my two sons. My older was in the fifth grade and my younger in the first grade.

What an adventure! I immediately ordered a well known curriculum for each of my boys. I wanted to be sure they received all that they needed and that I wasn't cheating them of anything. Being with them was a joy, but they didn't enjoy the curriculum I ordered for them, and neither did I. Adding more unit study approach projects livened things up quite a bit.

Then came the challenge. A well respected English teacher in a town near here had to take a semester off to have a baby. She wanted me to be her substitute (I am also certified to teach English). I turned the job down once, and then was offered such a marvelous salary, I couldn't resist. So, I put my boys back in school for a semester—the last semester that they were in school. My oldest son is very creative, and was penalized for writing a fabulous short story about a piano duel between Bach and Beethoven instead of finishing a story that was on a copy sheet. He went the extra mile and did extra work creatively, but was penalized for it. My other son was miserable as well. God showed me that money was not worth what it cost my boys in neglect to their education. The art curriculum I had written (and my husband put together) was a wonderful business on the side. Through that, I could teach my boys and still keep my feet in the teaching business.

Through many trials and errors, I have discovered the learning styles of my boys, and we all have enjoyed the wonderful learning adventure. My older son has been taking classes at a local college since he was 15. He loves learning and enjoys reading great literary classics, studying Greek and science, and repairing computers. He has even been paid to fix computers at the public school. He also DJ's at a Christian radio station (he started as an apprentice). My younger son is quite an outdoorsman. I enjoy teaching him, and, at 13, he still needs the extra help. I thank God for the wonderful privilege of really teaching and being with my own children. I can always work with other people's children when mine are gone from home.

A very wise lady, Kathleen Kutsch, once told me, when I had a great opportunity dangling in front of me, "You only have one chance to be with your own children. After they are grown you can do what you want."

There are so many homeschooling parents who have been teaching their children for years, and who are so much wiser than I. I just thank God for the wonderful opportunity of being a part of it!

For This Season:
Lavishing Your Children with Time

─────── *Jody Gutierrez* ───────

Jody writes, "I'm 37 and proud of it. I earned each silver strand on my crown. Those strands can be attributed to my farmer husband of seventeen years. Tender shoots of wisdom, understanding, long-suffering, and joyful giving are just a few of the seeds planted by God's grain drill: Eddie Gutierrez. The Eddie model was born in Lemitar, New Mexico, in 1957, and still is in great working condition. I was from the big city of Albuquerque and spotted this 'Deere' model on a drive through the countryside. A lifetime contract was drawn up on February 14, 1981. We have been farming by the sweet of our hearts ever since. Father God blessed the fruit of our womb with twin girls, Amaris Rose and Vania Rose, in September of 1986. (Not only the rabbits were having multiples that year!) Gloria added baby's breath to my growing garden, breaking ground in the spring of 1988. In the summer of 1990, Andres breathed wonderful colors of love, joy, and peace into our lives. We watched our little garden grow, wondering what our Lord would have us do with such exotics. Homeschooling was His answer."

Having run with the "tares" of the world, Jody feels qualified to spot all those counterfeits. Not having a higher education has intimidated her, but her "Counselor" is more than able to direct and point out the direction she should follow. Sometimes God uses Magdelenes, Sauls, and Matthews to lead the way through dark alleys of the unknown.

What do I—the farmer's wife—have to share with anyone about homeschooling? Among the many things, one that stands out—used as a foundation and built upon continually is—TIME.

Personal Time

In this season of our lives, as parents, absolutely nothing is more important than lavishly spending time on our children. Our Lord spends His love on us in the morning and His faithfulness at night. His thoughts towards us are innumerable. Parents are meant to be living representatives of our heavenly Father. Moms and Dads are to be the example of His love and faithfulness. Are my thoughts toward my children? Or am I rushing through my "duties" so that I can do what I "really" want? Am I driving my children like cattle towards the front door? And when all is said and done, do we even know them?

When they were "popped off the bottle," they still needed to be close to my bosom. What was the "Bosom of Abraham"? It was paradise, a place of happiness. Our homes need to be a place of happiness and security for everyone in our family. That's up to me, the mother of the household. What is my attitude towards my children? That is the question the Lord has given me as a plumb line to keep myself in order. Quite often my Lord swings that plumb line down, and I often get tangled up in it before realizing what is happening. Untangling myself from the knots of self-appointed duties is one of my regular problems. Do I find myself resenting these "blessings from the Lord?" Sometimes they do not seem like blessings, but more like millstones, heavy and awkward. Am I willing to pick up my cross and follow Jesus and the high calling He has given me for my life? Have you and I been placed here and now for such a time as this? Are other thoughts bombarding my brain—vain imaginations perhaps, seeing myself giving lectures, or in Caprice and never coming back.

Our children love and admire us more than anyone they know. Their thoughts toward us are innumerable: love, new every day, and faithfulness given undeserved. They laugh at our attempts to be funny, and really mean it. They are touched by our infirmities more than we can imagine. We are accepted by them just as we are, no fronts. We don't even have to try. Just like Jesus. How often do we find ourselves trying to win the approval of friends and acquaintances? So why are other people so much more significant? Our children are people, too, and I do not have to persuade them to think I'm clever or important. For all the acceptance I receive from my children, they deserve my TIME.

Unveiling the hearts of our children doesn't take much: a ride alone with you to town on errands, lying in bed with you until your spouse comes, or a walk on the irrigation ditch bank (my son's favorite). Our last walk took about forty minutes—one I had been promising (avoiding) for weeks. He has, since, brought that walk up so often as, "one of the best times I've had." What a compliment! Take time, look into their eyes, and see how much they love you, just the way you are. Sometimes you can see how lonely they can be in the midst of the hubbub of life. Listen to what they say; life is new and exciting to them. Bored? Take TIME to look at life with your child (science is a great place to try). Tap into their wellsprings of life. I've noticed little ones get up in the morning excited about life and the new day. Wow! That's a challenging one for me. A child will lead. Lord, help me become like one of these.

Discipline Time

Take the time to discipline. I have learned more about discipline by reading dog training books than child training books. Be Mommy-on-the-spot with those little pups. Children need to know that when you say "stop," they better—it could very well be life-saving. I do not spank with my hands because the Lord said, "rod." My hands are for serving, loving, healing, and teaching. "Sit-stay" is a great one for church, dinner, and school. "Speak" a kind word and it will turn away wrath. Out of the heart the mouth speaketh. I have learned even more about training children from God's Word than puppy training manuals. We train up our children the way they should go, God's way, and He will see to it that they will not depart. His Word tells us everything we need to know on child training, and it is readily applicable to our lives as well.

Training Time

Don't worry if you do not get through that school schedule you spent so much time putting together. It probably looks pretty good—one that would impress the school district office, if they happened to be in the neighborhood. However, did God create Eve to be an executive or a help-meet? Do our girls know how to run a household, or are we leaving that up to their husbands? Wasn't Eve perfect when Adam received her? Perfect, as in a condition of excellence, skill, or quality. What quality of helper is your daughter going to be? Give her that edge. What sense does it make for her to self-train after she gets married? Does an Olympic champion train without a trainer? Our boys: are they willing workers? How do they treat their sisters? or mommies? Do they pout to get their way? Are they lazy? Think women: would you want to be married to a couch potato who needs to be warmed, salted, and buttered before he smiles?

God's Time

I wish I would have known before I started homeschooling, to spend much more time in God's Word, instead of reading so many manuals on training homeschool mommies. It's been almost seven years, and now I think I've got it—well, maybe. Our Lord God must come first, before academics and in academics. What will my Lord tell them when my children stand before Him? "Good job, you got perfect grades"? No, it better be, "Well done my good and faithful servant." Know that He is able to lead and guide you in the way they should go. Do not compare yourself, continually, with the other homeschoolers. God gave those children to them and yours to you for a divine purpose. Just like their fingerprints, even with twins, each one is fearfully and wonderfully made. He has a purpose for all of them, and He will tell us if we ask Him. Spend that TIME with Him concerning everything to do with the raising of your children. Seek Him diligently and He is faithful to answer, always and every time. He will bring about the completion of His work, if you will let Him—in His TIME, of course.

Planning to Be Spontaneous:
Letting Love Spill into Every Task

——— *Candy Summers* ———

Educator, author, speaker, and leader, Candy Summers shares that her greatest accomplishments are being a wife and mother, while her most cherished blessings are her husband and four wonderful children. Homeschooling since 1980, Candy still sees each day as a gift from God to enjoy her precious children and to nurture their minds, bodies, and souls.

An honors graduate from the University of Missouri, St. Louis, Candy received a B.A. in elementary education. She and her husband, Jon, became leaders of the North County Christian Home School Association in 1988, which soon became the largest support group in Missouri, with over six hundred families. Jon and Candy are leading with a vision—training up godly generations for His throne room.

Author of There's No Place Like Home, *a unique collection of love letters written to homeschooling families to help them love their children and train them up for God's calling, Candy has also published a monthly newsletter since 1987. Guest speaker on radio and television, and at homeschool conventions, conferences, support groups, and colleges, Candy loves ministering to God's people.*

Candy's newest publication, a magazine entitled There's No Place Like Home, *contains a wealth of inspirational and informative articles on child training, marriage, educational materials, how-to's, and the blessings of homeschooling.*

We all have the same amount of time; it's short, but what we do with it makes all the difference for all generations to come. The enemy of our souls loves to distract us and keep us from our most important appointments, so we must learn by reflecting on past mistakes, and adjusting our perspective to more closely fit God's.

God never rushes; His timing is always perfect. He took time to enjoy all He created; He took time to sup with friends and those in need; and He continually takes time to nurture and love each of us, His children. Wisdom prevails when we emulate His ways, so plan to spend time with the precious children He has entrusted to your care. Take time to enjoy and nurture and love.

Before you begin this pursuit, journey back over the path you took last year. Reflect on the way you spent your minutes and hours. Were they mostly spent in the car traveling from one event to the next; separated from your loved ones by activities dominated by strangers; in tasks that kept you so busy that they took precedence over, "Mama, hold me," "Mama, smell this flower," "Mama, play with me," "Honey, sit by me"? Were they spent in frustration over chaos, with frayed nerves, ending in yelling? What took precedence over loving, nurturing, and enjoying the blessings that should make your heart soar?

If frustration and yelling have taken the place of peace and gentle leading, life has gone astray from God's design. Reflect in your heart! Determine the causes, then ask your husband to help you rebuild the broken foundation so the lasting impressions you impart are those of love, gentleness, wisdom, and peace.

It is time to make promises to God, each other, and yourself: promises to spend more time with God and with the people you care about most. You must make radical changes, adjusting your life to God's design, now, or it will never happen. You must take hold of the pen that inks in how your family's moments will be spent, or the enemy will.

Maintain a plan book for charting your family's life, and begin planning sentimental days filled with the fullness of God's beauty, grace, wisdom, and delight.

Plan to spend time alone with God each day to nourish your soul and soothe your spirit. Then, with your husband, pray for God's protection and guidance to set each day's course aloft with His direction and blessing. (Single moms, God is your husband and father to your children. Ask Him to give you direction and wisdom, and He will.)

Right after your devotions, plan your meals for the week. Then, first thing each morning, you will know what you are making for dinner and can prepare accordingly. Set a timer, if need be, for each phase of the preparation.

Plan to meticulously sculpt a heart for God in each child by daily imparting God's Word to them, praying for them, working out their bents, and living a truly godly life, instead of, "Do what I say, and not what I do." Children are like tiny sprouts that need rich soil, fresh spring showers, the warmth of our love, and the light of God in our lives. So, plan to pray and play with your precious ones throughout the day.

Plan to heartily embrace your children every day with direct eye contact, open arms, and adoring smiles, carefully tending to their conversations, needs, and dreams. Touch, pat, and hug throughout each day. Look, listen, and learn all you can about the incredible, marvelous gifts God sent in these soft, sweet, little bodies. Cultivate their insatiable curiosity by seeing through their eyes, listening to their questions, and "doing" with them.

Create pleasure among the daily tasks of life by planning surprises. "Surprise" means unexpected, so plan to do them at unexpected times: in the morning, in the middle of a hard lesson, or at bedtime—just plan something for every day. In the morning, have teddy bear parties, special breakfasts, days off for fun, a walk or game before lessons, a surprise guest for the day, or an adventure away from home. In the middle of a hard lesson have root beer floats, a milk and cookie break, fudge making, a game outside, a call to grandma, a concert with wooden spoons on the bottom of your cooking pots, a kazoo marching band, hide 'n seek in the basement with flashlights, a good wrestle, a game of charades, a sing-a-long, or a laughing contest. At bedtime, allow extra time for a game, popcorn and movie, more books, a tent raising for a sleep-out on the floor, or a night walk around the block.

What will Mom and Dad think of next? The possibilities are endless: picnics in the living room or at a new park, fishing trips on school days, baking in the middle of the day, painting, water fights, hiking, tea parties, finger painting in the bathtub, bubbles in the kitchen, obstacle courses throughout the house, school in a tent, a treasure hunt to find school books, lunch with the seals (a picnic at the zoo's seal area at the time the seals are fed), a bike ride around the park with dessert at the ice cream shop, pillow fights, tag while hopping on one foot, patty-cake, and peek-a-boo. Plan them, plan them, plan them into each day.

Include your children when you cook. Some moms say that they can't stand the mess, or they can't stand having someone else in the kitchen, probably because their mothers couldn't. Break that cycle of selfishness and teach your children the joy of working together. I never think of my children as being underfoot; rather, I encourage them to play merrily at my feet.

Frequently, plan to give thoughtful gifts just because you love them—things they want, or unexpected treasures. The monetary value does not matter, just the thought. Wrap and personally give the gift, or hide it some place they would never expect. My children get excited over finding new toothbrushes at bedtime, new underwear or socks in their drawer, new jammies on their pillow, a pretty pencil in their pencil box, flowers on their table, or pretty soap on the vanity. And don't forget endearing notes.

Plan to welcome Dad home with hugs and kisses, candlelight and music, a note on the door, pleasant odors from the kitchen, and then time alone with you for a heart-to-heart talk. Plan a candlelight rendezvous for appetizers, tea and dessert with a great read aloud book, a stroll in the park, and romance.

Plan to convey your love, appreciation, admiration, and fondness to those loved ones, near and far, by planning letter writing times. Set aside time when you alone write a letter, note, or card to someone in your home for a surprise treat, and also times when everyone sits down together to write several someones.

Also, plan regular times for preserving your lovely memories in a journal. Do not neglect polishing those memories by retelling them, sifting through pictures, and visiting relatives to hear them talk about the past. Plan special gatherings of family and friends, too.

With every breath you take, breathe in the sweetness of everyday life: the laughter of your children, the pitter-patter of their feet, the melody of their voices, the sound of your husband's voice, the strength of his arms, the smell of clean clothes, a clean house, cooking, the stillness of the night, the warmth of each day. Tune your thoughts to strike the same chord, rejoicing in each other's pleasures and mourning each other's woes. Let your love spill over into every task, allowing its fragrance to envelop and penetrate each child's thoughts. No greater treasure could be handed down through the generations.

> I do not ask that Thou shouldst give me some high or noble task. Give me a little hand to hold in mine. Give me a little child to point Thy way, over the strange, sweet path that leads to You. Give me a little voice to teach to pray. Give me two shining eyes Thy face to see. The only crown I ask to wear is this, that I may teach a little child. I do not ask that I may stand among the wise, the worthy, or the great; I only ask that softly, hand-in-hand, a child and I may enter at the gate.
>
> —Anonymous

Run along now, you have promises to make and planning to do.

"Planning to Be Spontaneous: Letting Love Spill into Every Task" is *adapted from* There's No Place Like Home *by Candy Summers. Used by permission.*

Accomplish What Is Important

——— *Joy Schroeder* ———

Joy Schroeder was raised in a Chicago suburb with dreams of someday seeing the mountains of the West. She graduated from Oral Roberts University in Tulsa, Oklahoma, in December 1975 and taught in the Tulsa public schools for almost three years. More dreams came true than simply going west when she joined a Youth With A Mission team doing evangelistic outreach in Yellowstone Park in 1977. She met Dick Schroeder, who was the team leader, and they were married the next summer. Joy joined Dick in campus ministry at Montana State University in Bozeman, and they have served there ever since. They have two teenage children, David and Mandy, whom they have homeschooled since birth.

Joy was in a tragic car accident in 1987. Her neck was broken, and she is now paralyzed from the chest down, and her hands are paralyzed. At the time, David was 4 and Mandy was 14 months old. Through a worldwide network of relationships, Joy and her family received a tremendous outpouring of love and practical help that carried them through this difficult time.

Joy remains actively involved in the campus ministry and homeschools the children. She is often invited to speak to community and church groups. In 1996, she coordinated the Montana State Homeschool Convention in Bozeman.

Recently, I asked my 15-year-old son, David, what he thought would have been different if I had been able-bodied when we started homeschooling. He thought for several seconds before answering, "We'd do the same things we did anyway."

My son's pragmatic answer told me that, despite the wheelchair, the important things are being accomplished in our family and in our children's lives. The important things are that our children know God's loving character, learn to obey Him, love one another, and love learning. In order to meet these ultimate goals, we must make daily choices and face obstacles that carry potential frustration. Instead of letting frustration—or the threat of it—overwhelm me, I use it. It points to the real problem or the real issue. What needs to change? I open up my situation to God—the most creative and loving Being in the universe—and expect Him to show me the way out. Then, through my problem-solving technique, I break apart frustrating situations into segments which are easier to evaluate and handle.

What does this problem-solving technique look like? It has developed into a six-step procedure: (1) identify the problem; (2) decide what important goal is involved; (3) list the options; (4) make a plan; (5) engage the plan; and (6) adjust. I ask a set of evaluating questions that lead me through these steps. First, what is frustrating me? or, what needs to change? Second, what is important? or, what do I want? Third, what are my options? Then, I devise a plan, put the plan to work, and adjust the plan if it does not work. The entire process is done from a heart position of asking for God's input and expecting His miraculous abilities to kick in.

Seven months after the car accident that landed me, once so vigorous and active, in a wheelchair with paralyzed body and hands, we finally returned home. David turned 5 the next day and Mandy was 21 months old. Hundreds of important things clamored for preeminence, but one issue carried the greatest weight. It was vitally important that my children would come to believe in the goodness of God's character as they processed the trauma of my accident. My plan to accomplish this important goal involved very deliberate preparation. I considered the likely questions regarding suffering and the goodness of God. I practiced simple and succinct answers on my doctors, nurses, therapists, fellow patients, and friends during the months of rehabilitation. I did not realize how soon I would need those answers for my children.

One afternoon, David and I were chatting and, after a pause in the conversation, he said, "Mommy, I don't think God is ever going to heal you." *Oh, God, help,* I thought. *This is not just a theological puzzle of whether or not God heals today. My son is questioning God's loving character. And he will know whether or not I really believe what I'm about to say. He'll see in my eyes whether those questions have been settled in my own soul. If he sees that I am at peace with God over this tragedy, then he will have that foundation to build on while he learns to know God and His character for himself. And I can't wax eloquent—he's only 5.*

"God is going to heal me either in this life or in heaven," I said. "This life is not all there is. We will live forever with Jesus. Sometimes bad things happen to good people, but God promises to be with us. He's a loving God and He will help us." He seemed to accept that and wandered off to play.

When we first returned home, I was no longer physically able to make sure that 21-month-old Mandy would obey me when my husband, Dick, was gone. Obviously a problem existed. It was profoundly important that she do what I told her. She was in a formative stage where she would be learning to obey or not to obey. Because of consistent, deliberate training, David had, to a great extent, internalized obedience. Mandy was in a vulnerable season, though. If she learned to obey me, she would obey God. That was the ultimate goal and the issue that hung in the balance. I needed to plan a way to teach her to obey.

What were my options? My best options were devoted Christian friends who worked with me and helped me in my home. They agreed to cooperate with my detailed plan. They were not to give the children directives or to correct them. (That would ultimately not help—David and Mandy only needed two parents.) If they saw the children doing something wrong, they were to tell me, and I would administer the correction. If Mandy needed follow-through on a directive, they were to be my hands for me, but let me be the mother.

"Mandy," I said one day, "It's time to pick up the toys." She looked me squarely in the eye. Then, very deliberately, returned to her play. I could feel her intuitive understanding that I could not do anything to make her obey.

I called my helper. "Don't say anything to Mandy. Not even, 'Mandy, your mother says pick up the toys.' Let me do all the talking. Now, take her hand and pick up the toys with it."

"Now, Mandy," I repeated, "It's time to pick up the toys." The plan worked! From then on, Mandy knew that I would find a way to make sure she did what I told her.

In homeschooling the children, it was important to me that they love learning. I wanted them to have as many hands-on experiences as possible. With paralyzed hands and being in a wheelchair, this was an intimidating prospect. I began to search for options. I discovered that a close friend of mine was starting a homeschool co-op that would meet once a week to do field trips or hands-on projects. For the next six years, we made the co-op plan work, and adjusted it many times when it did not. My co-op friends pushed me into a sheep barn to watch the shearing, around the dirt roads of a potato farm, and dozens of other places too difficult for my children to assist me. They took my children to a bronze foundry, an artist's studio/farm, and other hopelessly inaccessible places where I wanted my children to go but could not take them. The co-op accomplished for me what I felt was important.

This year, with two teenagers and a demanding schedule of retreat speaking and evening meetings with the campus ministry, we could see that family time was in danger of being eclipsed. What was important? It is a priority to maintain a family identity. What were the options? Examining the calendar showed us that Mondays and Tuesdays were consistently available. Then we made a plan and made it happen. We set aside Monday nights for Dick to study Proverbs with David and for me to read about what to expect from adolescence with Mandy. Tuesday night was blocked off for game night. We take turns planning the evening, we all agree to participate without complaining, and everyone is allowed to be very silly. It meets the goal of cementing us together in love.

Accomplishing what is important in homeschooling, child-raising, housekeeping, ministry, marriage—all the plates I keep in the air—means overcoming obstacles. I use frustration, or the hint of it, to help me determine what needs to change. Then I ask, what is important? What are my options? And I make a plan, make it happen, and adjust it if necessary. I pray prayers full of the belief that God is just waiting to be asked to intervene with His miraculous abilities and new ideas.

Reduce Your Rigorous Roster and Optimize Your Opportunities

——— *Cindy Wiggers* ———

Born and raised in Evansville, Indiana, Cindy married Josh Wiggers on leap year day in 1980, just two weeks before his thirtieth birthday. They have been blessed by God with three great kids, each with unique talents and gifts: Libby (17), Hannah (15),

and Alex (12). In 1989 the Wiggers began homeschooling in Colorado, where they lived for fourteen years. Although they dearly loved life in Colorado, they moved back to Evansville in 1997 in obedience to God's call to honor their parents.

God has used Josh's and Cindy's very different personalities to form an interesting home and family-based lifestyle. Josh's fun-loving character and innovative spirit are the perfect balance to Cindy's serious, studious, sequential nature. The family's ministry to the homeschool community reflects this diversity. They attend homeschool conferences all over the country as a vendor and workshop speaker. Cindy teaches informative workshops on geography while Josh enjoys the crowd in their booth, playing games, telling jokes and showing how their products will make school just as fun.

The Wiggers' business, Geography Matters, produces and sells several products used by educators, both in the private and public sector, including outline maps and timelines. In 1998 Libby developed a wonderful set of color-coded historical timeline figures. The Wiggers, with Maggie Hogan, just completed a K–12 geography curriculum called The Ultimate Geography and Timeline Guide. *This book is a comprehensive guide with loads of reproducibles to instruct parents and teachers in using geography to enhance many different subjects.*

◖▭▭▷ Homeschooling has totally revolutionized how we view our children and forever changed our lifestyle. We used to say, "Get out of the way while I finish this project," because the job could be completed more quickly without little hands in the way. Now, we willingly draw our children into every kind of project under the sun, knowing that the time spent with them learning something new has much more value, and brings many more marvelous opportunities for building relationships, than the time saved doing the job ourselves.

In fact, homeschooling by its very nature is chock full of opportunities just waiting to happen. If we resist the temptation to organize our school day like a regular school—strictly adhering to the schedule—exciting and unexpected learning moments await us just around the corner. So, if you have already made out that schedule for every hour of every day for the whole year, and have settled in with the exact curriculum you will use, take some advice from someone who's been there: throw out that rigid schedule right now and replace it with an adaptable plan! You should keep your heart open to being flexible regarding your curriculum, as well.

When I first yielded to the call to teach my children at home, I transformed our family room into a classroom that looked exactly like the one I had in first grade. I remember the many hours I spent organizing and supplying that room, planning a rigid school schedule complete with lunch break and recess. Each minute of our school day was scheduled and posted in the room: rise and shine, 6:30; breakfast and chores, 7:00–8:00; Bible, 8:00–8:25; math, 8:30–9:15; and on and on. I had established exact, page by page assignments from our "canned" curriculum for the entire school year. I even showed up for school the first day in a dress! I thought it would set the right mood and respect for authority in my classroom. I wondered if I should pack an apple in my daughter's lunch box to give the teacher!

Our strict schedule gave me a safe feeling that I was covering it all, but school was boring, and the goal of developing the hunger for knowledge in the hearts of my children would never be met in this way. I stuck to those workbook assignments without any consideration for each child's individuality. At that time, I was totally unaware of the diversity in learning styles and did not realize that, for Hannah, I was choking out any desire for learning. Fortunately for Libby, her learning style is perfectly suited for workbooks. But Hannah!—bless her heart—was forced to use the hand-me-down books that Libby had excelled with, even though she learns best by doing activities, not filling out workbooks.

If I could do it all over again, I would use one of the many excellent unit study curriculums available. These allow assignment choices that are suited to the individuality of the student as well as providing opportunities for teaching several grade levels of students at once. Hannah was never fond of school before and could not perform up to the level I thought her capable. No wonder! Instead of the curriculum being a tool, I was expecting it to be the teacher. I have changed curriculums often as I have grown in understanding of the ways in which each of my children learns and as we allow their natural interests to guide us. Hannah can now enjoy school because the unit activities stimulate her learning abilities.

I suppose you have figured out by now that, although it is necessary to have a plan, my rigid schedule had to go! In exchange, I have established a framework of order, allowing for the day by day events of life to teach us as well. As I lighten up and allow for spontaneity, God is faithful to set us up for unique learning opportunities. One time God sent a bird to our back yard on the same day Alex's nature reader described it. While Alex was drawing it in his nature journal, his sister jumped up screaming with delight for us to look out of the window. There on the picnic table—the Brown Thrasher itself!

Another time, in the same week that we were reading a novel depicting the slaughter of a hog, and describing its many uses, we were invited to the rural home of a family to watch their annual hog slaughter. The children even had the opportunity to dissect the eye of this animal and to make a balloon out of its bladder, just like we had read in our novel. All right, all right! This is where I must admit that this mom, before homeschooling became a part of my life, would have been grossed out by the very suggestion of such activities, instead of glorifying God for His provision!

When we first started homeschooling, Josh was working for a map company, so we had some excellent geography-related contacts. We had also become aware of the need for geography resources for homeschoolers. Our little company has grown tremendously since those days and is now a full-time family-operated business in which all five of us participate. The opportunity to earn some curriculum money blossomed into a whole new direction for our family.

This flexible lifestyle allows us to camp and to travel during the spring and summer months of the year. We take advantage of the opportunities to visit places of historical interest, attempting to choose those sites which support our studies. From exhibiting to camping, we have established friendships with the some of the most interesting people you could ever meet, and our children have friends, pen pals, and e-mail buddies all over the United States. We have learned that even camping trips provide valuable, lifelong educational experiences coupled with fun. We have often headed up the mountains in our RV on a "school" day and studied the beautiful bounty of nature God has provided us.

When we traveled to conferences, we were usually in our 1979 Class C, twenty-four-foot motorhome. Although very reliable mechanically, this vehicle also stretched our family in the area of patience with its many irritating breakdowns. The stories Josh can spin, and the opportunities we experienced from being on the road, are worth their weight in gold. Once, we had a flat tire just before the exit to an amusement park. After a grueling schedule and many miles behind us, we were delighted to get to spend the day enjoying amusement rides and having our picture taken with a Ferengi, Bajoran, and Klingon (only Trekkies will understand) while our camper was fitted with a couple of new tires! God's provision for us during many other situations has been a wonderful testimony of His faithfulness for our children.

Even the children have learned to take advantage of unique opportunities that present themselves. Alex made a good sum of money during one such incident. A new twenty-four-inch water line was being installed down the middle of our street, bringing a host of thirsty construction workers to our neighborhood daily for over three weeks. Alex would go out every day with a cooler in his red wagon to sell pop to these men for fifty cents a can. His business grew to include potato chips and cookies. They started watching for him each day, and even began requesting breakfast burritos! Alex learned more about economics from firsthand experience that month than he could have ever learned from me back in the days when I expected a schedule and a well-prepared plan were all I needed to teach my children.

I now allow for a lot of flexibility in our schedule. We take off from "school" whenever we need to, or whenever a great learning opportunity presents itself. In fact, rather than to say we are in school, I prefer to just think of it as a learning lifestyle. Learning is going on everywhere: in the kitchen while baking or preparing meals; in the living room where we gather to read historical novels or the next book in the Narnia series; at Grandma's, visiting or serving; on the road attending conferences. Anywhere learning takes place is school. This is our life.

Opportunities abound, and the homeschooling lifestyle just seems to be cut out for spontaneity. Be flexible; stay flexible. Rigid schedules can spoil some of the best chances to live in the abundance homeschooling has to offer!

—— *Part 4* ——

God's Involvement

Someone Has Been Here Before Me

——— *Clay and Sally Clarkson* ———

Clay and Sally started their relationship as friends when they met in 1975 while both were involved in the ministry of Campus Crusade for Christ. Sally went overseas to Eastern Europe and Clay stayed stateside, but six years later the friendship became a marriage when God brought them together in Denver, Colorado, where Clay was working toward an M.Div. from Denver Seminary. From the start of their marriage in 1981, they made the decision to homeschool their children. Sally even taught a class on homeschooling a year before she had Sarah, their first child!

After Clay's graduation, they ministered on church staffs overseas (Vienna, Austria), in California, and in Nashville, Tennessee. In each ministry, God continued to strengthen their convictions about Christian parenting and home education.

In 1994, the Clarksons moved to family property in central Texas to begin Whole Heart Ministries, their home-based non-profit ministry. Their desire is to equip parents to disciple their children in the Lord, and encourage them to educate their children at home using real books and real life. After publishing their book, Educating the WholeHearted Child, *they began speaking nationally, and launched a national children's books catalog,* Whole Heart Catalogue. *They have since published* Our 24 Family Ways *(for character training and devotions),* Seasons of a Mother's Heart *(to spiritually encourage homeschooling mothers), turn-of-the-century reprints, and others. Sally also ministers to homeschooling mothers through her WholeHearted Mother Conference. The Clarksons live in Fort Worth, Texas, with their four children, Sarah, Joel, Nathan, and Joy.*

Sarah, my first child, took off reading at 5 years old and never looked back. After having a child who was so easy to teach, I still shake my head in amazement that it was so hard for me to think about teaching her. I had a college degree and a teaching certificate, but, as a young homeschooling mother, I had to fight off a gnawing fear that I was not capable of teaching my child to read well. I was convinced that it required special gifts or knowledge, advanced training, or a secret method or resource.

Of course, like most idealistic, first-time homeschooling moms, I wanted only the very best education for my child, so I assumed that meant buying the best materials. About three reading programs and six hundred dollars later, though, I was feeling like a failure, not because my child was not reading yet, but because I could not keep up with all the tapes, games, cards, toys, and gimmicks that I was supposed to be using. Fortunately, I was introduced to a fifteen-dollar book that allowed me to painlessly and effectively introduce Sarah, and subsequently my other children, to the wonderful world of the printed word.

That whole process opened Sarah's eyes to words on a page, but it also opened my eyes in a different way. I had come to homeschooling with the mistaken notion that I was somehow responsible for teaching my child how to learn. I felt I not only had to teach her knowledge, but that I had to give her the ability to acquire it. I was not sure exactly what it was I was supposed to do, but I felt responsible to do something. I guess some of the secular philosophies about children being born with a mind that is a "blank slate" had crept into my thinking about my role as a home educator. I was overwhelmed by the thought of having to fill that slate with the right information. As I observed the learning process in Sarah, though, God began to show me that in the task of educating my children, He has gone before me.

Now, ten years and three more children later, I am relaxed and confident as a homeschooling mother. This is partly because I am more experienced as a home educator, but primarily because I began to look at my children through the eyes of biblical faith, rather than through the eyes of secular educators. The spiritually untrained eye may see a blank slate, but the eye trained by biblical truth sees that Someone has been here before me. The "slate" is already written upon.

It is funny how we can sometimes read the Scripture and not realize the full impact of it. Consider the implications of Ephesians 2:10: "For we are His workmanship, created in Christ Jesus for good works, which God prepared beforehand that we should walk in them" (NKJV). That does not sound like a blank slate to me. If God has prepared my children from eternity past to do good works for Him as adults, it seems only logical that He has also prepared them from eternity past for the time they will be children with Clay and me at home. Let me share with you three ways I believe God has already prepared your children.

God has prepared your children to learn.

No one really knows how a child learns to speak. Parents do not have to go through a beginning speaking curriculum, or take them to a special school of audio-phonics. It just happens. Researchers and scientists have tried to explain it, but, in the end, all they can say is that, for the early childhood environment, the more verbal it is the better. Children come already wired for speaking and for learning.

When you realize that God has pre-wired your child to learn, not just language skills, but all knowledge, it throws a whole new light on teaching. I look at beginning reading much differently now. The ability to read is not a skill that I must somehow instill; it is already written on the slate. My children are prepared from eternity past to read. My role as a parent-educator is not so much actually teaching my child how to read, as it is creating the environment in which that inherent, God-given ability can find root and grow.

There is a hunger and thirst for knowledge in your children that you did not put there, and that your children will, of their own accord, attempt to satisfy. It is God's design. Your role is to make sure they feed on wholesome foods and drink from pure wells. This is a very liberating idea to someone burdened by doubt about their ability to teach.

God has prepared your children to learn at home.

The family structure is not a sociological accident, an experiment, or a necessary invention of some nomadic people at the beginning of history. It is completely God's design. In fact, it is the first and only institution designed and implemented by God before the Fall. Though corrupted by sin, it is nonetheless God's foundational institution of human relationship, without which the later institutions of government and the church are incapable of functioning properly.

Your children are designed by God and prepared by Him in eternity past to learn from within your family structure all they need to know in order to live righteously and well. God did not somehow forget to include the institution of school in the Scriptures: it is not there because it is not needed. God intended from the beginning that children would live and learn within a family. That is already written on the slates of their hearts.

When a family and home is functioning as God designed it, learning will not be something that is somehow "added," but will be a natural part of family life. It is natural for your children to want to learn from you, and for you to want to instruct and guide them. It is natural to want to be with your children every day of their lives until they leave your home. In contrast, it is unnatural to send your children to strangers to do for them what God designed you and your family to do.

God has prepared your children to learn at home
from real books and real life.

We are a nation hooked on experts. Like co-dependents, we believe we need them to tell us what to do, and they need us to have someone to tell what to do. Nowhere is this more evident than in education. We become dependent upon textbooks, workbooks, and curricula to teach our children, and experts create more and more of them to reinforce our dependence on their "expertness."

God has prepared your children to learn all they will need to know from books and from life. We are already "people of the Book"—the Bible. God's Word and words are eternally preserved in a book. We need no earthly mediator to explain the deep mysteries of eternal salvation and divine purpose contained in that book. God's preparation of us from eternity past to learn from His Book enables us to learn from all books. It is already written on the slate of every child. They learn from books because God has chosen to communicate to us through a book.

We also learn from life as naturally as we learn from books. The Proverbs overflow with this principle. The great *shema* of Israel—the great "hear and pay attention" command—in Deuteronomy 6:4-9, still repeated daily by pious Jews, emphasizes the foundational importance of passing along righteousness to our children through the common, everyday events of life. You will never run out of materials in the classroom of life. God has designed every child to learn from life experiences, especially within the home and family.

Do I still need to plan, prepare, guide, and direct the living and learning process that goes on in my home? Of course I do. That is what God designed us as parents to do (Eph. 6:4). How I wish I had known that first year that God has gone before me in my children's hearts and minds. They are not blank slates, but spiritual and intellectual creatures of God already prepared and ready to learn. As bearers of God's image, they come to my home possessing intelligence, curiosity, and creativity.

Your children will seek out knowledge and develop skills because that is what God has designed them to do. Your role is not so much to control, manage, and manipulate their learning through a variety of teaching devices, but to create a learning environment, offer guidance and insight, and let them learn. You are not responsible to fill up a blank slate. You are privileged to accompany your children, as they cooperate with the God who made them, in the marvelous process of learning and growing. He has been there before you.

From Confusion to Confidence:
Making Choices in Curriculum

——— *Camilla Leedahl* ———

Born into an Air Force family, Camilla spent her first fifteen years in cities, living around the world. When her father retired to a small farm in northwestern Minnesota, she thought that this time they had moved to the end of the world. Working in Fargo, North Dakota, Camilla had big dreams for her career as a registered nurse. When she married Arlo in 1977, she traded her nurse's cap for a pair of chore gloves and became a partner in their farm and ranch in southeastern North Dakota's rugged sandhills. Arlo and Camilla have been home-schooling their three children for eleven years: Jonathan is 18, Melody is 16, and Peter is 12.

Camilla is an enthusiastic advocate of home education in the state of North Dakota, speaking to civic groups and the media, writing how-to articles, presenting workshops on a myriad of topics, counseling homeschoolers and support group leaders, and serving as a support group leader in the Fargo area.

She recently established Hearthside Productions and published her first book, The Homeschool Support Group.

⟨▭▭▭▰⟩ "You seem so confident and your children are remarkable. What curriculum do you use?" As homeschoolers earnestly look for the direction they need, this is the most common question they ask me. It is also the most difficult question to answer. It is difficult, not just because each child is an original or because each family situation is unique, but because books and curriculum are not the central issues to the success of home education. The confidence I have is not in myself, nor in books. It is assurance in the Lord and His direction. The pleasant results others observe in my children are fruits of their relationship to Christ. These things I learned the hard way after misplacing my reliance onto methods and curriculum, rather than on the light of God's Word.

Eleven years ago, I approached this new venture of home education with my naturally methodical, researching ways. With a "Lord, help me!" prayer, I gathered, organized, and digested all the information I could find. I subscribed to magazines (there were only a few back then), read books, and examined curriculum catalogs and what reviews I could find. I busily wrote out my philosophy, determined some goals, and set up my record keeping. I visited a curriculum fair and purchased my books. I did everything I understood a prudent homeschooler should do. A few months passed as we pursued our system, until the latest how-to books arrived. These were filled with new ideas and new systems, so I changed approaches, altered goals and bought new curriculum. In preparation for the state mandated annual achievement test, I focused on the checklists. I "taught to the test," because I wanted my children to measure up. To secure the best possible education for them and the best possible outcome from them was my quest!

However, despite my knowledge, and despite purchasing and using the newest and best that the world of home education had to offer my children, uncertainty pursued me. Like a wave of the ocean, I surged upward with each new approach to learning, then sank down as my hopes were not fulfilled. With the second year rolling to a close, my plight became apparent to me: I was awash in a sea of curriculum confusion.

One early June day, I looked with distress at yet another new strategy to implement for the next year in front of me. Why was I not at peace? In our homeschooling efforts, had I not been trying to serve God and obey Him? Overwhelmed, I hastened fom the house, and swiftly walked down our pasture lane. Striding furiously along, I wept, "Lord, something is not right with my homeschool planning process. I don't know what to do next!" I stopped under the welcoming shade of an old cottonwood tree. The tranquil beauty of our meadow stretched before me, the hills and the river beyond. The words from a psalm came repeatedly to mind. "Be still and know that I am God. Be still and know that I am God. Be still and know that I am God." I sat quietly, the Creator ministering to me through His creation. A portion of another psalm came to mind, giving voice to my heart, "Show me Your ways, O Lord; teach me Your paths. Guide me in Your truth and teach me. My hope is in You all day long."

My heart was pierced as He revealed to me the futility of my human efforts. I had been researching and planning so hard, but, instead of submitting to God, I had been maneuvering Him carefully into my plans. I had been hurrying along on my own timetable, not waiting for His leading. How could I have received counsel from the Lord under those limitations? I needed a discerning eye to see through the fog of popular homeschool choices. I needed a purified set of goals, a new standard with which to judge progress. I no longer wanted to do it my way.

The words of Romans 12:2 gripped me; I was not to adapt myself to the pattern of the world, but to be transformed by the renewing of my mind. Only then could I know His good and perfect will. In my heart, the Lord counseled me to take my focus away from my favorite authors' and speakers' insights, and away from my own understanding, as well. Those human props must be set aside before the Spirit of God could do His transforming work in me.

It was a precious summer. Every morning I would get up early and search the Word, then work in the garden with a fervent and unceasing prayer in my heart. The rhythmic routine of weeding and cultivating, pruning and harvesting gave my mind room for meditation. Day after day, I focused on what He was revealing to me from His Word, enlightening me on purpose, on education, on learning, and on my children's gifts and abilities. I became a student of my children, desiring to know them intimately, purposing to know their hearts, their hopes, their dreams.

The cultivation of the Word in my heart bore its fruit. I began to know what was necessary for my children. They needed to understand what they were learning, not just master the content. They needed to possess the tools of learning, so they could learn for themselves as a way of life. Most of all, they needed to long for the Lord. Academic requirements needed to become secondary to spiritual goals, for pursuit of discipleship in Jesus Christ would vault them far beyond what man could ever offer.

As I planned for my children's studies, I allowed time for the Lord to confirm within me the course of action for each child, determined by their particular needs. Waiting was not easy, since I am a "do it right now" type of person. September came, and I was concerned the children might "get behind." I need not have worried, for the Lord provided richly during this interim. They happily did projects in topics of interest to them, with limited guidance from me, learning more than I could have imagined. I decided that I could go ahead and use many of the books I had previously purchased. However, instead of letting those books be the substance of our education, they now became merely tools in our toolkit of learning. The how-to books and academic guides showed themselves useful, but they were now subjected *first* to the illuminating light of God's Word, speaking to my prepared heart.

While acquaintance with Christ and the renewing of my mind is an ongoing process, that summer of concentrated time, separated to God's Word, was the change that made the difference in our homeschooling lifestyle. As the years go by and adjustments are made for the changing needs of our family, He continues to show Himself to be our reliable and primary source of direction.

Watching expectantly what the Lord is doing in the lives of my children, I quietly marvel at my Teacher, my Guide, my Provider. The joy is unspeakable. Nothing, nothing in this world can compare with walking in the Light.

His Burden Is Light

———— *Margie Gray* ————

Margie Gray was born on a Navajo Indian reservation in Arizona where her parents taught. When Margie was eight, the family moved to Barstow, California, where she finished high school. Although she had many exceptional teachers, Margie began to see the "social agenda" of the educational system. Seeing the problems her parents faced within their profession, she chose a nursing degree. After college, Margie moved to Mountain Pass, California, where in 1983, she met and married her husband, Owen, a heavy equipment operator.

In 1990 Owen and Margie moved their family of six to Arkansas to be nearer to relatives. Margie's grandmother lived with them the last three years of her life.

After she died, Owen and Margie longed to move west. So in 1997, with hopes of employment nearer to home and a better climate, the Gray family moved to Silver City, New Mexico. Owen and Margie have always homeschooled their five girls, ages 14, 11, 9 (twins), and three. The academic benefits of homeschooling have been wonderful, but greater joy has been in the strengthening of family relationships. Because of this, Margie participates actively in the leadership of local homeschool groups to encourage the hearts of parents toward their children.

In 1993, Margie self-published the literature-based curriculum, The Prairie Primer. *She is currently writing a dual project,* Academics and Anne *and* Anne's Anthology, *a unit study and reference work, respectively, based on Anne of Green Gables.*

As I strolled down the San Diego street contemplating the beginning of our first actual year of homeschooling, I was enveloped in fear—and it was only kindergarten! Janell's whole education depended on me. In fact, how could I possibly think that I could teach my children?!? I knew that a tutorial, one-on-one education was ideal, but would I be able to teach my daughter everything she needed to know?

The decision to homeschool came early. By the time our first daughter, Janell, was born, my husband and I had been reading books by Dr. Raymond

Moore, and were convinced that for a child to spend all day behind a desk surrounded by peers was indeed exhausting and unnecessary. We were thoroughly convinced of the rightness of homeschooling, but I imagined that everything in my children's education depended on me. This burden was so heavy that I staggered under it, but Jesus says that His yoke is easy and His burden is light. If I had to do it over again, it would not be so much a program or a method that I would change in our homeschooling, but more the recognition and acknowledgement of who is in charge. Over time, this truth became a reality in our homeschooling. But, as I walked along that day, I wondered, "What on earth have I been thinking for the last five years! What if there are gaps in her education?"

I was past the point of caution, or even normal concern—I was fearful! My consolation came in the form of 2 Timothy 1:7: "For God hath not given us the spirit of fear; but of power, and of love, and of a sound mind" (KJV). Truly my fear was not of God. I pictured my girls' video of Psalty singing, "I can do all things through Christ that strengthens me." I realized then that whatever was needed, God would supply the strength. As I look back on this incident, I chuckle at the thought of being petrified to homeschool kindergarten. I never even attended kindergarten, yet went on to graduate from college!

Panic departed, but was replaced by concern and resolve to provide (single-handedly!) everything Janell needed for an excellent education. So, as I began homeschooling—while breast feeding newborn twins and with a toddler in tow—I was determined there would be no holes in MY kindergartener's education! I could do it all! And we did: I covered reading, writing, arithmetic, art, history, Bible, and arranged for both piano and swimming lessons. The stress, though, of "doing it all"—being mother, teacher, cook, janitor, bus driver, secretary, and nurse—became more and more burdensome. Eventually, productive tutorial time with Janell was also hindered by the increasing educational needs of the younger children.

Then the gaps showed up. After five years of homeschooling, the holes I had feared were becoming obvious. On her fourth grade standardized exam, Janell scored post–high school in reading, but ranked at only a first grade level in spelling. (This was in spite of going through several spelling programs.) As I was ordering vitamins one day, the salesclerk asked me about our reading program and then promptly informed me that my child would be a terrible speller because of it! It was confirmed: I had ruined her! I entered depression. My worst nightmare was upon me: GAPS! How would I ever fix this?

At this point the Lord comforted me with a friend who reminded me that I had eighteen years to instill what was needed. Janell was very proficient in reading, she had a good foundation in math, she knew the discipline of learning and could learn what she needed to. Moreover, we had plenty of time to work on spelling. Perhaps, all was not lost.

Oh, but then there were other holes. Like the one in the area we call "practical living." There was the day I asked Janell to fill in for her sister on dish washing. She had been trained the year before and knew what to do. Somehow, though, when she couldn't find the right dish washer detergent, she thought the liquid dish washing soap would work. It was hard to be calm as the soap oozed and bubbled out onto the floor, but I reminded myself that her memory only needed refreshing; that she would have dish duty again next year; that I still had the remainder of her eighteen years at home to instill this, as well as so many other things. There was still hope.

There was comfort, too, in Solomon's words from Ecclesiastes: "Of making many books there is no end; and much study is a weariness of the flesh. Let us hear the conclusion of the whole matter: Fear God, and keep his commandments: for this is the whole duty of man" (Eccl. 12:12–13; KJV). If, as the Preacher says, there is no end to knowledge or the making of books, then knowing everything is indeed impossible. No one educational program will be complete. My own public school education had many holes. (One of the fun things about homeschooling is filling in some of those gaps—like learning parts of history that I had never learned.) There will always be gaps—areas inadvertently missed, consciously avoided, or those which are presented but the children never quite master, and so have to be brought back for round two.

To prevent gaps many people stick rigidly to a scope and sequence, a list of subjects to insure they "cover all the bases." They find themselves plodding faithfully through a set curriculum, knowing their children will cover the standard areas at the "right" time. But, is this real insurance against gaps? And whose scope and sequence should you follow? The biggest hole in my education was that I had not been taught to fear the Lord. According to Proverbs 9:10: "The fear of the Lord is the beginning of wisdom, and the knowledge of the Holy One is understanding" (NKJV). I should not fear holes in my children's education, but fear God and allow Him to lead us in our schooling.

God is faithful. He has His ways of providing, once we recognize that we cannot do it all. For instance, at a hectic time in my life, my mother's unsought assistance became a blessing as she shouldered part of the burden of homeschooling the twins. She was cheered by the challenge of teaching Jessica and Karissa to read. This freed me up for other demands and was a tremendous blessing to me. God also provided a music teacher who would come to my home, giving more time for academics and less time playing shuttle-bus. He provided outside children, whom I included in our homeschool part-time, so my girls could develop friendships. Spelling was the difficult area for all my girls until I found a non-threatening spelling curriculum which finally made improvement attainable. As I saw God provide, I felt less compelled to carry the burden of filling the "gaps" myself.

As my children have grown, they have begun to fill in their own gaps. It is delightful to have them tell me things I never taught them. My eldest taught me about ball lightning, which is probably the strange phenomenon mentioned in the *Little House* books. While I was researching *Anne of Green Gables*, my girls told me how Florence Nightingale was a nurse during the Crimean War. These were things they had studied on their own, independent of our academic program. Janell can work and grade her own algebra. They occasionally need an explanation or a reminder of a principle, but I am thrilled that they have learned how to learn.

Perhaps I am taking a child to the doctor, or cleaning up red powdered Jell-o on the white linoleum floor, or helping one of the girls fix a challenging meal—my unavailability does not bring school to a complete halt. The children are trained to move on in their studies, even when Mom doesn't. They have learned to be inquisitive and to find answers on their own. Schooling has become easier, more natural. For science we read books together, or I assign them as free reading. For history we visit historical sites, or look up places on a globe or map as we read about them. We talk about the characters in stories and relate them to the Bible and to life. This more relaxed atmosphere helps the children retain information better.

As for me, I do not feel the pressure that I will make or break their education. Although I am their only teacher, their education is not solely my responsibility. God continues to fill the gaps. I do my best and prayerfully remind God He is to do the rest. As He has said, His "burden is light."

Home Educating for Eternity

——— *Ed and Kathy Green* ———

Ed and Kathy Green were married on December 21, 1974. Two years later (to the day!) their first daughter, Cara, was born. During the next five years, three more daughters would follow: Megan, Shannon, and Brittany. The Green family began to home-
school in 1981. *They have been ministering to the homeschool community ever since. Ed and Kathy are the founders of Homeschoolers of Maine (HOME), an eight-year-old organization established for the purpose of support and encouragement to home educators in Maine. The "Heart of HOME Bookstore" supplies the community with a wealth of titles by favorite authors.*

Pride. We parents are the worst offenders. And home educating parents are no exception. When it comes to our children, how can we help it? Of course, they are so bright, so witty, so talented, so cute, so…GREAT! What are parents to do with such GREATNESS?!

We were faced with this dilemma when it came time for our oldest daughter, Cara, to attend the local public kindergarten. She was already reading, and we hoped to continue this educational fast track all the way to college. The sooner she got there, the better. In order to speed the process along, we opted to teach her at home.

Fortunately, God is wise and wonderful. He smiled at our immaturity, and proceeded to teach us little by little all that we would need to know. He knew what was best for our family, and created a desire within us to listen. Slowly, we began to understand His ways, but it took some time. After a little research, we chose a curriculum. In our first years of homeschooling, there were not as many choices as we have today. The research did not take long. Our "box" of curriculum soon arrived, complete with ruler, pencils, and crayons. We could not wait to begin. A little red desk built by Dad was ready, and a classroom corner was established. Cara, always an eager student, worked dutifully at her little desk for hours each day.

For Mom, though, it was a heartbreaking sight. It seemed so isolating, so confining, and so dull. We wondered if her eagerness to learn would soon fade in an environment such as this. This was not at all what Mom wanted for her bright little girl. God was teaching and Mom was listening...at least a little. The curriculum went back into the box. We did more research, chose another curriculum, and found more heartbreak. This cycle went on for months. Cara absorbed everything happily, while Mom continued to feel unhappy and terribly guilty. What were we missing?

Then a miracle happened. Well, not really, but it did change our home-school approach forever. Mom came down with an illness that required bed rest for several weeks. Enlightenment! With Mom out of commission, the chores had to be shared, right down to the youngest child. Believe it or not, this was a new idea in the Green family. When the chores were finished, school commenced, right on Mom's bed!

During those weeks we read book after book, played educational games, listened to music, talked, and cuddled; and we giggled when the school bus drove by. We were growing in love and care for each other. Quite by accident (or by God's design?!), our family had discovered a peaceful rhythm. Mom was still sick, but she was *happy*, and the family was "cozy." God was teaching, and Mom was listening...a little harder this time.

When life got back to normal, we made a conscious effort to keep a gentle rhythm to our lives that would enhance and not hinder our educational growth as a family. There would be a time for chores, a time for more structured learning, a time for creative projects, a time for play, a time for activities outside of our home, a time for reading together, eating together, and praying together, and a time for quiet. It is not always easy to keep a gentle rhythm: the phone does ring, the baby does cry, unexpected company does drop in, family members do get sick, etc. Even in a crisis, though, that rhythm can have a stabilizing effect on the family. And the effort to keep the rhythm going produces worthwhile results in the end. The family emerges from the home with an obvious harmony. A spirit of contentment is visible in each of its members. Even strangers will note the difference.

Our formal home education years are drawing to a close. The girls are now 21, 20, 18, and 16. They are as different as can be. Except for some things that are strikingly similar. We think that these can only be attributed to the gentle daily rhythm that home education has provided for them. The most obvious similarity is their love for each other. One would hope that all siblings would share such a bond, but there is no doubt about it among these four. It is not uncommon to see them walking arm in arm whenever they are together. Then there is their love for learning. Over the years one of our favorite answers to any of a multitude of questions (whether we knew the answer or not) has been, "Look it up!" It is comical now to see the girls looking things up automatically, in so many situations—to settle an argument, to provoke further discussion, or simply to appease their curiosity. Visiting a new place without checking out the historic sites? Well, it just is not done! The sun and the beaches in Mexico are nice, but we can't leave without learning something (preferably everything!) about the area, its people, and its culture. Every inch of the ancient ruins nearby will be happily explored, while engaging the tour guide in some lively conversation. Quietly, at the end of a busy day, impressions are noted in journals.

Finally, the most striking similarity of all is their love for the Lord. Not one of them is perfect. They make their share of mistakes, but the surety that they have in God's love is a comfort to us as parents. Their willingness to serve Him with their own unique giftedness is what we have really wanted all along. God was teaching us every step of the way. Only by looking back can we see a little more clearly what He was wanting us to know at the outset: they are His; He has a plan for each of them; as they gradually discern His will for their lives, HE will accomplish His work in and through them (however great or small).

Are we proud parents? You bet! Did we accomplish OUR will for our children's lives? Not really. But when we finally allowed the Lord to do His work, we found that He accomplished greater things than we could ever have imagined—things not measured by the world's standards. God was teaching...and the gentle rhythm that He provided for our lives allowed us to learn from Him (Eccl. 3:1–8,14).

The Compass

—————— *Janice Southerland* ——————

Janice's childhood home was Richardson, Texas. She and her husband, David, met at Texas Tech University and moved to Colorado Springs where they were first introduced to homeschooling. Now in Oklahoma, they continue to homeschool their daughters, Kellie (13) and Amy (11). "Homeschooling has changed our life for the best. It's one of the best decisions we ever made because it has whetted our family's appetite for a lifetime of learning!"

Parenting means teaching. To teach, one must be able to learn, and Janice has studied under the best: her mom, who introduced her to inductive Bible study.

Janice has led twenty Precept Bible studies in homes, churches, and at Ft. Carson. Out of a need for inductive materials that would teach students how to learn in the context of Scripture, Janice began writing inductive studies for her own children. Their family ministry, Children's Inductive Bible Studies (CIBS), began in 1994 providing inductive Bible studies for students who can read (third grade and up).

Through CIBS, Janice has presented more than sixty workshops at church and homeschool conferences, instructing parents and church staff how to teach inductive study methods to children. She has also written articles for Eclectic Homeschool Online.

Sometimes it is difficult to get our bearings when we move into unfamiliar territory. We began homeschooling with the perception that it would be "school at home." We attended a homeschool conference in the spring of 1990 (surprised that these people were normal parents!), and selected a curriculum that looked good. I insisted on having a blackboard, a flag, and desks for the three of us (myself and our daughters, ages 5 and 3). We began to learn a routine that gave structure to our school day, but soon realized that school at home was more all-encompassing than a "routine"!

Gradually, over the last several years, we have learned that "school" is not confined to a room and a time. It is a vital, growing aspect of family life. True education is learning how to learn; learning about yourself, your family, the world around you; and, most importantly, getting to know God and His awesome plans for you in His world. I began homeschooling with the idea that I would teach our girls the things I had been taught at their age. God continues to teach me that true education is not merely facts, formulas, dates, and field trips (although those are necessary building blocks). True education is seeing that these things are parts of God's world, created to help us begin to know Him. True education is a lifelong journey, available to anyone willing to learn.

These are some of the trail markers of effective homeschooling we are discovering along the homeschool journey.

Trust God in All Things

When we began our homeschool journey, we were easily overwhelmed by all kinds of advice, curriculum choices, methods, learning styles...in fact, the more we read about schooling, the less competent I felt about teaching. Fortunately, as we began, I heard a speaker explain that parents are qualified and able—even without formal degrees!—to teach their own children. We CAN teach them because God provides all we need for what He requires. How true! And yet, we must continually go to Him with our questions and be willing to sit and hear His advice. God is the only expert worthy of our full attention because He created the precious children that we have, and He knows best how they will learn.

It is a simple, yet powerful truth to remember: make time daily to read God's Word and pray. Many times I have been too busy, and have waited until the day unraveled before stopping to ask Him to guide us and make our attitudes right. I often have to stop and remind my girls that I am learning to be a better parent and teacher, as they are learning to be good children and students. Recognizing that we are all learners helps us realize who the real Teacher is!

Glean All You Can

Resources abound explaining the hows and whys of homeschooling. One of the most important is your local support group. They will provide that family-to-family contact as you venture into unfamiliar territory. Read, observe, and listen to the advice of others with experience. As you do, remember to not compare your bad days, or areas of weakness, with another family's pinnacle of success: it brings despair and it clouds reality. Search out other homeschooling families, and be open to share with one another. In getting to know the uniqueness of other families through their choices and experiences, your family will be enriched and challenged. Listen to others who are walking this road of home education, and your eyes will be opened to areas of value and beauty that you might not have considered on your journey.

I wish I had known when we began that there is more than just one right curriculum, and more than just one right way to homeschool. It is OK to change your plan as you and your family grow. As you begin to gather lots of great ideas, or hear about a fun project to do, remember that it does not ALL have to be done this year. There will be time to work in some things later. Keep a simple file drawer with notes about those great ideas under general categories: science, math, history, music, etc. Later, when you need something new and different, or when you are planning the next semester, the ideas will be there close at hand.

Be Aware of Perspective

As we began, it was tempting to make choices based on another person's opinion or on someone else's values or perceived expectations for our family. Trying to live up to the expectations of others has not always been wise. When we pause to consider that other person's perspective, we might realize that our values differ greatly. What is absolutely essential to one person may not be important to another. What do they value? What do you value? Whose standard do you live by? Are you determining your values based on truth in context with the whole counsel of God's Word?

Because it is so easy to be sidetracked by someone's comments or enthusiasm, we frequently need to monitor our own perspective. Our pastor explains perspective with the illustration of a person who picks up a small piece of green glass. If he holds it to his eye, he will declare that all the world is green, because all that he sees is colored by that glass. True perspective is found by holding the glass at arm's length. Then we realize that, although the piece of glass is green, not everything in the world is. Take time to evaluate what "glass" may be influencing you. Sifting the influences, and holding them in perspective, will help to keep you on track.

Follow God's Priorities for Each Day

It sounds easy in theory, but this is where I struggle the most. I make "to do" lists, and then find myself asking God to bless what I have decided to do...ouch! That would be the same as having a young child make decisions about issues that are beyond his ability and comprehension. In a study of the book of John, it became apparent that Jesus' example was to always seek His Father first. Jesus had very full, productive days, ordered by His Father. He also had time for rest and relaxation. Amazingly, Jesus was not stressed! How was this possible? Jesus avoided stress as we know it because He followed God's priorities for each day. He did not add his own agenda to the work of the day.

I have often crawled along this part of the journey because of my unwillingness to let go of my "to do" lists. Some days lead us in a totally different direction than we had planned: a friend has a pressing need, illness strikes, fatigue overwhelms, a doorbell announces a surprise visit, or we wrestle with a math concept and then with each other! Whatever the detour, when I remember to trust God to know what to put in and take out of each day, and yield to His guidance, He never fails to bring good out of it all. There are no such guarantees, however, when I hold too tightly to those "to do" lists. Trusting God to order each day brings peace and greater satisfaction than any completed list ever will.

What is your destination? When we began the journey of homeschooling, our first goal was to get through the year with good grades. We have since realized that academics will come with daily diligence. Time on the trail has taught us that our life here on earth is simply "boot camp" for eternity. A lifetime of learning is but a brief preparation for life in eternity with God. Our goal now is to invest our days in building relationships and developing character, which have eternal value, as we master academics. Proverbs 3:5–6 has been described as God's compass for life. It is a practical travel guide for the journey of homeschooling as well. It says:

> *Trust in the Lord with all your heart,*
> *and do not lean on your own understanding.*
> *In all your ways acknowledge Him,*
> *and He will make your paths straight.* (NAS)

In homeschooling, as in life, the compass you use to reach your goals and destination will determine the course of your journey. I encourage you to make each day count for what you value. Enjoy the adventure!

Moses Didn't Feel Qualified, Either!

————— Nancy Robins —————

In 1979, after completing his residency in family practice, Lanny Robins and Nancy were married in her hometown of Two Rivers, Wisconsin. Nancy worked as a registered nurse in the neonatal intensive care unit, hoping to acquire skills for their new jobs in Castañer, Puerto Rico. It was there that the Robins' first son, Ethan, was born. When Lanny's time with the Public Health Service ended in 1981, they returned home, ultimately settling in the beautiful Northwoods. Ethan was soon blessed with a new brother, Robbie. Several years later, God sent David, Emilie, and just a few months ago, Anna Marie. Ethan is now 16 years old, Robb is 14, and David and Emilie are 7 and 3.

The Robins family has homeschooled since Ethan was in kindergarten, less one very "educational" year when Ethan attended second grade and Robbie entered kindergarten at the local public school.

Like most young women in the seventies, I dreamed of finishing college and launching into a wonderfully fulfilling career. I would then marry the perfect man, have two children (a boy and a girl, of course) and, when they were both in school full-time, would resume my career, and we would all live happily ever after!

Two sons later, that dream was altered just a bit! But, in a few short years, the boys would be off to school, and I could resume the rest of my dream. Then the time came for Ethan to enter kindergarten. I remember thinking, "But he's still such a little boy, and not yet ready to be in someone else's care. They don't know him like we do, nor do they love him enough to be sensitive to his subtle needs for encouragement, tender words, or hugs. They won't get excited about his accomplishments, other children may be unkind, or he may not understand something and be too shy to speak up." And on and on my mind went. But, they have to go to school; that's how it works.

It was during this period that God called me to Himself, and I began to grow spiritually. As a new Christian, the desire to have Ethan and Robb "well educated with a healthy self-esteem" seemed to lose its importance as the prime focus for their education. We began to understand that as parents, with our heavenly Father's help, we were to teach our children to love God with all their hearts and to be unafraid to stand for what is holy and good. We were beginning to realize that our children did not have to go to school after all. Now, however, a new fear set in—how could we teach these things to our children if we weren't living this way ourselves? Was God asking us to homeschool so that we would grow closer to Him, as well?

In order to help our family put God first, we made Deuteronomy 6:6–7 a guidepost in our home: "These commandments that I give you today are to be upon your hearts. Impress them on your children. Talk about them when you sit at home and when you walk along the road, when you lie down and when you get up" (NIV). God has entrusted our children to us to train—not to school teachers, coaches, music teachers, or even Sunday school teachers. Certainly they have a place, but that place must fit into your overall plan. God will hold each of us parents accountable for how well we have "trained up" His children. Never does He want us to throw up our hands saying, "It's too late," "I'm not smart enough," or "What choice did we have?" If our children leave our home loving God with all their hearts, souls, and minds, and sharing that love with others, I feel they will have received an outstanding education.

Having shared this background with you, I will try to answer the question, "Things we wish we'd known our first year of homeschooling." First of all, I wish we had known God. I wish this for your family as well. Your homeschooling efforts will be merely that unless you see the task ahead as an assignment given to you by God. Then, when nerves are frazzled (which, at times, they will be) and you wonder what you have gotten your family into (I must have been crazy!), you need only look heavenward and know that the God who has called you to this task is the same God who will enable you to do whatever needs to be done. Much heartache, frustration, and wasted energy would have been avoided in those early years had we focused on God's desires for our children rather than our own. As a Christian, never doubt your competence to educate your children, no matter what your educational background may have been. I believe that when you doubt your own abilities, you are doubting God's power to equip you to do all that He has called you to do! Don't forget, Moses didn't feel qualified, either! No one is adequate for this awesome responsibility except God himself!

Secondly, I would have prayed for wisdom regarding all the decisions we made. After many false starts and spending too much money and time on products that didn't produce the results we had hoped for, we finally realized we first needed to discover God's goals for our family so that future plans, teachings, and purchases would have a clear focus. Then, as we set out to educate ourselves about homeschooling, we would have been better able to separate truth from trend. I found it helpful to read many of the classic books by experienced homeschoolers to help clarify my reasons to homeschool. Explore the various ways children learn and the several approaches to teaching children. There are many, so find the style that best suits your family. Homeschool magazines like *The Teaching Home*, *Practical Home Schooling*, and many others have reviewed these in past articles. Mary Pride's "Big Books" along with Cathy Duffy's curriculum manuals have been so helpful to me. After thoroughly gleaning what wisdom you can from experienced homeschoolers, join with your spouse to prayerfully determine the goals God would reveal for your family. Only then will you be ready to formulate long-term and daily plans.

Practically speaking, I encourage you to remember that homeschooling is not an eight to three job, but a lifestyle. You will find educational opportunities in everything from daily living and child care, to home and auto repair, to interpersonal relationships, crisis management (like spilled oatmeal, skinned elbows, or sibling disagreements) and, importantly, flexibility! A great revelation came when I realized that "abnormal" is "normal." If you happen to have a school day go exactly as planned, consider it a special blessing, but don't get discouraged if it doesn't reoccur for another month!

If your family is anything like mine, you will need to constantly remind yourself to "do the best we can with the time and resources God has given us." You will rarely feel that twenty-four hours are adequate. One of the best time savers I can suggest is orderliness. Everything needs to have a home. Then each morning, as part of the school day, everyone pitches in to put things back where they live. You will find much peace working in an environment where everyone can quickly find what they need. In the long run, it will take much less time to maintain than to overhaul.

Answering machines are essential to homeschooling families. Telephone calls, doorbells, and too many house guests or outside activities will steal away time meant for your family. We are not to separate ourselves from others whom God would have us serve, yet we must carefully evaluate all of our commitments. "There is a time for everything, and a season for every activity under heaven…" (Eccl. 3:1–8; NIV). In this season of raising our families, we need to push out anything else that would interfere with our call to homeschool. Remember, even though there are many worthwhile causes, they are not necessarily calling to you for attention. Keep focused on the job God has for you. This is an incredibly grand task, and Satan would love for us to fail. He does not want anything to hinder his work, and strong, godly young people are definitely a hindrance!

The third thing I wish I had known is to have been regularly evaluating what we were doing with our day. It may be a wonderful curriculum, or an approach that fits our family philosophically, but is it continuing to work for the needs of our changing household? What might have succeeded for our family of four might not be effective for our family of seven.

Finally, I wish we'd known that, if, with our Lord's help, we lead each of our children to a personal relationship with the Lord Jesus; instill within them godly character, a servant's heart, a solid grasp of the Three R's, and a love of life and learning; then we will have given them the tools with which to learn anything they set their hearts toward for the rest of their lives. Let your family's decisions be made in light of God's principles, seeking the wise advice of others, but always weighing it against the goals God has given to you for your unique family situation. Then, march forward in faith and confidence knowing that God will honor your obedience. "Trust in the Lord with all your heart and lean not on your own understanding; *in all your ways* [italics mine] acknowledge him, and he will make your paths straight" (Prov. 3:5–6; NIV).

Becoming a Confident Homeschooler

———— *Debbie Strayer* ————

Debbie Strayer is a south Florida native. She and her husband Greg met as college students at Florida State University, and will celebrate their twentieth anniversary this year. Debbie is the mother of two: Nathan (14) and Ashley (11). The family resides in Tampa, where they have been homeschooling for the last ten years. The Strayer family has been active in various ministries, with Greg pastoring a church for several years. Being a sports-minded family, they are often at baseball games watching Nathan play, or at a pool, watching Ashley practice with her synchronized swimming team.

Having received Bachelor's and Master's degrees in education from Florida State University, Debbie began a teaching career, including three years as a special education teacher, three years as a second grade teacher, and one year as the assistant administrator of a remedial math and reading program. As a Florida certified teacher, Debbie has evaluated homeschooled children and assisted their parents for the last seven years.

Debbie is one of the co-authors of the Learning Language Arts through Literature *series and the author of* Gaining Confidence to Teach. *She was the editor of* Homeschooling Today *magazine for six years, and is currently working as the editor on a book of questions and answers for homeschoolers by Dr. Ruth Beechick, due out in May 1998. Debbie is a frequent speaker at homeschooling conferences, and the Strayers will continue their ministry to homeschoolers through the family-owned business established in 1990: Family Educational Services.*

Homeschooling is a walk of faith. You work with what you know to be true in your children, encouraging qualities and abilities that are as yet unseen, going into many days more keenly aware of their failures than their successes.

Looking at it from the natural point of view, you may feel you have a great deal of work to do—maybe too much to be accomplished by any human parent.

After all, Suzy's children all read at 3, and yours still holds the book upside down! Her children do chores at 6 A.M. cheerfully, while yours whine and cry at having to get dressed. Are you sure you can do this thing called home-schooling? After all, Suzy's closets are straight and sweet-smelling, and your children paw through the dryer for their clothes.

When I began homeschooling ten years ago, it was my desire to be the very best teaching parent I could be. Since I was already a teacher by training, I felt (and so did other people) that our homeschool should be creative, thorough, even awe-inspiring, and should produce advanced students who loved things like classical music and using a dictionary. I worked very hard preparing lessons, poring over catalogs so I would not miss anything newer and better than what I was using, and diligently trying to whip my little charges into shape. If I put in the right ingredients, out would come the model children I saw at conventions and heard speakers describing. If I chose the right curriculum, like a recipe correctly done, out would pop children who were smart, kind, and diligent. Then something strange began to happen.

Contentment with our school was nowhere to be found. There was always more I could do. If my child read some new words, or learned a new skill in math, there was always another homeschooler who was ahead of him. My husband was pleased with our work, but I still did not have the housework under control like I wanted, and I don't even want to talk about exercise. What was happening to this teacher turned homeschooler? What had seemed so logical and easy to do in theory had become a great weight, and I could feel myself getting weaker underneath it all.

It was in this state that my husband found me one afternoon—lying face down on the couch. The small boy had been banned to his room for some crime which awaited Daddy's personal attention. I had *had* it. Dinner was not even a part of my conscious thought process, and I lay there feeling miserable. My husband came in and bravely asked how I was doing. Out came a torrent of my inadequacies and failures, closely followed by the children's. Then came the list of things my homeschooling friend did better than me, finishing with the fact that I thought she had even made curtains during the early stages of labor with her fourth child. I was completely unhinged. Surely, he would see the logic in my case and decide to relieve me of the burden of homeschooling.

What he said stunned me and changed my life. "I don't want her (my homeschooling friend) teaching our children," he said. "You're the perfect person to teach our kids. God gave you the personality and gifts that are just right for our children; no one could do a better job than you." How could he say these things? Couldn't he see that I was not measuring up? Then he made the comment that was to put my stress to an end. He said, "God will show you what to do that will be right for our kids," and off he went to deal with the small offender in his bedroom. I was in shock, yet I knew that what he had said had penetrated my fog and was enabling me to think again. Like water to a dying African violet, his words had a rejuvenating effect on me. If what he said was true, then this homeschooling thing required a real change in outlook from me. I had been seeing it as something that I had to do myself, and I was either doing it right or not, with woeful consequences if I were not. He was talking about something completely different—something God would do through me, faults and all. He was talking about receiving the power from God to walk in the calling God had given to us as a family, and to me as the primary teacher.

What I experienced in the following days was nothing short of a miracle, in my opinion. I felt peace. I felt confident about our homeschooling because it was no longer me that I was trying to be confident in—it was the Lord. After searching the Scriptures and looking at the way others had handled their callings from God (Jonah springs to mind), I felt comforted. I was not the only one who had struggled to do something that was impossible through my own strength, but which was very possible through God. I realized that the successes up until then had been divinely inspired, and that the mistakes were not capable of undoing the work of the God of the universe. Now, the weight of my homeschooling responsibilities seemed bearable, even light in comparison. A Scripture I read during that time has become the foundation of our entire homeschool experience: "The one who calls you is faithful and he will do it" (1 Thess. 5:24; NIV).

Since that time I have seen my children learn to read and think, develop character, and enjoy God's creation. I have known that His hand has been guiding in every decision. He has opened doors of opportunity and provided answers in times of need. Certainly nothing we have struggled with has been too small to bring to His attention, or too big for Him to handle.

As my son began ninth grade, I experienced some of the old fears again. What if I do not do it right? What if my transcripts are not acceptable? What if I ruin his life? I think you know what the answer was to my new struggles: "God will show you what to do"—the same as He had years before, because the good news is that God has not changed. He is still faithful to those He calls, and He will see us through each new phase of homeschooling life.

God has also been faithful to provide helpful and encouraging resources along the way, such as the work of Dr. Ruth Beechick. Her books are understandable, yet profound in the way they explain educational concepts and grade-level goals in each subject. She has a deep faith in God that forms the basis for understanding how children learn, and, thus, she gives reasonable and practical ways to teach. The result of reading her works has always been the same for me: peace. If you are just beginning to homeschool, or if you are a discouraged veteran, the best resource for you is the practical wisdom found in books by Ruth Beechick.

God has shown us that homeschooling success is not what is measured on a standardized test, or even in how our children compare to other home-schoolers. Success comes in our house by seeking God, and then doing what He leads us to do. This has translated into being patient with a boy who was not very interested in learning to read. It has meant altering the standard math curriculum to fit a daughter who is very intimidated by even the thought of math. It has meant treasuring the precious moments of love and kindness and revelation that I have shared with my children. Hearing our daughter confess Christ as her Savior as a response to our devotions still has to be the most amazing event of our homeschooling time.

All of us have been humbled during our homeschooling years because each family member has been known by the others as we really are—the good and the bad. My children have been able to witness our struggles and God's victories. They have had a course in real life management, and, because of God's grace, we have come out of ten years of homeschooling with love and respect for each other, and with God-given goals for each person's life.

I can say with confidence that I am sure I could not have continued to homeschool in my own strength and on the basis of my own knowledge. I could not have borne the awesome responsibility for shaping my children's lives and future success based on my making all the right decisions. I am so grateful that I did not have to be the designer of the plan, just one of the vessels for carrying it out.

Fear Not, for I Am with You

————— *Gail Schultz* —————

Gail grew up in Minneapolis and attended a private Christian high school. Her husband Tony grew up on a dairy farm and acquired a love of math from his older sister. They met at the University of Minnesota, where Gail earned a Home Economics degree, and Tony a Computer Science degree.

Tony is currently a software engineer at Lockheed Martin Corporation. They live in Burnsville, Minnesota, where they enjoy intense games of Monopoly with their children Christie, Joseph, Andrew, and Timothy.

Gail developed a unit study curriculum for her children. They had so much fun with it that she decided to publish it. Her three guides, Lessons from History: 1400's–1700's, Lessons from History: 1800's, *and* Lessons from History: 1900's, *help families organize their study of key historical figures through biographies and other literature. She is currently working on* Lessons from History: Creation to 100AD.

✏️ I had a mission. Determined to find the secret recipe that would make my children's homeschooling education excellent, I wanted to find the best curriculum available. I started wading through the swamp of good educational material looking for the best—that perfect plan that would guarantee success. I didn't find it. Almost everything I looked at was good, but each program promised to work better because it employed this feature, followed this theory, or that method. The further I waded into the educational jargon and opposing theories, the more my fear grew. I figured one must need a four-year degree just to make sense of it all. Sure, there were glimpses of light here and there, but how could I be certain that I would be covering all the bases, since all these experts could not even agree?

I studied, read, and interviewed other homeschooling moms. Then, I took a deep breath, and bravely stepped into the frightening world of kindergarten. OK, so kindergarten wasn't that tough. It was nothing but a series of common sense baby steps toward reading and math, building within my daughter an excitement for learning new and interesting things—no big deal. Perhaps first grade would reveal an unsolvable mystery only deciphered by education majors. But no, just the next small step in reading and math, with a little basic information in other subjects. The more I read and paid attention, the more I understood my daughter and what she needed in order to learn. I began to see that whenever I encountered a difficulty, God was ready with an answer. God was teaching me that He is my helper in time of need.

The one subject that did spook me was history, mostly because I knew so little. I had been taught all the Sunday school stories, and knew a few dates, such as "In fourteen hundred and ninety-two Columbus sailed the ocean blue," and that the Declaration of Independence was signed in 1776. Beyond that, history was just a jumble of unrelated names and places. I decided that I had better get a handle on this history stuff, or my children would be seriously impaired (like me). I went to the library and found a general book about history in the adult section. It was about four inches thick—and I am not a great reader. I remember sitting in my front yard with this book, watching my babies play (they were one, 3, 5, and 7), and being amazed to discover that Napoleon began as emperor of France just after George Washington finished as President of the United States. Now, you may be thinking, "how silly—everyone knows that," but I didn't. Here I was a mother of four, a graduate of a Christian high school, with a baccalaureate degree from a state university, but I had never put this together! Bible history, world history, and American history were three distinct subjects; I had never even tried to connect them before.

Well, I was hooked. I began poring over timelines. No longer just because I wanted to be a good homeschooling mom, but now, just because I was curious. Names, places, and events started to make sense. Galileo was studying the heavens about the same time the Pilgrims were coming to America (1620s). Mozart was composing music about the same time as the American Revolution. What a blast! My excitement and enjoyment has been rubbing off on my children. Currently, they can't wait to find out if Hannibal will survive his duel with General Gisbo during the second Punic War.

I had been afraid because I knew so little history. God knew that need and met the need. My anxieties have decreased, and God has shown me that He has a plan. God is in control, and He is gracious. He knows me, He made me, and He gave me my teaching style. He knows my children. He made them with their individual strengths and their own learning styles. He also chose me to be their mother.

Similar fears are expressed by new homeschooling parents. Not all are so scared about kindergarten. Usually, their fears involve more advanced subjects, like biology labs and algebra. God has made it very clear, though, that we are not to worry! "Therefore do not worry about tomorrow, for tomorrow will worry about itself. Each day has enough trouble of its own" (Matthew 6:34; NIV). This is not just a nice idea; this is a command. He is God. To Him we have entrusted our finances, our health, our eternal security. Surely, we can trust Him to gently show us how to homeschool.

Mission accomplished! I have discovered the secret ingredient in the recipe of successful homeschooling: "Trust in the Lord with all your heart and lean not on your own understanding; in all your ways acknowledge him, and he will make your paths straight" (Proverbs 3:5, 6; NIV).

Relax; it's not that complicated. Don't worry about the educational debates. Pay close attention to your children, and pray. Then read the homeschool guides and explore the educational options. God is faithful. He has blessed the homeschooling community with lots of helpful information about learning styles and teaching methods. There is so much good curriculum available. Trust Him as you do your research to show you which methods and materials are best for your family. God is the best educator there is. He is able to masterfully tailor a curriculum to meet the needs of your children.

God continues to meet the curriculum needs in our family. My children pore over the atlas looking for the answers to our computer geography game. They race each other to build up points quickly by answering the most math problems in their math game. Now, I have heard that some children love flash cards, but, if I had decided that my children should sit down and increase their speed in math with flash cards, it would be as dry as week-old toast. But God knew the need (learn the multiplication tables) and met the need: a fun computer game with a little friendly competition.

God made my daughter. She loves to read and write poetry; at 12 years old she is so delighted about Shakespeare that she giggles while reading it. I certainly would never have picked this out for a seventh grader, but God knows best.

God made my oldest son, who is two grades ahead in math. He likes to have the directions laid out clearly, step by step, and doesn't enjoy creative writing. God has plans for him, and is tailoring an education to prepare him for these plans.

God made my middle son, who struggles to read and understand math, but who sees life through an artist's eyes, always coming up with creative alternatives.

God made my youngest son, who seems capable of anything—way ahead in reading and math—but who sometimes forgets to put his pants on.

How could I customize an academic plan to challenge their strengths and shore up their weaknesses? "With man this is impossible, but with God all things are possible" (Matt. 19:26; NIV). Do not worry about what you do not know. Keep studying and walking in the path that God is showing you. One step at a time, God wants you to keep depending on him. Work diligently in the tasks He gives you, and trust Him.

"Fear not, for I am with you" (Isa. 41:10; NKJV).

Can I Homeschool without Commitment?

——— *Frank and Debbie Schaner* ———

Frank and Debbie Schaner were born and raised in Montana. The day after their wedding in 1981, they moved to Louisiana so Frank could begin his chemical engineering career with an oil company. After fourteen years spent in southwest Louisiana and Houston, Texas, they returned to Montana in 1995 to establish family roots and to grow their business for helping homeschool families. Ranging in age from 6 to 15, their four children, Daniel, Rachel, Anna, and Amanda, have always been homeschooled.

The Schaners used Frank's chemical engineering background and Debbie's registered nurse training in a unique way when they started Home Training Tools in late 1994. This business was begun to help homeschool families develop an understanding and a love for God's creation through science. Through Home Training Tools, the Schaners provide homeschool families easy access to a great variety of affordable, and often hard to find, educational science products. They have also provided parent workshops to promote science and have taught science workshops and courses to groups of homeschool children. Two articles written by Frank, on selecting microscopes and telescopes, were published in the July-August 1997 issue of The Teaching Home *magazine.*

"Commit your way to the Lord; trust in him and he will do this: He will make your righteousness shine like the dawn, the justice of your cause like the noonday sun" (Psalm 37:5–6; NIV).

We were excited when we began, eleven years ago, homeschooling Amanda, our oldest child. The city we lived in had just expanded kindergarten to an all-day program, and we just couldn't bear the thought of handing over our joyful 5-year-old for six hours of structured classroom activity. Homeschooling was becoming more visible at the time, and that seemed like a good alternative. After a quick evaluation of the options, we made a decision to homeschool Amanda for one year. What a great year that was! We had so much fun, and even learned a great deal.

Summer came and we debated again: "Is our firstborn now ready to enter the ranks of the dutiful, marching off to the local grade school?" Again, we thought God was calling us to keep Amanda home. We spent the year reading many books to her, and Debbie taught her to read with a supplemental phonics program. Our school was very unstructured, loosely planned, and we had no long-term goals. Our main objective was to protect our precious child just a little longer, while adequately preparing her for "school."

During that second year a dramatic change occurred—one that eventually affected almost every aspect of our lives. Debbie read a magazine article encouraging parents to discern whether God was really calling them to homeschool, and, if so, to be fully committed to that calling. We didn't need anyone to convince us of God's total sovereignty over our lives, or of our responsibility to teach our children the "fear of the Lord." However, Deuteronomy 6:4–9 now raised many questions that we did not have before. What did it mean to teach our children God's commandments "when you sit at home and when you walk along the road, when you lie down and when you get up," and to "write them on the doorframes of your houses and on your gates" (NIV)? As we searched the Scriptures, prayed, and counseled with friends, we became convinced that we were doing the right thing in homeschooling Amanda, but for the wrong reason. God was not glorified in our non-committal, year-to-year approach. At that point, we became fully committed to the homeschooling lifestyle.

Our family is benefiting greatly from making homeschooling an integral part of our lives. To begin with, we think and plan for the long term: not the next year or two, but the next generation or two. We are preparing our three daughters to be godly wives, mothers, and homeschool teachers, who will give of themselves to their family and to Christ's church. We are preparing our son to glorify God as a husband, father, homeschool overseer, church elder, and business owner, who will provide for his family while serving others. With these long-term goals, it becomes easier to make major decisions, like where we will live, go to church, and work. It is also much easier to make other decisions, such as what areas to study, what skills to develop, and how to invest the time and monetary resources God has provided us.

We see two major results of committing our family to a homeschooling lifestyle: first, starting a business to help homeschool families; and second, moving home to Montana. As we prayed about and explored the many options before us, we thought God was leading us to move back to Montana permanently, and to start a business helping homeschool families teach science. Frank's engineering job had required us to move every few years and had kept him many long hours away from home. The frequent moves had made it difficult to teach our children the importance of establishing roots in family, local church, and community. Further, we saw many benefits in owning and operating our own business. Not only would we choose whom to employ and whom to serve, but we would teach our son necessary business skills, and employ our daughters, prior to marriage. As a result, we now live in Montana, where we operate our own business.

Committing to a homeschooling lifestyle also requires sacrifices. Financial sacrifices are obvious: needing to buy many extra books and materials while living on a single income and still paying public school taxes. It means learning to be content with less. In our family, we have given up the nice vacations, newer car, meals at restaurants, visits to the beauty shop, and costly new clothes. Time sacrifices are even more significant. Focusing on the areas of study more necessary to meeting our goals, we have given up many of the tempting, fun, outside activities that are abundant in homeschool groups. Many evenings are spent preparing Latin or high school math and science lessons, rather than just relaxing, or pursuing our own interests.

The rewards of a homeschool lifestyle are many and significant. We spend time together, real quantity time. Our relationships with each other, and with our children, are much closer. We function as a family unit when we work and when we play. We can accomplish more working together, and we are able to work out right away any problems and differences.

Watching our children grow in wisdom and stature, becoming more like Jesus Christ, is a tremendous reward. Because we know our children well, we are able to pray for God's grace to grow in very specific areas of their lives. We are also able to adapt our teaching to address either specific or broad areas of study. Instead of just "preparing our children for college," we delight in learning all we can about literature, history, art, and science, and seeing God's work in it all. We think every part of life is an opportunity to learn and to teach: our daily tasks, walks together, hospitality, gardening, visits with friends, serving others, even watching a good video.

The homeschooling lifestyle we have chosen also helps us focus on doing the day-to-day work well, to the glory of God. When we have a bad day or a discipline problem, we have to deal with it rather than threaten to put our children in another school. If our children are not learning what they should, we know that we are responsible. We are teaching our children and making these necessary sacrifices, not just for today's rewards, but for the sake of our grandchildren and great-grandchildren. Obstacles are easier to overcome with this long-term perspective, so that we no longer feel like quitting on the bad days. We have also learned to plan and schedule our days, yet remain sufficiently flexible to absorb the many unforeseen events that occur weekly. Proverbs 16:3 has been a great help to Debbie: committing our ways to the Lord helps our thoughts to be established. During those first two years we homeschooled, we were very much like a builder who starts to work on a house without a plan and without counting the cost. We were digging holes for the foundation without knowing how the house was going to look. We were ready to quit anytime it got tough, or the cost became too high. Being fully committed to a homeschooling lifestyle has meant developing a plan, calculating the cost to complete it, and working diligently every day, building according to the plan. We experience much joy and satisfaction in building this house together, and in looking back each day, week, and year at the lasting progress. We see our children growing spiritually in wisdom and knowledge. We see teaching and learning that will carry over to the next generation. We delight in a growing capacity to minister to others.

We are totally inadequate to undertake this commitment in ourselves, but by God's grace we can do all things through Jesus Christ. In all that you do, may your family also be fully committed to the ways of the Lord, for His glory.

Part 5

Christian Character

The Heart of the Child:
Homeschooling's Highest Objective

———— Monte and Karey Swan ————

Monte was born and raised in Wisconsin. He is blessed with wonderful Christian parents and a spiritual heritage that has borne abundant fruit and happiness. He has a degree in geological engineering from Michigan Tech and a Masters in geology from the University of Arizona. He is vice-president of MagmaChem Exploration, Inc., a geologic research and exploration consulting group.

Karey was born in Salzburg, Austria and raised in Colorado and Arizona. Her Christian parents were always there for her and encouraged her to develop her creativity. She studied nutrition and landscape architecture at the University of Arizona. Karey is a lifelong learner and has studied harder after her formal schooling teaching herself subjects ranging from beekeeping to theology. Her greatest creative passion is textile art.

Monte and Karey were married in 1975 and settled in the Colorado mountains in 1983. They decided to homeschool before their first child was born and now spend fifty percent of their time ministering to homeschool families. Thousands have been touched through their books, albums, concerts, and speaking. Most of all, they believe homeschooling should be a family-builder, focusing on education of the child's heart.

Not long ago we were talking to Monte's cousin, Bekki, who lives on a dairy farm in northern Wisconsin. Monte had just asked Bekki for her definition of "the homeschool lifestyle" when she began laughing. Monte asked her, "What is so funny about my question?" Becki said, "Oh, it's not your question—it's the answer." When she quit laughing, she painted a vivid picture of her 18-month-old son, Moses, sitting on the linoleum floor pouring a gallon of maple syrup over his head, and then happily splashing, slapping, and trying to swim in it. Rather than panicking, Bekki was savoring the sweet moment. Now, we do not recommend that parents provide their children with jugs of maple syrup to experience sweet moments. However, Bekki's answer illustrates the wisdom of a wonderful homeschool mother romancing her son's heart and protecting his sense of wonder.

Our own children would have had more sweet moments if, in our first year of homeschooling, we had understood the truth of Dr. Ruth Beechick's statement: "The missing ingredient in most educational approaches is the heart of the child." It took us years to realize that the highest objective in homeschooling is the education of our children's hearts. This is also referred to as character development, or conforming a child's image unto Christ—the process of sanctification. It is what Proverbs 22:6 is all about. The Hebrew expression, "train up a child," includes the idea of starting a child along a particular way— the way of wisdom. A deliberate choice is made by the child's heart between the two ways. Will the child choose wisdom or folly, righteousness or wickedness? In this context, the words "discipling," "shepherding," and "mentoring" have been used. But, since we are dealing with a heart that has a free will, we like to use the word "romancing" because it emphasizes the winning of that heart. This is consistent with the original love story of Calvary—the greatest romance. Proverbs is not about teaching the intellect, but training the heart. It is about aiming the arrow, not sharpening its point.

During our first homeschool years, we tended to focus on the academics— unknowingly embracing the Greek method of education which concentrates on the intellect at the expense of the heart. Homeschooling became a time of day, a room in the house, or a hat we put on. We followed a specific curriculum with Karey assuming the primary role of teacher—leaving Monte on the periphery. However, when we made the heart of the child the primary objective, both of us came to the very center of the homeschool. In this way, homeschooling encompassed the whole lifestyle of our family—not just a desk and textbook—and the world became our year-round classroom.

Homeschooling is a romance of our children's hearts as we draw them and woo them to God's Truth. The primary way we do this is with story. The story is told through our lives unfolding before our children's eyes, and through the story in great books and narratives. The vehicle of story carries the cargo of Truth better than any other teaching method because it is the language of the heart. We should follow Jesus' example. He not only taught through parables, but He kept His followers with Him so they could observe His life and story.

Here is a practical example of story in books. In a textbook we might read that in the mid-1860s, doctors began giving their patients anesthesia before operating. Then, we might read of doctors discovering the need for steriliza-tion. To summarize, we might require memorizing facts for a test. From our own experience, though, we know that little of this information will remain in memory. On the other hand, if we read a book, like the biography of Joseph Lister, we learn that it was a status symbol for pre-1860s doctors to wear dirty, bloody lab aprons, but that the majority of their patients died of gangrene. We read of a patient's fear that he would never come out of surgery alive. Though a dentist in America had written about anesthesia and Louis Pasteur had writ-ten about germs, these were discounted by the surgeons. However, Joseph Lister pulled it all together. He ordered his ward's bedding cleaned between patients and his tools sterilized between uses. He anesthetized his patients dur-ing surgery so he could work carefully and cleanly. His patients walked out of the hospital alive and well. But...the surgeons still ignored his research.

Our children read this biography, and realized that much suffering would have been alleviated had Lister's ideas been accepted prior to the U.S. Civil War. Moreover, they experienced the drama, felt the patients' pain and Lister's frustration, and were inspired by Lister's passion. They will never forget his story because it moved their hearts.

Unfortunately, our culture has been losing its story ever since the Enlightenment philosophers dismissed the idea of a divine Author. As a result, modern education is reductionist, which means it is characterized by islands of specialized information surrounded by oceans of interdisciplinary ignorance. We lose the whole in the parts. Facts alone are inadequate, as the failure of public schools dramatically demonstrates. In contrast, story is the vessel that enables us to sail the oceans between the islands of information. It provides a web of meaning, or a big picture, where facts can be hung, shaped, and inter-preted. Then the flow of history, the processes of the ages since before the beginning of time, becomes a passionate drama—Creation's epic—God's story. This connects history, science, art, and theology into a purposeful framework of romance, because God is not only the Author but also the Hero of the story.

When we feed our children knowledge that has been fragmented into hour-long class subjects, it makes little sense to them. They need the context and the story. Would we be reported for child abuse if we made our children eat a cake by the individual ingredients: salt, raw eggs, baking powder, flour, etc.? Yuck, we would never do that! It only makes sense to eat a cake whole, baked and frosted. It tastes better and does not cause indigestion! The same is true for education.

As we live the story of our lives before our children's eyes, it is easy to lose the larger perspective if our story becomes just the "random days of our lives." For example, homeschool mothers can become so wrapped up in the "school-ish" part of homeschooling, that they put their own lives and interests on hold as a sacrifice to their children. As noble as this seems, Karey has identified it as a sort of negligence: withholding who she is—the best part of herself—from our children. How can she give our children the part of her life that can romance their hearts if she is running on empty? Has Karey's life's story been just a tale of maintenance (cleaning, laundry, and ironing), or has it told a drama of creative passions and of a whimsical love for exploring the beauty of God's creation? Has her life been attractive to her children? She now tries to live beyond maintenance, and our children know her as a person as she crafts a dried flower wreath, extends hospitality to a tired friend, or picks wild raspberries for lunch. They are kindred spirits, and enjoy a deep, wonderful relationship. Karey's life romances their hearts.

Romance requires relationship, which is the most fundamental part of Creation's story, from the inter-relationships within atoms to the relationship of the Triune God of creation with His children. In our lives, relationship with our children is woven throughout our homeschool. For example, our home is designed around food, music, and books for the purpose of facilitating hospitality. The people who have stayed at our Singing Springs Bed and Breakfast, in a sense, have brought the world to our home. Reality is not found in front of a TV, it is found in relationships around a dining room table. That is where some of our best education takes place.

Recently, we hosted a homeschool family camp and tasted the sweet results of romancing our children's hearts. On a still, moon-lit Colorado night, as our high school age children were talking and singing around a campfire, we parents lay in our beds listening to their conversation and observing a page of their story unfold. They were passionately sharing with each other how to protect a girl's heart. They discussed free will and election. They sang in harmony, accompanied by violin and guitar. They discussed making their way into the world—"planting their fields and building their houses." We shed tears of joy that night as we realized that we had reached our highest objective in romancing our children to God's Truth—we had won their hearts.

Curriculum and Character

———— *Barbara West* ————

Barbara West, a graduate of the University of Colorado, has been homeschooling for over ten years. She and her husband, Bruce, an Air Force pilot, married in 1979. They have two daughters, Tiffany (15) and Heather (12). The emphasis in their home is to instill biblically based character qualities in their children. The West family currently resides in Stuttgart, Germany.

While living in South Dakota, Barbara served on the board of Western Dakota Christian Home Schools, authored legislation, and testified before various education committees to successfully change the alternative education law to abolish home visits. In another political arena, she was narrowly defeated in her campaign for a seat on the Rapid City School Board. She was also a popular convention workshop speaker.

Barbara started HEART (Home Educators Are Real Teachers) for Germany to serve U.S. and European homeschoolers in Germany and other European countries. She and Bruce also serve on the board of their local home education group, Stuttgart Area Home Schoolers.

Like all sane people, when I first heard about homeschooling, my gut reaction was, "No way!" My husband and I knew we wanted a biblical foundation for our children's education, and, to us, that meant Christian school. However, the Lord impressed upon my heart that my sights needed to be realigned. I yielded, and the Lord focused my attention on personally training the children He had given into our care.

I broached the subject with Bruce. He thought this might be fine for others, but not for his children. Bruce and I had been leaders academically, socially, and athletically in school. We had been overachievers and rarely, if ever, challenged. We liked to compete and excelled at whatever we did. Bruce was unsure if the homeschooling avenue could provide a challenge or an opportunity to excel.

Another concern was that the children would miss out on socialization. This was a pivotal issue when the Lord began a work in Bruce to change his attitude toward homeschooling. When we learned that the content of many classes at the school dealt with nonacademic issues—sex education, drug abuse, gangs, guns and violence—Bruce realized that "missing out" on socialization was not a bad idea.

We spent time in prayer. We sought the Lord about which curriculum we were to use, what course of study we were to follow, and how we were to accomplish homeschooling. The conviction we received to homeschool was a long-term commitment, never a year by year trial. It was a call from the Lord. We could not just turn it on and off.

We researched homeschool kindergarten options and chose a full program, rated A+ academically. To us, a good education was equivalent to strong academics. We began, and in less than six weeks had whizzed through the entire program. I thought, "Homeschooling is not so tough!" Looking back, I know now that a subtle change occurred. Academics became paramount. With each new level mastered, higher academic achievement became the goal. When the academic results were excellent, that equated to doing a good job in homeschooling.

I felt a personal responsibility to prove the effectiveness of homeschooling. Homeschool research publicized the success of homeschooling, and I wanted to make sure I did not discredit those reports. I watched other homeschoolers to see how they operated. I compared myself to other moms, and I compared my child to their children, even if their children were older. I put tremendous pressure on myself—and my child—to outperform them. It became a competition to see who was "the best." This attitude lasted for a few years.

We wanted the Bible as the core of the curriculum, but, in reality, academics had become our god. I was so busy trying to prove homeschooling was the best, that I failed to keep the Lord and His vision for homeschooling in front of my eyes. I would say, "The Lord is in the center of our homeschool," but He was not.

Before beginning our studies one year, the Lord impressed upon me that I was also a student. He broke my heart through a series of questions. Do you like being home? Do you enjoy your children? Do you want to teach them? Do you have contentment in your heart? These questions should have brought an immediate affirmative response, but they did not. I was miserable.

The Lord then showed me how comparing my child or myself to someone else is wrong. I can always find someone doing it better, and that will make me feel inferior. I can also find someone who is doing worse, and that makes me prideful. I need to remember that my measuring stick is the Lord and not someone else.

The Lord then challenged me to wait on Him that year. He would choose the curriculum, the time to introduce new concepts, and when to begin. He would take the burden. I eased back from the academics. We memorized portions of Scripture, went on walks, played games, read books, took field trips, and had fun being together. We were having a wonderful year. I relaxed—which is no small feat! Relaxing and easing back are terrible struggles for me.

That year our "academic" school year never began. I waited for the Lord to prompt me to tackle the core of my curriculum: math, language arts, history, science. When the prompting never came, I panicked! I had to force myself to trust Him. With my limited vision at that time, I felt we were not doing anything; we were not accomplishing anything; we were not reaching our goal. We were not going to finish the books because we had not even started yet!

In our state, mandatory testing using the Stanford Achievement Test was required every year. I steeled myself for poor test results that spring. I could not have been more surprised. The scores were high. I had not "done" any school, so how had this happened? The answer: "Seek ye first the kingdom of God and his righteousness; and all these things shall be added unto you" (Matt. 6:33; KJV). It was an earth-shaking object lesson for me.

The Lord used my weaknesses to bring about His ultimate good. Our homeschool has transitioned from "school at home" to a lifestyle. The focus in our home has shifted from academic emphasis to spiritual and character development—truly a twenty-four-hour a day teaching job with the ones I love! This emphasis on spiritual and character refinement encourages them to be Christ-like, use their God-given talents for good, give the glory for their achievements to God, and use their lives to serve the Lord.

Curriculum is important, but it is not the main thing. Curriculum goes beyond academic subjects. Learning, exhorting, correcting, and teaching are all vital. Patience, obedience, and truthfulness are character lessons tackled every day, whether I want to include them in our curriculum or not! God is dealing with me in these areas as well, which is a humbling experience. This is the "big picture" curriculum.

My biggest challenge is balancing the desire to provide enjoyable learning situations with trying to do something that resembles "real school." We strive to do well academically and cover all the core subjects, but it is easy to get caught up in "just getting through the books" and lose sight of the original goal—training our children to spend an eternity with Him. It really does not matter whether we finish the books.

I still struggle. If I look too far down the road I will push, start "speeding-up," or try to accomplish too much. By keeping my eyes on the children right in front of me, I tend to stay on course. A homeschool mother of four said it well: "I have really had a bit of a personality transplant lately—instead of being so goal-oriented, I am really enjoying the moments. Sure, it gets totally crazy sometimes, but I refuse to be one of those people who later says they wish they had enjoyed their kids more. Of course, I may have to break down one of these days and actually attack the laundry pile—which is often taller than I am!"

To maintain the perspective that my children are gifts from God, I work to keep some memories fresh in my mind. Remembering the thrill when I first knew I was pregnant. Recalling the awe I felt holding that newborn babe in my arms. The overwhelming feeling of unconditional love. Am I overcome with these same emotions today? I try to be. It helps me maintain a "heavenly" perspective.

I know that giving my attention, time, and love to my children is the most worthwhile thing I can do. The more I invest in my children, the more of a blessing will be reaped. I have learned to enjoy our children and appreciate their value. I venture to say we must not look at our children as "products" that are to come out a certain way. We should work our academic and character curriculum around these special, unique human beings whom God has placed with us.

What Is Education?

—————— *Karen Andreola* ——————

Karen was born and raised in New Jersey. After high school she attended the Boston Conservatory of Music where she majored in modern and classical dance. She married Dean in 1979; they have three children. During the last nineteen years, Dean and Karen have traveled extensively while working in Christian publishing. They began their homeschool experience in 1986 while serving a mission term with Operation Mobilization in Bromley, England. It was there that Karen began her research on turn-of-the-century British educator Charlotte Mason.

Upon returning to the States, Dean and Karen began the Charlotte Mason Research and Supply Company with the re-publication of the six-volume The Original Homeschool Series, *followed by* Simply Grammar, Hints on Child Training, *and* Beautiful Girlhood.

Her feature articles on the Charlotte Mason method have appeared in Mary Pride's Practical Homeschooling *magazine,* Homeschooling Today, *and her own* Parents' Review for Home Training & Culture. *(Back issues are kept available for six years.)*

Along with conference speaking and reviewing homeschool products, Karen has just released her latest book: A Charlotte Mason Companion: Personal Reflections on the Gentle Art of Learning.

✐ *"The finest of all the fine arts is the art of doing good and yet, it is the least cultivated."*—T. DeWitt Talmage

How do you picture education? A schoolroom crammed with bored children? A teacher idly lecturing about things that the children will soon forget? Education is thought of as an affair for teachers, a major in college, something that requires a large amount of brains and has very little to do with ordinary people.

Over ten years ago when I first began homeschooling I felt the need to have a new and different concept of education. My prayers were answered when I read the writings of the nineteenth century British educator, Charlotte Mason. If Charlotte were with us today, she would use the old Saxon phrase "bringing up" to express her educational ideals.

We all wish our children to be well brought up, and when we have come to understand what that means, we know that we need to go beyond simply fitting the child with the basic skills to make a living. Making lots of money is not identical with success, and a person who succeeds at making lots of money but has not the moral attributes, cultural niceties, educational background, or self-knowledge to use his wealth wisely will find his life empty indeed. Every person must achieve his own kind of success, and such success is far more important than how much money he or she makes.

First and foremost in importance is to have the power to live the life God has given in the way God intended. In order to have this power, a person must be at his best in his heart, mind, and soul. He must know how to choose good and how to refuse evil.

We, as persons, are not enlightened by means of multiple-choice tests or grades, but rather by relationships with other people in our lives that we come to know, admire, and love. We are educated by our friendships and by our intimacies. For instance, think about how the actions of someone you admire have such an influence on your behavior. Similarly, think also of how a boy's interest is sparked by a hobby he loves, and how he devotes all his time and effort to it. Whether it be gardening, keeping house, or governing a state, love of work—like love of people—teaches things that no school, no system can.

Children are inspired by relationships, and this helps form their personality. And so, throughout their educational lives, we put them in touch with persons, places and things.

Providing Opportunities

What is the best curriculum for a well-brought-up person? Whatever the specifics of the curriculum used in your home, be sure that your children each day have:

- Something or someone to love
- Something to do
- Something to think about

Something to Love

Whether it be parents, brothers, sisters, friends, a cat, dog, rabbit, or hamster (in some homeschooling circles it seems that sheep, goats, chickens, and pigs are also coming back in style), everybody needs someone and something to love. There are opportunities for love in every home. There are also many ways to provide services (labors of love) to others if we look for them.

Something to Do

By "something to do," I mean of course "something *worthwhile* to do." A child staring passively at a television screen is not really doing anything worthwhile.

When our children complain, "There is nothing to do!" they really mean, "Please, amuse me." Amusing oneself with idle pastimes all day is not really doing anything. A little amusement is fine, but boredom will be transformed into real interest when your children are given meaningful tasks of recreation or of service. They like to see and measure results of their activities. A frequent request at our house is, "Mom, look what I made!"

Such "things to do" could be:
- Sewing doll clothes, quilting, learning to make a mitten
- Planning or tending a garden
- Helping stamp and stuff the support group newsletter
- Peeling vegetables for soup or salad
- Learning ten new French words from a French song
- Listening to little sister read aloud, or teaching her how to "jump in" at jump rope or pitch a stone at hopscotch
- Putting together a model Roman villa, or pyramid, or castle
- Writing a play to put on with family members, or recording a radio play with sound effects, or making puppets for a puppet show.

Something to Think About

"Something to think about" gets left out in so many homes, yet it is one of the most important parts of living. Thinking is quite impossible without *something to think about*. It is enjoying other peoples' ideas and thoughts and jokes…noticing beauty in music and pictures…enjoying country sights and sounds, birds and flowers. Children's horizons of thought need to be wider than their workbooks. Children who are not given something to think about grow up, at best, with two ideas: to work hard and to amuse themselves when they are not working.

Everyone needs a certain amount of amusement, but amusement is not an adequate substitute for something to think about. People who enjoy using their minds do not rush off to every kind of amusement, or get hooked on routine visits to the video store.

When you give your children a Charlotte Mason-style education, you will be endowing them with the substantial things of our culture; and their interest in these things will naturally spill out—like a cup running over—into their leisure activities, even as they enter adulthood. When children are guided to seek after something to think about during their home life, they will continue this habit throughout their lives.

So where do we find something to think about? Charlotte Mason often said that ideas to grow on are present in books—real, "living" books. And it is we as parents who are responsible for giving our children a taste of the finest, so that they will acquire a taste for the best our civilization has to offer.

The power of finding joy and refreshment in reading is an incredible resource! Charlotte wished all children to be equipped with this power, a power that was more than just finding out the sense of printed words but making the written thoughts and experiences of great men and women their own. This is why she used narration from quality books. The child learns to dig out the ideas by relating a passage in his *own* words.

Whatever curriculum you use, remember to give yourself and your children three things: something to love, something to do, and something to think about. Accomplish this and your goal of having well brought up children will be much advanced, and you will be experiencing, as well, the educational life of which Charlotte Mason spoke.

⊞⊞⊞⊞⊞ *"What Is Education?" is excerpted from* A Charlotte Mason Companion: Personal Reflections on the Gentle Art of Learning *by Karen Andreola, and is used with permission of the publisher.*

Character Building Is Whose Job?

──────── *Maxine and Ronnie Harris* ────────

Ronnie and Maxine are more in love today than when they married twenty-seven years ago. Their oldest, Anna, worked for Intercessors for America and now for Great Christian Books. She is happily married to Christopher Wise, a music minister. Anna looks forward to homeschooling their children when they come! Betsie graduated a year early to attend nursing school. After obtaining her R.N. degree, she secured a hospital position as a cardiac nurse. She plans to continue her education, and also knows the Lord has called her to the mission field. The Harrises' first son, Matthew, also graduated early and is in a sort of vocational school as an apprentice with a blacksmith from Holland. Their youngest, Joseph, is in third grade and is doing extremely well academically and personally. He is their joy in their old age! Ronnie is a game warden for the state of Maryland and gardener extraordinaire.

Maxine works for Great Christian Books (Homeschool Warehouse) as a customer consultant and product reviewer. More non-Christians are starting to homeschool along with the Christian parents who feel called to the task. "Mine is the opportunity of guiding them through the uncharted waters of curriculum selection. It is a responsibility I do not take lightly; I am thankful for the occasion to help." In order to accommodate the first-time homeschooler, GCB has allowed her to design curriculum packages as an aid to the novice. She also sits on the editorial committee of Holly Hall Publications.

Maxine: Aiming school time, specifically Bible time, at character building and "fruit inspection" consumed large quantities of our efforts the first year or two that we homeschooled. No one ever told me to expect that. I had this wild idea of congenially working together to accomplish our academic goals. Academic goals, ah yes—the ultimate to strive for in order to give our children a quality education. Don't get me wrong—academics are very important to us. Our three oldest children who have all graduated from our homeschool can attest to that. However, building godly character reigns supreme on our list of why we homeschool. If character is lined up with the Word of God, or if we are at least attempting to line up to it, then cooperation on school work will follow.

We can remember Bible time lasting for hours—yes, a couple of hours—many days, as we worked together on important areas of godly character. Some of our sessions concerned issues such as: how to be considerate of sibling feelings, how to die to self, obedience to God and His authorities, etc. Was this time wasted, or ill-spent? How could time spent on such a vital aspect of our lives be a waste? What happens to your lesson plans when all this character building is going on? Change your lesson plans on those days. Eliminate a subject if you need to in order to make room for it. Be diligent and not slothful in academics, but be flexible enough, on a day when it is deemed necessary, to allow character building to have preeminence.

My job in the homeschooling community affords me the privilege (and I seriously consider it that) of leading many first-time homeschoolers through the process of curriculum selection. For some of the parents I advise, it is almost amusing to hear their expectations that the books they purchase will be the solution to all their child's problems. Here is where I am often able to explain the importance of building character and of putting the Word of God into their lives. Head knowledge may get you far in *this* world; disciplines of the inner man are the true riches. Character: it is worth building—every time!

And guess what! Do you think my children were the only ones experiencing an overhaul on their attitudes and character through our homeschooling? Oh no, God is so big he does the entire family at the same time! Why didn't somebody tell me I would frequently find myself lying, sitting, or standing in the bedroom crying out to God for mercy, grace, and anything else that was handy? The "crying out to God" part is not just an expression—it was real crying. "Lord, make it clear to us that we are on the right path. Help us—please, help us! Father, encourage me today."

I did not know that other homeschool moms cried and wondered about whether they really were doing the best for their children by homeschooling them. Keep in mind, our children were 14, 11, 8, and newborn when we began to homeschool. They were accustomed to the ways and activities of Christian school. We experienced a sort of culture shock at bringing them home, just like many of you. Yes, the first few years were not a breeze. I will never forget, though, the girls' prayers one day while we were having Bible class. They each thanked God for us and for the fact that we loved them enough to homeschool them. Then there was the day when Anna, the oldest, who has always been the most desirous of marriage and children, asked me if I would help her homeschool her children when they come along. Do I need to tell you I sat and cried? All those times in the bedroom crying out to God—He was listening all the time!

Have we, or our children, attained perfection? Ha ha ha ha ha hee hee ha ha ha! Come on! We are real people, like you, who have to eat, breathe, etc. But we press toward the mark for the prize of the high calling of God in Christ Jesus (Phil. 3:14). Are we pleased with our kids?—you bet! Would we choose to homeschool again if we were given the choice?—absolutely!

Ronnie: When Maxine and I began homeschooling, we experienced great uncertainty. There were not very many homeschoolers or support groups. We stepped out in faith that the Lord was indeed guiding us. Now our three oldest have successfully graduated from our homeschool high school. They are walking into the areas that the Lord has picked out for them. Our youngest is learning to love homeschooling.

I teach science and history. These are two subjects that I enjoyed while in school, and they are my strengths. However, the most important thing that I can do as a father is to be in proper relationship to the Lord Jesus Christ, and to love my wife as Christ loves the church. If a father were to do these two things first, and be diligent in them, everything else would fall into place. I do not mean to imply that you will not have any problems—they will come. However, the Lord will give you the wisdom when you ask Him for it. By honoring Jesus first in our lives, He does go before us, is with us, is behind us, and lays His hand upon us as He says He will do in Psalm 139. I remember being told the story of a great evangelist who won many to the Lord, but his own children refused to believe because of the insincere life that he led. I want my children to remember, "Dad was always there for us. He made time for us and pointed us toward God."

We have learned many things over the years. The teacher does learn more than the pupil. Take homeschooling one day at a time. Do not fret about tomorrow, for tomorrow will take care of itself. Maintain a good sense of humor; do not take yourself too seriously. Character building is far more important than the academics. Bible should be your most important subject, and developing a strong relationship with Jesus Christ is the most important thing that you can have and teach.

Aiming for a Heart of Wisdom

─────── *Robin Scarlata* ───────

Robin Scarlata is a homeschooling mother of seven children in Nashville, TN. Four of her children have graduated and two are married with children of their own. The Scarlata children are Belinda (25), Rebecca (23), Victoria (22), Daniel (21), Regina (12), Anthony (7), and Michael (4). Robin operates the Heart of Wisdom Publishing Company, and is the author of several acclaimed books, including What Your Child Needs to Know When, A Family Guide to the Biblical Holidays, *and* Far Above Rubies Lesson Plans *(four volumes). She has authored articles on education for* Homeschool Today *and* Teaching Home, *and she is a regular contributor for the* Home School Digest. *She has been the keynote speaker and provided popular presentations at conferences, workshops, and meetings since 1989. Robin prefers speaking on the Hebraic roots of Christianity.*

Robin designed the Heart of Wisdom teaching approach. This teaching approach focuses on the Bible to teach all curriculum. It is actually a combination of teaching methods based on God's Word and utilizing: Ruth Beechick's language arts teaching methods; the integrated unit study method; the Lifestyle of Learning approach; Charlotte Mason's philosophy; phonics instruction outlined in Teach a Child to Read with Children's Books; *and a writing-to-learn philosophy similar to that used by* The Principle Approach. *You can find out more about the Heart of Wisdom teaching approach through Robin's web site.*

Our homeschool journey began with a desire to teach our children God's Word and the necessary academics to prepare them for life. But somehow we drifted off course. I believe this happens to most homeschoolers—either the original destination is chosen poorly, or, somewhere along the line, a wrong turn is taken. The original goal of teaching our children God's ways mysteriously transforms into teaching what the state or "world" requires. I pray the story of our journey will encourage you to reexamine your own journey to be sure your family stays on course.

We began homeschooling with four school age children and a toddler. We prepared to go forth on our new journey by praying, setting up a schoolroom, choosing a curriculum, and planning a schedule. The classroom was fully equipped with bookshelves, desks, American flag, etc. Each child had a separate Bible, history, science, math, spelling, and English workbook. School rules were enforced—the children were not allowed to talk unless they raised their hands. We were "doing school."

The journey progressed as planned except for one unexpected obstacle. I, the leader of the expedition, was exhausted. I spent each evening planning six subjects for four grade levels. I spent so much time planning school that I did not have time to interact with my children. School became little more than a sticky note on the outside of a textbook. During the day I sat at my desk, graded papers, and spent countless hours writing scores in miniature boxes, and, if I had time, answering questions about school work. We were "doing school."

When a mother becomes exhausted, she begins to see things in a different light. Little things become huge; she becomes irritable. A child's normal amount of time to learn a fraction concept can become distorted. A few misspelled words seem overwhelming. Suddenly, it appears that the children have very little intelligence. When some of my children's papers reflected a lack of comprehension, I panicked. We spent more time in problem areas and increased the amount of school time. I was determined we were going to "do school."

An Alternate Route

Since I was so busy planning that I was not teaching, I redid our schedule, changing from a textbook to a unit study approach. This allowed me to teach all Bible, history, and science to all the children at the same time. I worked separately with them on math and language arts. My planning and grading times were drastically cut. The children and I interacted, we read aloud together, worked on projects, and they were really learning. The children were doing well academically. We were actually looking forward to school. We were homeschooling instead of "doing school."

Better, but Still Bumpy

The children were learning academics, but, somewhere along the line, when I was not seeing things in perspective, I replaced Bible study with math, spelling, or history. A quick evaluation of our school time showed a very limited amount of Bible study. Our curriculum was Christian, and we read an occasional Bible verse, but we were not spending time in God's Word. It was time to inspect the map to see exactly where we were headed. God's Word, our map, is alive. It can quickly reveal a wrong path and put it on course.

"For the word of God is quick, and powerful, and sharper than any two-edged sword, piercing even to the dividing asunder of soul and spirit, and of the joints and marrow, and is a discerner of the thoughts and intents of the heart" (Heb. 4:12; KJV).

One Needful Thing

In the Bible story of Mary and Martha, Martha was busy with preparations while Mary sat at the feet of Christ. When Martha complained, Jesus said to her, "Martha, Martha, thou art careful and troubled about many things: But one thing is needful; and Mary hath chosen that good part, which shall not be taken away from her" (Luke 10:41–42; KJV).

The lesson is simple: only one thing is necessary. Everything else is extra. The most important thing we can ever teach our children is to sit at Jesus' feet and hear His word. Sensible Martha had many accomplishments, but worry and trouble were her rewards. Mary, on the other hand, was praised for choosing "that good thing" which was itself her reward, and which would not be taken away from her.

Martha's preparation work was not wrong; in fact, it was important. It was Martha's focus that was wrong. It is your focus that makes the difference. Social achievement is important, but it is nothing without Christ.

Academics (math, language arts, history, and science) matter, but only as they sharpen your focus on the Kingdom of God and His righteousness. The academic subjects are important tools to help in the journey, but they are not the goal. The moment academics redirect you or cloud your view, to whatever degree they slow your pursuit they move from helpful tools to what Jesus calls the "cares of this life."

Back on Course, Directed towards One Needful Thing

I purposed to accomplish the "one needful thing" daily by committing to reading the Bible before any schoolwork. I set aside strivings and anxieties and purposed to teach my children who Christ is. We began to spend time sitting at His feet and feasting at the table of His mercy, forgiveness, and peace. We began to learn the unseen things of God. We began to learn true wisdom.

True wisdom is having the ability to judge correctly and to follow the best course of action, based on knowledge and understanding. Knowing the facts in a situation (economical, mathematical, scientific, etc.) is not enough to make a godly decision. To make a wise decision one must know what God says about the situation. Almost anyone can gain scholastic achievement to become a doctor, businessman, etc. But is the achievement truly achievement if they are a crooked doctor or businessman? What good is it to know how to speak five foreign languages if one does not have tongue control? What good is it to be proficient in accounting if one cheats on income taxes? What good is it to know the names of every bone in the body if one does not know how to give a kind word?

Our family now includes seven children. The four children from the beginning of this story have grown, graduated, and some have children of their own. Today, I am teaching three younger children. Over the years, I changed how we studied, but maintained the purpose to always put Bible before other studies. Through the years, this included different daily devotions, Bible study curriculum, focusing on one particular book of the Bible, reading a certain number of chapters per day, or reading Bible stories. Honestly, I must say that at times it has been a struggle. It is very easy to slip back into "doing school," but each time I slipped, God gently reminded me of the one needful thing, and we would get back on track.

After twelve years of examining teaching approaches, learning styles, and, most importantly, what God's word says about teaching children, I designed an approach to teaching based on Psalms 90:12; "Teach us to number our days aright, that we may gain a heart of wisdom" (NIV). Not only must we renew our thinking about the context of what is taught, but, also, the method by which it is taught (Josh. 24:23; Prov. 3:5–6; Matt. 6:19–21). The Heart of Wisdom centers all teaching on God's Word. I can use it with any curriculum.

Heart of Wisdom

The most important part of the Heart of Wisdom approach is the Bible reading. This is an active, ongoing project: reading through the Bible every year. (We use Bible story books for younger children and the Bible with Bible study aids for older children.) Each day we read and discuss a section of Scripture. After the story, the children work on a project to demonstrate, according to their ability levels, what they have learned. Writing, spelling, grammar, capitalization and punctuation, handwriting, vocabulary, and critical thinking skills are learned, not as separate subjects but integrated into each study. A younger child's portfolio will contain drawings, handwriting samples, memory verses, dictated summary pages, photos of a play costume, pages from a Bible coloring book, etc. Older students' portfolios will contain character and event summaries, research papers, essays, computer printouts, timelines, maps, sketches, etc. (History, science, and math are added, either through a unit study or textbook approach.) Students keep all work in a Bible portfolio, consequently, they have their own Bible Storybook at the end of the school year.

The one thing I wish I would have known the first year of homeschooling is: put the Bible first. It is the one needful thing—everything else is secondary. Acknowledge Him in all your ways and He will direct your paths.

Plants, Pillars, and Palaces–Psalm 144:12

——— *Bonnie Ferguson* ———

Jim and Bonnie were both born and raised in Pennsylvania. Before they married, Jim announced that he wanted a large family. Thus far, God has been gracious in blessing the Fergusons seven times. Sean is the eldest. At 19, he is proficient at building computers and fixing glitches in the systems.

Lore (17) is the only girl. Bonnie wasn't sure that Lore (or her mother) would survive until adulthood, but since she gave her life to the Lord several years ago, God has been molding her into a beautiful young woman. Daniel at 15 is a very promising young entrepreneur. Andrew and Joseph (12 and 9) are the last of the "first" set. After six years, Jim and Bonnie started anew with Joshua (3) and Aaron (1). The Ferguson family started homeschooling in 1986. The Lord has brought many other families into their life through their homeschooling family business. God has used this to develop the gift of hospitality in them. Some of the Fergusons' greatest blessings have come in recent years as they have opened their home to families from across the nation.

In 1991, Jim founded Ferg N' Us Services, a desktop publishing company. He designed The Homeschooler's Journal for homeschooling records keeping. Soon word got out, and the focus of Ferg N' Us changed to a resource supply company based out of the home. Jim also serves as chairman of South Eastern ARea Christian Homeschoolers (SEARCH) of Pennsylvania. This group sponsors an annual Homeschool Conference and Book Fair just outside of Philadelphia.

Homeschooling as a lifestyle was introduced to our family by a dear, sweet woman, Grace Wommer, about to retire after more than thirty-five years as an elementary school teacher. I will never forget that initial meeting. Grace was passionate as she described how institutional settings and the "Sesame Street mentality" were instrumental in tearing down the family structure and instilling the attitude of, "I want it fast, and I want it my way!"

Being the product of the American educational system myself, I know that my school years lacked the great example of godly leaders. My parents were only somewhat "religious" (my mother became a believer in her later years), and most examples of godly leadership were obliterated from textbooks by the 1960s. It has been a struggle for Jim and me to be the kind of examples we wish for our children, and to keep secular indoctrination out. God has taken two sinners and done a mighty work in each of our lives, but struggle is always there.

The problem is: American people are fast-tracked. We have become an "instant" society. The technology we use (e.g., cars, TV programs, computers, kitchen appliances) all are based on saving time by doing everything in the fastest way possible. Our fast-paced culture has infiltrated the roots of home-schooling. The prevailing winds of change are showing in our movement's character: impatience, irritability, ingratitude, and an unwillingness to be a godly example to this next generation.

Character training in our homes *begins with our example*. Our children, yours and ours, will be the first generation in over one hundred years that will finish high school without a state-approved diploma. Our children have the opportunity, collectively, to make an impact, with far-reaching implications, on this nation. Shouldn't we then, collectively, be encouraging and inspiring them to greater mission fields and service opportunities than our self-indulgent generation knew? If our calling is to train up our children in the home, then we should be an inspiration to others who have the same calling by encouraging them to start with *character*—their own first, and then their children's.

Let me back up and explain why we have this concern about the direction of homeschooling. What Grace Wommer was encouraging Jim and me to do was to slow our pace, rely on the Lord, and launch something radical, to say the least: educating our own children with a focus on character.

Oh, how scary this scenario could have been as we began in 1986: there were no protection laws for homeschooling in Pennsylvania; only one major Christian curriculum supplier would even talk to us. There were no such things as curriculum fairs. We were on our own. We have an all-knowing, gracious Lord, however, who knew all of our needs and supplied them. The first couple of years were a struggle, yes, but oh what glory comes from trial!

They say necessity is the mother of invention. Without textbooks, we certainly did a lot of inventing. We learned how to take an encyclopedia and develop a "unit study." (I had no idea they were called that at the time). The Bible was our only course in character training. Math and language were definite trials. Working with used books from library book sales stretched me. Thankfully, I did not need to have answer keys for the lower grades!

The times have definitely changed. We now have thousands of choices in resources, curriculum, unit studies, getting started manuals, how-to books, organizers…well, you get the picture. These tools are great. They have helped us to organize; we now have more time to develop those lost skills of communication, to slow our pace, and, maybe, focus on character training for our children. But, do we?

Jim and I firmly believe that, once biblical character has been built in, a child will *want* to learn. That is not to say that we have a bunch of Einsteins running around—we don't! However, I want to stress that their own desire for learning eventually takes over, and, then, more than half of the educational battle is won.

With a concern for the character and the future of our children, we began our home business. All of our children serve in the family business. Our oldest, Sean, has taken over a major part. He is receptionist, bookkeeper, shipper, receiver, and all-around computer problem solver. Lore answers the telephone, keys data-entry, and fills orders. All of the children help in the daily job of bookbinding. Jim and I have dedicated our children to the Lord, and pray for Him to use them. Sometimes this means keeping their testimony pure when answering rude telephone calls from mean-spirited customers. (I can't help but wonder about the children of those customers, and the example those parents are setting.)

I will tie all of this together by saying that our children will, Lord willing, be the second generation of a homeschooling trend. Homeschooling has changed from its radical roots. We must, therefore, surround our children with godly examples and cover them with prayer—prayer for God to use them as He sees fit, and for them to be listening for His call.

Also, if I see that they are interested in a particular subject or in training in an area which Jim or I can not provide, I pray that God would raise up a specific godly person to fill that need. Sean expressed a desire to learn woodworking several years back. Jim worked with him as much as he was able, but it still was not meeting the need. We prayed for God to bring someone into Sean's life to be a role model and that Sean could apprentice under. God, in His infinite wisdom, brought just the man to us, and as it turned out, we were an answer to this man's prayer as he was looking for a church for his family. Sean was able to apprentice under our friend for a year and a half. What a great double blessing God had in store for our families!

When we pray for God to use our children, we had better be prepared for changes to take place in their lives and ours. Lore was 11 when she became very interested in horses, a subject in which I have little to no knowledge or interest. Lore has been the most strong-willed of our children, and, at that time of her life, she was experiencing a bit of rebelliousness. God waited until just the right moment to answer our prayer for this one. One day Jim helped a beginning homeschool mom who had locked her keys in her car. In the course of conversation, she shared that she had several horses that, unfortunately, were rarely worked due to time constraints. Would Lore perhaps be interested in helping by babysitting and cleaning, and, in return, receive free riding lessons? This mom was not a believer, nor was her husband. God brought us together as families. He used us as His tools for leading the whole family into His presence, and gave Lore an opportunity of a lifetime. Lore became a member of the local 4-H club, rode extensively for four years until her favorite horse died, and gave lessons for two years. The disciplines that were learned in her years as an apprentice we could not have duplicated here at home.

Godly character cannot be overemphasized. Academics will follow if the child's heart is right toward God, if their character is submissive and hard working, and if they, along with this rest of us, are praying for their future. Let us join and lift these young people as they move into the second generation. Let us pray that we will see our children's children serving the Lord. Then we will know that we were successful parents.

Part 6

The Blessings

The Habit of Listening

─────── *Michael and Susan Card* ───────

Michael and Susan Card have been married for fifteen years. Susan has a degree in nursing from Western Kentucky University where she and Michael met. Michael is an award-winning singer/songwriter holding a Master's degree in biblical studies, concentrating in Old Testament. He is known as a Bible teacher who carefully crafts lessons in the poetry of song. The Cards have four children: Katherine (11), Will (9), Nathan (5), and Maggie (3). They have been homeschooling for the past six years and make their home in Tennessee.

Susan left the nursing profession early in their marriage to assist Michael in his music ministry. They have worked together over the years for Michael to produce numerous albums and books. His recent children's books include Close Your Eyes So You Can See *(a 1997 ECPA Gold Medallion finalist) and* Sleep Sound in Jesus. *Susan wrote her first book in 1997 entitled* The Homeschool Journey, *which includes chapter reflections written by Michael. They have been featured in several articles concerning homeschooling in magazines like* Homeschooling Today, Virtue, Home Life, *and* Partnership. *Their business is called Michael Card Music.*

Michael and Susan are committed to quality education and have partnered with Dr. William and Brenda Lane in establishing a Biblical Study Center in their hometown.

⊂▭▬▶ The decision to homeschool was never really a struggle for Michael and me. We knew beyond a shadow of a doubt that it was the best educational choice for our children. We relished the first days of school with great joy and excitement. Hindsight has revealed, however, that school was happening long before the first letter of the alphabet was taught, or the first number was identified on a page. Our children's education began in their infancy and grew in complexity as they grew. We began to realize that the habits of learning were "tapestried" into our daily living. Without always being conscious of it, we were establishing what would become the spontaneous routines of lifelong learners.

I did a great deal of reflecting, along with Michael, in preparation for writing this article. What do we wish we had known our first year of homeschooling? There is one issue we are firmly united in, and that concerns developing a lifestyle of listening. This idea of a lifestyle of listening was formed into Michael's life by his professor and mentor, Bill Lane.

Michael wrote in our book, *The Homeschool Journey*, "The framework for who I am as a Christian man was largely constructed during weekly walks with Bill Lane, my mentor from university days. Though I was in my early twenties, he could walk me into the ground and seemed to enjoy doing so—twice around campus at a breakneck pace, rain or snow or shine. I vividly remember one time when the snow piled up on his great bushy eyebrows. There were a few phrases Bill repeated again and again. They were his special discoveries, made over a lifetime of listening to his own life. He repeated them endlessly, or so it seemed to me. One of his favorites was, 'Timing is of the Lord.' That was his response to, among many others, my agonizing questions about whom I would marry and when. Another phrase he loved to bellow with a booming voice as he strolled around the classroom, handing out another nearly impossible test was, 'Lo rachamim!' (no mercy). Even now I can taste the fear in my mouth at the sound of those mischievous words.

" 'Let it simmer on the back burner of your mind,' he would say when we would talk about some prospective topic for a paper. I found it was indeed true. When I was perplexed by some exegetical problem, I would often go to sleep with it 'simmering,' only to wake with the solution.

"One of his common phrases still simmers on the back burner of my mind. 'You must develop a lifestyle of listening,' he would often say when we would speak about some difficulty I was having with some person or another. 'The best way to show someone you love them is by listening,' he said once on one of our walks. Twenty-five years later I have finally begun to understand the wisdom of those words. That's a long time to simmer!

"The best way we can show our children our love is by listening to them. Susan has taught me this powerfully from her example. When it comes to our children, she is a great listener. Not only does she listen to their words, but to their silences as well. One of the first things we must learn as listeners is that children, as well as adults, often don't mean what they say. This makes becoming a listener even more challenging.

"The ability to demonstrate love by true listening is one the greatest pluses of a homeschool education. Many times, due to overcrowding and lack of time, other educational systems can become a 'dialogue of the deaf.' The teachers speak without really listening either to the students or themselves.

But within the freeing confines of home we have the greatest opportunities to listen to our children's lives and hear most clearly what they need and who they are.

"We need to nurture in our children the ability to truly listen. To help them become listeners is to convince them that the best way to show others you love them is to listen to them. And those others include God Himself. If indeed we truly love Him, we will listen to Him, listen for Him. For He speaks to us in His Word and in prayer as we silence our hearts." (Excerpted from *The Homeschool Journey* by Susan and Michael Card. Used by permission.)

Developing the habit of listening to your life does not come easy. This is a deaf culture. We seldom listen to each other. How much more difficult, then, to learn to listen to your own life and the lives of your children. Yet this habit is at the heart of homeschooling. The whole business is a matter of listening—of listening to our children's hearts, their needs, their fears. It is, also, a matter of teaching them the habit of listening to life, to the world around them, to books, nature, their siblings, their parents, and ultimately, of course, to God Himself.

We began modeling habits of lifelong learning for our children from infancy. The habits of curling up silently to read a book; of holding a child in our arms and exploring together the wonder and mystery of the written word; of journaling together at bedtime; of browsing the shelves out of delightful curiosity; of developing personal libraries; of researching questions; of responding to the beauty of nature with faith and enthusiasm and integrating our relationship with the Lord into our academic studies. We learned the value of "living books" and witnessed our children responding to their pages with a hunger for more.

We discovered together that the best teacher was the experience of life itself. What was called for was developing the habit of diligently looking and listening for lessons in truth that life had to offer. Like the woman who swept the house clean looking for the precious coin, we discovered that we were looking for something of great value that had seemed lost when, in truth, it had been in our house, underfoot, all along. And, like that woman, we found it on our knees.

When asking myself, "What were the things I wish I'd known my first year of homeschooling?" the recurring theme for me has been, I wish I had listened less to fear and more to the voices of comfort: my mentor who was encouraging me; my husband who supported the idea and stood on the sidelines cheering all my efforts; my children who were crying out to be heard in a multitude of ways; my own intuition that kept telling me this was the right thing to do. Most of all, I wish I had listened to the Word and the silence of prayer, for, if I had, I would have heard a most supremely encouraging Voice telling me, "Never will I leave you, never will I forsake you."

If we develop the habit of listening, we will be freed up to enjoy the often difficult work of homeschooling. Joy often results from freedom, in this case the freedom to nurture, to train, and to educate our children. I remarked to Michael once, when the children and I were on tour with him, how unbelievable it was to have the kind of freedom that would allow us to spend all our days together, if we so chose: to be able to go to his concerts when we liked and for as long as we liked without the blessing of some authority. God is so good!

"Why does it surprise you," Michael responded, "that God would make the desires of your heart come true?"

He was exactly right. I had not been listening. Had not God Himself "told me," and put the desire in my heart to homeschool my children? This recurring revelation is one I wish had been highlighted as we started our homeschool journey. There is so much "noise" to contend with when teaching your children at home. One wears so many hats that one forgets the importance of listening. If I were just starting, I would ask for more grace to learn the habit of listening—to my children, whom I love so dearly; to my culture, which demands my response; to my community, which encourages me to invest in my children for the sake of their future; to the Word, which promises, "if you train a child up in the way he should go, when he is old he will not depart from it"; to the silence of prayer, where I gain the strength to continue on in this joyful, arduous process; to my heart, through whom the Spirit speaks so gently and reassuringly. And, once I began to get a handle on it, I would pray to be able to pass on to my little ones this habit of listening.

The Blessings of Time

——— *Carol Singleton* ———

Born in San Francisco to a family in the United States Army, Carol spent the first eighteen years of life traveling all over Europe and the United States. She settled down to study science at the University of California, then started moving again after graduation.

Carol has had lots of terrific jobs over the years, such as theater costume construction, florist, fruit picker in Colorado, wilderness camp worker in Yosemite, botanist at the Nevada Test Site, botany laboratory instructor at Indiana University, and research technician in plant physiology, medical genetics, and soil microbiology labs. She married Colin, a Canadian, and moved to Canada in 1982.

The Singletons began homeschooling their two daughters in 1990 and continued blissfully until Carol was widowed in 1995. Because Carol loves books and had trouble finding materials when they were getting started, she and Colin began Maple Ridge Books to supply Canadian homeschooling families with books. Carol and her daughters continue the business from their home in rural Ontario, where they have a beautiful view out every window.

Time. If I had to name the most valuable homeschooling dividend, it would be time. Shakespeare wrote of time as an enemy who would age his lady love. Busy people speak of time as money, and say there is never enough of it. Einstein speculated that time slows down as we approach the speed of light. Time, with its myriad of clichés and constraints, is hard to describe, yet inexorably effects us all. I view time as a gift we receive when we are born. We each have a certain amount of time to use during our life. We can give it and sell it to others, or keep it for ourselves.

If I had known in 1990 what I know now, would I have ever started homeschooling? Definitely! I lived in the suburbs of Toronto, had a husband earning well in the six figures, a car of my own, a university degree, and two school aged daughters. What made me decide against claiming the six hours of freedom each day which most of my contemporaries were claiming? Why go off the beaten path? It is simple: I was in love with my children. I enjoyed their company as well as their insights and excitement. I delighted in their expanding vocabularies. I treasured that they were best friends and allies. I didn't like the tears before school, the tired depression after, and the rigid schedule. I watched the creative spark being extinguished in my 6-year-old daughter, and declared, "No!"

When we began our homeschooling, I planned the days and carefully categorized our activities. We had reading lessons, writing lessons, and hands-on math. We played with words and made up rhymes. We created terrific unit studies. After we watched sheep shearing at the Royal Winter Fair, we brought wool home, dyed it with onion skins, and spun it. We made life-sized, three-dimensional human body posters with all the organs. We grew plants and ran experiments on them. We cooked and shopped. We went to Dad's photography studio and watched the "photo shoots." We did arts and crafts. We went on field trips and nature hikes. Evenings were spent reading memorable classics aloud for hours. I was with the girls all day, every day. They learned to read well, and the door to a world of knowledge opened for them to pass through. They *ran* through! They gained a strong sense of how greatly we valued each of them. It was idyllic.

However, always in the background, the timer was ticking. Time was running out. My wonderful, fun-loving husband had cancer. We had learned about it shortly after we were married and had lived with the disease for fifteen years. When Colin went to the hospital for surgery or therapy, we simply packed up books and shifted our lives there. Those girls could play and read quietly anywhere. I had told Colin that if he ever became very ill, I would care for him at home. When that came to pass, the four of us pulled even closer together. This was the real education—learning to love unselfishly. It required new skills to be partners with someone no longer handsome and fun, but haggard and cranky. We learned to serve cheerfully, to speak our minds honestly, to follow our hearts promptly, and to offer love unreservedly, in spite of certain pain. There was not time to do otherwise.

After Colin died, we moved out of the city to our new home, surrounded by fifty acres of rocks and trees. We operate our mail-order homeschool supply business from home and continue to be together all day. The togetherness is different, now, because I am working, and the girls are responsible for many things previously done by me. They have assumed new responsibilities for animal ownership and for a small business. Occasionally, I struggle with fatigue, loneliness, and finances, and wonder if I should just find a real job with a real paycheck and send the girls to the local schools. I cannot do it. I think of the time it would steal from their day—at least eight hours—and I just can't do it.

These are hours which they use productively studying, dreaming, and working at home. I cannot take that away from them. Soon enough, they may be off in the outside world where there will be serious claims on their time. For now, I will do all I can to protect this freedom for them.

Through all this allocating of time, the person last on the list to receive seemed to be me. The children were young, Colin was ill, the business was demanding. There were always urgent reasons to push my own interests aside. Things are changing, now that the girls are older and understand that their help is of real value. They spontaneously lift burdens off my shoulders when they sense the need. When an extra large project is added to my jobs, I have awakened from a much-needed nap to find the table set and dinner ready! While poring over bookkeeping, I have received a nice neck rub. There is, occasionally, a customized, encouraging screen saver to greet me when I sit down at the computer. This is nice.

I am also finding the resolve to claim short periods during the day for my own pursuit of health, knowledge, and beauty. I make time to walk in the woods. I read a little for my own interest, rather than for lessons or for book reviews for the catalogue. I practice music in the hope that I will be able to play beautifully some day. Because of the heavy investment of time made in the children's early education, I am able to find a little time for myself now. When the girls are grown, of course, I will have too much time to do with as I please. Then, I will recall this busy period wistfully. Time is the greatest gift I am able to provide to my daughters through homeschooling. Time to have known their father, to dream their dreams, to really listen, to study what interests them.

Has the path I've chosen been easy? No, not easy. But, it is still simple: I am in love with my children.

The Importance of the Father's Leadership in the Homeschool

—— *Wade Hulcy* ——

Wade Hulcy is a native of Dallas, Texas, and a graduate of East Texas State University, holding a B.S. in biology and physical education. He is the father of four boys, ages 22, 18, 15 and 10. His real claim to fame is his wife, Jessica Hulcy, his first grade sweetheart and co-author of the KONOS curriculum. The Hulcys currently reside on a 125-acre farm outside Anna, Texas (population 904). They are in their sixteenth year of homeschooling, having sent the oldest two on to college. "That's two down and two to go!" A former public school teacher and coach, Wade worked for five years in the underprivileged schools of Dallas. He was in private business for ten years before taking over the day-to-day operations as CEO of KONOS, Inc. in 1989. KONOS is a major provider of homeschool curriculum. Wade teaches physical education to 150 homeschoolers each week and also serves on the board of his state homeschool organization, the Texas Home School Coalition. Wade is a believer in the Lord Jesus Christ and seeks to honor Him in all of his endeavors.

My first year of teaching, back in 1971, was spent in an underprivileged elementary school in Dallas, Texas. There was a group of sixth grade boys who always hung around after football practice. Each Friday afternoon, I would take them home with me. One Friday night my wife and I had other plans, so I told the guys that they should go home after school because I was busy. When I got to my car, there they were! Tersely I informed them, "I told you guys to go home. I cannot take you home with me today." They sadly mumbled acceptance, but, as I glanced in my rear-view mirror, I saw them lying on the ground behind my car. I could not back out without running over them! Of course, I capitulated and took them home with me that Friday night, too.

Even though I was not a believer at the time and not yet a father, I think the Lord was showing me that young people are hungry for positive adult leadership, especially male leadership, and they will do almost anything to have a relationship with a man. This need for male leadership is the central driving force in the gang problem throughout the world today. Our children don't want to join a gang or go home with the coach, they just want Dad to take an interest in them and be their hero. It is crucial for us, as fathers, to accept our role as leader in the home.

We must implement the last verse in the Old Testament, Malachi 4:6, which says: "And he will restore the hearts of the fathers to their children, and the hearts of the children to their fathers, lest I come and smite the land with a curse" (NAS). Sadly, our land is smitten with a curse. How do we, as men, accomplish this awesome job of fathering? It is essential that a man understand how important it is to give his time to his family.

Time

The most important advantage of home education is that it provides a vehicle for developing the parent-child relationship by increasing the amount of time parents actually have available to spend with their children. Education is truly discipleship. It is a process in which the teacher spends time with the student until the student becomes "like the teacher" (Luke 6:40). Jesus modeled this method with his twelve disciples. As fathers, we face a serious challenge in becoming a part of the home education/discipleship process because most of us are away from home for a major portion of the day! Yet, we must commit ourselves to spending as much time as possible with our families, demonstrating our love for them. Love is spelled t-i-m-e. We must be willing to limit our outside activities, no matter how good they are, and focus our efforts on family activities.

Responsibility

God's Word is clear that a man is to take charge of his home, and this certainly includes the education of his children. Fathers are always the first ones addressed as the teachers of children: "Hear, my son, your father's instruction, and do not forsake your mother's teaching" (Prov. 1:8; NAS). When judgment day comes and the Lord asks for an accounting of the raising of the children, He will not go first to our wives or our children—He will come straight to us. Therefore, character development is even more important than academic training. There is significance to the order of priority in 2 Peter 1:5 (NIV): "...add to your faith goodness; and to goodness, knowledge..." Knowledge is important, but less important than faith and virtue. The Hebrew (biblical) method is to train the heart. Most of us were trained under the Greek method, the training of the mind. The modern education system, both public and private, tends to emphasize the mind to the great neglect of the heart. Home education provides an excellent opportunity to return to a more biblical method of raising children. Sadly, many homeschooling families settle for the same text-books and teaching methodologies that are being used in many private schools and experience the same failure to develop character in their children. Above all our efforts, we must pray, because it is the Lord alone who can change the heart and make our children into godly men and women (John 6:44). Like our homeschooling wives, a homeschooling father has many responsibilities.

Dad as PROVIDER

One of our chief duties as fathers is to provide financially for our families. First Timothy 5:8 instructs us, "But if anyone does not provide for his own…he has denied the faith and is worse than an unbeliever" (NKJV).

There is a fine balance between not providing enough income to protect our families, and working so much that we don't have time to even see our families. Several years ago one of the richest men on earth died. The story goes that he called for his grown sons and daughters to come to his deathbed for one last visit. None came. One son said, "Hug your moneybags, Dad."

Dad as PASTOR

We, as fathers, are the spiritual leaders of our families. Every father has the same calling as father Abraham, about whom the Lord said, "For I have cho-sen him, so that he will direct his children and his household after him to keep the way of the Lord by doing what is right and just" (Gen. 18:19; NIV). God has promised that if we bring our children up in the proper way, they will not depart from that path (Prov. 22:6). Daily family worship ought to be one of the highest priorities of every father. If we do not acknowledge God together as a family each day, we are teaching our children that God is not truly preeminent in our lives.

Dad as PROTECTOR

We, as fathers, must be the defenders of our families. This protection is carried out on both a physical and a spiritual level. Dads are the ones who must see that their families are safe from the ever-present dangers they face in life. A father's defensive actions are even more vital on the spiritual plane. Every father is a gatekeeper whose role it is to decide who or what has access to his little flock, and to bar exposure to that which could draw them away from the Lord. We should know the name and reputation of the soccer coach, the bal-let teacher, and the Sunday school teacher before we even consider delegating to them some of the responsibility of training our children.

Dad as PRINCIPAL

Obviously, we, as dads, should assume the position as the head of the home education process. As principal, we should be the policy-maker and main disciplinarian for the family (Prov. 13:24). We should be involved in matters as diverse as what curriculum to use, what family schedule to keep, what the family practice will be regarding television, dress, sports, etc. It is our high duty and responsibility to provide for our wives the guidance needed to make these critical decisions together.

Of course, a good principal depends on a good faculty, his wife. His leadership is not dictatorship. It is a form of service (Matt. 20:25–28).

Often the wife is more knowledgeable and gifted than the husband for the role of teaching the children, but our wives need and want our help and guidance. This is a form of cherishing! It is essential that the husband and wife sit down weekly to have an uninterrupted time of discussion, planning, and problem solving. I've found that the television must be turned off, and you must actually face your wife!

Dad as PARTNER

It has been said, "The greatest gift a father can give to his children is to love their mother." We must love our wives as Christ loves the church (Eph. 5:25). This means sacrificing our comfort and convenience for their good. It means putting their interests ahead of our own (Phil. 2:3–4). It also means a healthy measure of physical affection. Showing love for our wives by demonstrations of affection is one of the most powerful ways we create a sense of security in our homes. Our children know they are safe when they see that Dad and Mom love each other and are tight and are not going to break apart. A good place to start is the fifty-second hug every day!

Conclusion

Homeschooling is not just about giving our children a better education. It is about extending the Kingdom of God and the Gospel of Jesus Christ—and we, as fathers, are the key players if God's model is to succeed. Be a godly father. Renew your family—and change the world.

Grandpa's Bus and Glowing Reports

—— *Jill Darling* ——

Jill Darling has resided in Warren Center, Pennsylvania, since marrying Pete in 1974. They've homeschooled for sixteen years. Their older son, Greg (20), a sophomore and mass communications major at Cambell University, North Carolina, received a $16,000 leadership scholarship. As an ROTC and Ranger Challenge Team member, he plans to become an Army officer upon graduation. A Civil Air Patrol (CAP) member for eight years, Greg is cadet commander holding the grade of LTC, advanced ranger, medic first class, and has received several CAP scholarships. He enjoys writing and was a national winner in the Editorial Division of Quill & Scroll's writing contest. Keith (18) is a tenth grader, and has done extremely well, despite physical challenges with cerebral palsy. He plays all positions on Little League Challengers, with his picture on display at the Little League Museum in Williamsport, Pennsylvania. Keith enjoys woodworking, inventing, and repairing things. He plans to pursue training in an apprenticeship program or attend vocational school.

Jill assists Pete in pastoring Faith Christian Fellowship in Apalachin, New York. In addition to administration and counseling, she is head of the children's department and puppet team. Jill has served as youth leader and directs a community-wide Christian skate night.

She is a member of Pennsylvania Homeschoolers and New York State LEAH, serving as a Pennsylvania contact person. In addition to writing numerous articles for these organizations' newsletters, Jill is a freelance journalist, published in Teaching Home and Real magazine. She contributes Christian-related guest editorials and feature articles to local newspapers.

◁▭▭▭▷ "You'll be riding on Grandpa's bus when you start kindergarten," I assured Greg as Grandpa drove his bus past our house each day. But Greg never joined Grandpa to ride his bus to school. In fact, he never went to school.

Christian principles and family unity were foremost to our child training, so we had reservations about sending Greg to school. The summer before kindergarten, I listened to a radio program featuring national homeschooling advocate, Dr. Raymond Moore. "Homeschooling? This may be our answer!" I quickly wrote down the information. We ordered and devoured Moore's books, and prayerfully considered the decision to homeschool.

When we began in the fall of 1982, homeschooling was virtually unheard of. We did not know anyone in the area doing it, and felt like lone pioneers embarking on an adventure. That is the way homeschooling started—just a handful of families across the nation blazing the trail with no support groups, statewide organizations, newsletters, or national magazines. Curriculum was limited, and a "used curriculum sale" was a dream to come. The only guides we had to go by were the glowing reports from other families we read in books. "Could we do it in our home?" we wondered.

Friends and relatives were shocked at our plans, and full of pointed questions. It was rather unsettling to them, the first they had heard of the concept. The usual questions were: Is it legal? How can you do that? Why would you want to? What about socialization? How are the kids going to make it in the "real world"?

A family friend and long-time teacher was skeptical about our venture because she had attended state-of-the-art literacy workshops. She had worked diligently to be certain her kindergarteners were reading by the end of the year. Using a box of phonics flash cards, we won our first homeschool victory. Greg learned to read not after a year of kindergarten, but after only a month into kindergarten! Our confidence level soared!

Another shining moment came when Greg, at age 8, wanted to learn how to type. I gave him my old typing book, and he raced through everything, skipping over tedious repetition exercises, moving on to the next lessons. I figured he could have his fun, and I would do the course properly when he got older. To my amazement, he typed each letter, using all the correct techniques, and did a beautiful job! He has been typing ever since.

Not every aspect of our homeschooling has been this remarkable. Multiplication tables, spelling, and advanced math problems, which the boys just could not understand, got so nightmarish that I felt like paying someone, anyone, to come in and help for a while. But, we forged ahead.

Even though we had trying days, the rewards have been wonderful. By having my children at home, I could catch and confront cheating with on-the-spot admonition from Scripture. I could discipline with consistency whenever troubles cropped up. I also experienced the harsh realization that I needed to improve in some areas—areas in which I had been so adamant while training the boys!

Every part of home life became a part of school: building, painting, cooking, sewing, even traveling. Our vacations turned into educational experiences: field trips! Learning was happening all around us. We would make a yearly plan, but if exciting opportunities came up, we'd "go for it." When we took an unexpected trip to Niagara Falls, it turned our sights to studying Canada. Using the library as our favorite and foremost resource, we watched videos about the falls, read books, and checked out travel brochures.

Civil War study came to life as we stopped at battlefields and museums en route to relatives we were visiting down South. We were able to personalize our history on that trip by using our family genealogy. While at Andersonville Prison in Georgia, we looked up ancestor Eugene Sleeper and later found a detailed account of his escape and of his testimony at the war crimes trial of the prison commander, Capt. Henry Wirz.

Opportunities to meet people from other countries came easily. We met visitors from Mexico and East Berlin through the Friendship Force, an international foreign exchange program. A Civil Air Patrol (military search-and-rescue organization) cadet exchange program brought an Austrian pilot into our home. Hospital visits, church missionaries, and our neighbor's annual sheep shearing allowed us to meet people from Poland, Puerto Rico, Africa, New Zealand, England, and Ireland.

Our first big socialization test came when Greg, then 14, went to an eleven-day Civil Air Patrol camp. Cadets could have no contact with their families, and Greg did not know a soul. We wondered how he would do with a bunch of strange kids. Would they like him? Would he be considered an oddball? Would he be swallowed up by it all? The eleven days passed so slowly before we were allowed to attend the camp's closing award ceremonies. At the ceremony, the announcer proclaimed, "Honor Cadet of Charlie Flight: Greg Darling!" Two of Greg's superiors made a beeline to shake our hands, greatly impressed with the "fine product" we had in our son. Hallelujah! Another homeschool victory!

In order to have more creativity and flexibility in our studies, we did not use a prescribed curriculum or textbooks, other than math, until the latter high school years. Using a scope and sequence (which is an outline, available from some publishers, of specific topics addressed in each grade), I created our own curriculum from a compilation of library books, inspired ideas, and intriguing finds. For example, instead of reading dry textbooks about a time period, we read historical fiction which projected us into vibrant accounts of those days.

Unit studies (subjects built around a particular theme), were used in our study of Japan. For that unit, we watched a "Reading Rainbow" segment and the show "Big Bird Goes to Japan." We read Japanese stories, wrote hiakus for English, attempted to grow bonsai for science, drew Japanese letters and made origami for art, and bought and cooked Oriental food. Dressed in Japanese-style costumes, we ate our special meal, complete with Japanese music in the background.

Written pieces never "decorated the refrigerator," but always served a purpose. Newspapers' inquiries, letters to the editor, and writing/art contests were perfect vehicles. We wrote letters to relatives, senators, and congressmen about pertinent issues, and made requests to companies who were touting their free or inexpensive materials. Our annual family newsletter for relatives was filled with accounts of field trips, homeschool happenings, and creative writing samples. Photographs became the impetus for writing essays in various styles, resulting in an archival photo-journaling album to keep as a family heirloom. Greg and Keith have had many articles published in the "Teen Page" of their local newspaper, along with articles in homeschool newsletters, magazines, and a book.

Whatever could not be accomplished within the home, we sought to accomplish outside the home. The boys attended drawing classes and conversational German courses where their classmates were the "over-fifty crowd." Talk about socialization! They have had co-op classes with other homeschoolers in which a hired teacher or a proficient parent teaches a course. One summer we hired a biology instructor to do labs with us. It was such fun as teacher, mother, and students swam around our backyard pond collecting samples of water, algae, and insect eggs to examine under a microscope. We identified in field guides a dozen different kinds of mushrooms found in the woods nearby. We had already dissected a frog on our own, but the biology teacher found some surprise critters to be dissected waiting in our freezer. There was a fish, a duck our dog had killed, and a snapping turtle we found freshly killed along the road. Our class was dubbed "road-kill biology!"

When subjects began getting more difficult, we decided to use a video program for the last two years of Greg's high school. We wanted him to get used to textbooks for college, and to have a general overview of science, history, and English courses to solidify what we had already done. In addition, courses such as chemistry, physics, trigonometry, and analytic geometry were beyond our ability to teach. The daily video tapes were expensive, but a definite lifesaver.

As we look back over sixteen years of portfolios, and at all the hard work put into homeschooling, in one sense it seems like a long time. On the other hand, it has gone so fast, as Greg so suddenly has moved on to college.

The homeschool route proved successful: we can now share our own glowing reports that others can read in books. The boys have emerged academically sound, socially adept, and solid in their Christian convictions. They have a purpose in life, and enthusiastically pursue the dreams God has set before them. The spiritual depth and family cohesiveness we have attained could never have been accomplished had they taken the journey on Grandpa's school bus. Praise God for homeschooling!

A Lifetime of Learning:
Have Books, Will Travel

——— *Tina and Bob Farewell* ———

Bob Farewell was brought up near San Francisco, while Tina was born and raised at Chalet Suzanne Restaurant and Country Inn in Lake Wales, Florida. Married in 1979, they now have five children: Elizabeth (15), Eric (12), Joseph (7), Rebecca (5), and James (2), plus two little blessings in heaven. Their residence is an old house they moved onto the property at Chalet Suzanne. They lend a hand at the Chalet whenever needed.

Tina has always loved and collected books, but after having her children, her thirst for great books, especially out-of-print books, became practically insatiable. Searching for the best "living" books for their children led Tina, in 1987, to found Lifetime Books and Gifts. *After compiling* The Always Incomplete Resource Guide and Catalog, *the Farewells' lives rapidly changed. Bob took over the business, and together they wrapped many a book in pretty pink tissue paper, wrote notes by hand to each customer, and licked a myriad of stamps for the packages, usually after midnight.*

Their Learning Lifestyle encompasses traveling in a motorhome with their children for six months each year; speaking at conventions, especially about the War Between the States, fathering, and the Learning Lifestyle; and sharing with home educators all over America. One of their goals is to take their family and their books to foreign countries to encourage home educators with stories of what God has done in their lives, business, and ministry.

Things We Wish We'd Known in Our First Year of Homeschooling
by Bob Farewell

...that our interior walls would become bookshelves
...that entire rooms would be converted to libraries
...that homeschooling was not schooling at home

…that it is most important to have well disciplined children

…that reading biographies is the easiest and best of all ways to teach history

…that taking a walk around the lake at midnight is something the whole family will remember

…that chasing an owl's hoot is the finest nature lesson we've ever had.

This is too much fun! We love it!!

✎▷ God's grace and wisdom prevail in our lives. We certainly did not plan to homeschool the way we do, but God did, and His thoughts are not our thoughts; His ways are not our ways. He had a better idea! We planned to do school at home, just like a regular classroom, until He intervened. Because we could not find great books in our area, I started a small book business in 1987. Bob took over when it soon became more than I could manage, and, after we wrote our resource guide, our lives changed overnight! We changed the way we lived, and the way we "did school."

We used to live a life of structure: prayers, Pledge of Allegiance, fifteen minutes of this, forty-five minutes of that, snack break, lunch break, and field trips for our kindergartener and preschooler. Now, our lives have become more like this: working alongside one another; discussing decisions; traveling six months a year all over the country selling books; meeting extraordinary people; studying history, geography, and science firsthand; and rejoicing in our children's desire for—and love of—learning. In other words, we traded the school desks for sofas, and a home address for a home on wheels.

Yes, we still cover reading, writing, and arithmetic—although reading is the most enjoyed subject. But, we wish we had planned this Learning Lifestyle from the beginning, rather than having it almost forced upon us by our Heavenly Father who loves His children more than we can ever understand. He knew what we and our children needed, and through our lifestyle and business, helped us conform to His plan. We are still astounded at His shaping of our lives, and how He brought it all about through our Learning Lifestyle.

Let me share just a few things that have taken place in our lives since we returned home from our homeschool book fair travels in September. This will show you what the Farewells' Learning Lifestyle is all about. Eight days after we arrived home, my father died after a long illness. Instead of letting professionals handle everything, my husband and brother, along with their sons, built Daddy's casket. The ladies of the family lined it with red velvet. We buried Daddy's "empty body-house" here on our property. Emotions were high, but there was such healing and joy in doing it this way. This was truly a learning experience. Soon after, we stayed for a week at my parents' cottage on a little island in the Gulf of Mexico. Some would call it a vacation—we called it twelve hours a day of marine science laboratory…and lots of reading aloud and game playing after dark.

Upon our return home, Elizabeth, then 14, attended a seminar held near our home. We hosted two other families whose teens were also attending, clumping seventeen of us together to fellowship and learn and play for nearly a week. This was an intense week of education and sharing for the three couples involved, not to mention all that the children learned! After everyone left we began our "schoolish" routine: normal chores, focused times of reading, writing, arithmetic, and reading aloud. Elizabeth and Eric (he was 11 at the time) put in gardens for the first time. Joseph (7), Rebecca (5), and James (2), spent many days catching and identifying butterflies. Hundreds of books flowed in, and we all did our part to read and review them for our catalog.

Next on our fall calendar, a home educating family parked their motorhome in our back yard for a couple of weeks before moving into their home. As much as we tried to stay in our routine, it just didn't always work—now there were five more people to fit into it! But, learning definitely took place—lots of it, and joyfully!

Then came Thanksgiving when we worked together in the restaurant and, later, hosted a huge family meal. My mother had asked Elizabeth to decorate the whole inn for Christmas—an enormous job that turned out absolutely beautifully. It was very difficult work, and included weeks of planning, physical labor, training others to help, and leadership skills. Elizabeth and her friends put up the decorations the day after Thanksgiving. The decorating was immediately followed by a celebration of National Bed and Breakfast Week at the inn. Each day Elizabeth helped serve many guests, while Eric gave tours of the historic property.

Next began the visits to doctors, chiropractors, and hospitals because I broke my right wrist (and yes, I am right-handed!) on December 15, before I had finished all those creative Christmas things I had planned. I was in a cast past my elbow for two months. Then life really got hard—I was confined to bed for months because of a miscarriage and a back injury.

So, do you think our children are learning anything this season of our lives? Are they learning to serve? Are they learning to rejoice in all things? Are they learning to get along with others? Are they learning to share their feelings about their losses and difficulties? Are they learning math skills? Are they begging their father, "Read more, please!"? You bet they are! And much, much more.

Nevertheless, I sometimes find myself feeling guilty that we are not more "schoolish" around here. But, then my mind and heart are quickly put at ease when I remember the benefits of our Learning Lifestyle. For instance, one day Eric received a fan letter from a sweet little lady who was on one of his tours of the inn. Thank you notes and roses came to Elizabeth for an etiquette seminar she presented to a local Brownie troop. James is frequently complimented for sitting still so long at church. Joseph's enthusiastic talk about lions amazed our 4-H club. Rebecca can learn any song she hears just twice. All these skills have long-term effects, which are not gained by simply sitting at desks in a schoolroom.

These children are living! They are loving! They are gaining wisdom and knowledge! They are communicating with adults and peers, and doing it well! They are reaching out to others and learning what real life is all about. They love learning and can't wait to learn more! They are being shaped by the Master's hands, and by ours. This is education. This is the real world.

In order to accomplish this, we must constantly focus on our goals, and we must develop a Learning Lifestyle in every area of our lives. We must prayerfully consider what God is calling us to do as we trust Him for the education of our children. We must create the atmosphere in which our children learn to live. We must nurture children who think of others first and truly desire to serve. We must seek to establish a thinking, reasoning, and wise generation of young people who yearn to serve their Creator and Master. These are worthy goals.

It all starts in times around the dining room table, in hugs and kisses in the morning, in washing dishes, doing chores, playing games, reading great books, learning together, and in praying and worshiping as a family.

Sometimes this flows in seasons, as does our Learning Lifestyle. When our family is traveling, things are much different than when we are at home, which is a great joy! All of us have seasons in our lives. Think about them. Pray about them. Ask God to direct your path, and don't worry about what others think or say. He will show you how to live through the seasons of your life, and, as you delight yourself in Him, He will show you what is important for your family. Rest in Him, and remember, in the words from an old hymn (which I wrote on my cast), "Fret not, my soul, on God rely."

Family Unity: A Letter from Beverly

——— *Beverly Thomas* ———

Beverly was born and raised in Baltimore, Maryland. In 1963, she graduated from Southern High School, then completed two years at Coppin State College, pursuing a degree in elementary education with a major in mathematics.

She and her beloved Alfred celebrated their twenty-fifth anniversary January 22, 1997. They met at a Maryland Army facility in 1968, married in 1972 and relocated to Detroit, Alfred's hometown, in 1973. The Thomas family consists of six children: Roy B. Griffin and his family live in Baltimore; Kirstie A. Hansel and her family live in Detroit; Daniel Craig lives and works in metro Detroit; Deborah Naomi is a missionary in Guatemala; and Simeon Nehemiah and Cynthia Cherisse are both at home. When the Thomases started their home training program in September of 1985, these children were 19, 11, 9, 6, 4, and 2 years old.

Over the past twenty-three years, Alfred and Beverly have attended and assisted the Detroit Committee with the Institute in Basic Life Principles seminars. They have volunteered and chaired events for Christian Home Educators of Michigan since 1993. Since attending in October 1995 they have been coordinators and volunteers for Family Life Marriage Conference, Campus Crusade for Christ. The Thomases have fellowshipped with Calvary Christian Church in Royal Oak since March 1986. There they receive a diet which equips them for their vision for strengthening marriages, encouraging families, and pursuing holiness in daily living.

I found an example of the home life I desired when I befriended a young Jewish mother and her children. She unashamedly taught and practiced the Jewish customs and ways. I envied the influence and results of their family interaction. The children attended a Jewish school where their mother taught classes several times a month throughout the year. How could I have that kind of influence? Being Jewish was not only her race but her religion. During our short time of friendship, I became increasingly desirous of having my Christian faith be the central influence over our children's lives.

My first effort towards having that kind of influence was to participate in the parent/teacher community group that addressed problems and made recommendations in our elementary school. At one point, I brought to their attention the alarming transitions away from traditional family values we had discovered in the children's textbooks. Response: these are the books the teachers must use. Slowly, as the months passed, peer pressure began to whittle away at the unity of our children's family relationships. Their hearts were being drawn away and their attitudes were being reshaped by their teachers and classmates. The same thing was happening to my children that had taken place between my siblings and myself. Would anything prevent this or even restrain it? What recourse do we parents have if the teachers are going to continue to teach from books that lead our children away from our values?

At a seminar, whose goal was to equip parents and their teens to have better relationships, I heard something that gave me hope. The ministry leader shared his vision for reclaiming Black youth, and for strengthening their families through home education. Though I had never heard of "home education," my heart burned within me. "Could this be the solution I am looking for?"

The proposed curriculum offered materials and guidance to assist in training our children to be godly men and women, committed husbands and wives, caring leaders and teachers, and loving fathers and mothers. Reflecting upon my own life, my questions about those areas of adult responsibility had received answers that were void of biblical direction. Shouldn't God's commandments be the foundation for our lives, not only for our faith but for our conduct as well, if we are Christians? These formative years, where we have a captive audience, are the best years to lay the foundation for those adult stages of life. It was with this curriculum that we began our journey.

The children were eager to learn. However, the weight of high expectations for academic achievement, whether real or implied, was frustrating. Finally, that fateful day came when I was ready to throw in the towel. When I cried unto the Lord because I was overwhelmed, God directed me to the neglected music portion of our curriculum. I do not remember how long we struggled over that first hymn, "My Anchor Holds," but, after prayer one day, it finally came together. WE REJOICED! WE PRAISED THE LORD! That was when, in my heart, the Spirit of God said, "If you will seek ME for learning your roles in the family as you have sought Me for learning your parts in this song, I will bring harmony in your home as I have brought harmony in this song." Why music? It was God's tool for encouraging togetherness, we could easily measure our progress, and it required the development of many disciplines and virtues. Second Peter 1:5 says, "And besides this, giving all diligence, add to your faith virtue; and to virtue, knowledge" (KJV).

In retrospect, that fateful day was a faithful day. God was giving us a principle to pattern our training. In our study of spiritual motivations we discovered that, just as each of us had good voices but limitations of vocal range, we also had our gifts and limitations of character. As we learned about strengths and weaknesses of character, we all seemed to gravitate to certain roles and responsibilities. Over time, through numerous challenges, we have developed the skill of attacking problems and seeing life through each other's motivation.

Let me share a little incident concerning my children's developing ability to see life this way. One Sunday morning the children had been invited to sing at a church in Ypsilanti, but our daughter, Cynthia, complained of a sore throat. We tried some ideas we thought would give her relief, but, after a short warm-up, we knew it was serious. Surely Simeon would fill in, since her part was within his range. That morning though, Simeon could not have held those notes in a bucket. The first selection went quite well. Were our home remedies working? The wideness of Cynthia's eyes into the second selection indicated that she was really struggling. Then it happened! Cynthia stopped singing and just stood in place as though waiting for a cue, but the harmony continued uninterrupted! The congregation was not even aware of the change. Simeon had reached beyond himself to God and had covered for his sister. We praise God for showing Himself strong on our behalf.

In any situation that involves more than one person there is the opportunity for chaos, but when each shares the burden of responsibility and absorbs the consequences through the gifts that God has given them, it brings order and peace. "Likewise, ye younger, submit yourselves unto the elder. Yea, all of you be subject one to another, and be clothed with humility: for God resisteth the proud, and giveth grace to the humble" (1 Peter 5:5; KJV). When your young people bring to your attention the behavior of a sibling, LISTEN!! If you discern that the one bringing the report has wrong motives, discipline them for it; if not, allow them to be their "brother's keeper." You will not be with your children always. Insist on obedience, not just to what you say, but to your wishes and desires. Teach and train them to care about one another, not just physically but spiritually. All too often an older sibling, puffed up by the pride of their good judgment and handling of responsibilities, can become an oppressor to a younger sibling. The older one becomes a problem, and you are not aware because you have been dependent on that one. Encourage, by your example, appreciation for the talents and gifts each child possesses, the younger and the older. By doing so, you will find that each works harder at developing that talent or gift.

In the pursuit of education, we must not forfeit the training for essentials of a godly life. During these years, our student/child is developing his or her ideas about jobs, friends, and God (not necessarily in that order). By God's grace we want to have instilled the importance of God's way being the "bench-mark" for every action, thought, word, and deed.

I offer a portion of our testimony as a guide, not a guarantee. So many variables are at work with every family and each individual. In spite of the challenges we have faced—and, even as I write—it is such a source of strength knowing that the Holy Spirit of God watches over and cares for each of us. God opens and closes the doors of opportunity. God provides resources and handcrafts our influences. God determines every outcome. May God richly bless you and yours as you seek Him and follow His lead.

Achieving the Right Results, or
The Cake Might Fall

——— *Debbie Ward* ———

Allan and Debbie Ward celebrated their twenty-fifth wedding anniversary this year. Since their marriage, they have lived in Birmingham, Alabama where they have reared their three sons: Neal (22), Clay (16), and Mark (14). They have homeschooled since 1990. Since 1994 they have served as administrators of their church school, The School at Cahaba Ridge, located in Clay, Alabama.

Debbie has served on the editorial staff of Homeschooling Today magazine since 1992, currently as the managing editor. She has written various articles for the magazine, and has been a regular contributor to the Living Literature *feature. She is also an author for Common Sense Press, including a number of the books from the curriculum, Reading Skills Discovery Series.*

Allan and Debbie own Award Marketing, a company that assists with the marketing and advertising needs of businesses related to the homeschool industry. Allan serves as an advertising and marketing consultant and Debbie as an editorial consultant to various publishers in the homeschool market.

I was just minding my own business one day, when the phone rang. It was a friend telling me she had just heard about homeschooling on the radio. I quickly informed her that I was certain it was illegal in the state of Alabama. Besides, there was no way I would homeschool, anyway! That was the end of that, or so I thought. Within only a month, I was hooked, and so was my husband. The homeschool adventure began to reel us in.

In truth, most of the suggestions I offer were shared with me by others before I began homeschooling—I just wasn't discerning enough to heed their advice. Like many lessons in life, I had to learn this the hard way, through experience.

Don't Bring School Home

Others had told me that homeschoolers didn't have to "bring school home," but that is precisely what I did. Since I had no background or training to let me know how to begin, other than my own public school experience, there I went—wading through homeschool catalogs, searching for the perfect curriculum. Then, I ordered massive amounts of workbooks and teacher's manuals for our sons, then in K5 and second grade. I felt secure knowing everything to say and do each day.

It took the whole first semester for me to realize that our children could function just as well, actually better, at the couch or breakfast table than at the school desks I had purchased. I also discontinued the rule to raise your hand before speaking...although there are days I wish I had retained it!

With time I grew confident. I realized each child has his own particular talent and bent. I incorporated unit studies into our curriculum, bringing more fun and less paper/pencil work. Our days became more relaxed. Learning became a more natural process, and I became less a taskmaster.

Chill Out

Within a few months, we brought our eighth grade son home also. Immediately I was surrounded by a houseful of men, twenty-four hours a day, as if I had stumbled into the boys dorm! No doubt, it had been easier when I dropped them off at school each day. I quickly learned that, in order to survive this homeschool adventure, I would have to relax and "not sweat the small stuff."

An example: in our home, morning hours are devoted to homeschooling, but there is always a distraction. The phone or the doorbell rings; the dog has puppies (thankfully, not too often!); someone has an appointment; a friend stops by. Even for a disciplined person, it is hard to keep a schedule. One has to learn to prioritize. What is most important? We decided that people and real life experiences are more important than schedules. We should plan our days, yet be open to respond to ministry opportunities, unexpected changes, and life's emergencies. Be flexible. Spontaneously meeting the needs of others offers invaluable lessons for our children. Unexpected guests offer great lessons in hospitality, along with crash courses in speed housecleaning!

Be Real

Getting to know your children (and their getting to know you) can be a convicting experience. When your children attend traditional school, it is easy to ignore character flaws. Being at home all day with your children can expose (for better or worse) who they really are, and who you really are. It uncovers blemishes in your character that you previously had managed to conceal. God has a way of revealing these and of convicting us about them

208 Debbie Ward

through our children. You must be "real" with your children and practice what you preach, for your children easily see your faults. You must learn to live in harmony, to "put up" with one another. The principle of "iron sharpening iron" becomes familiar. Instead of always viewing ourselves as the iron that sharpens, we sometimes become the iron that gets sharpened. Some days our home is filled with "iron filings!"

Put 1 Corinthians 13 into practice. Learn to be servants. As it says in Romans 12 and Hebrews 10, meet the needs of others, spur one another on to good deeds.

Sometimes the Cake Falls

Have you ever baked a cake—not a box mix, but a "from scratch" cake? You grease and measure; you melt, shake, sift; you mix and time, and check the recipe one last time. When you think everything is perfect, it goes in the oven. You rest assured you have done your best, and wait for the pleasing aroma to permeate the air. I wish I could say that, when these steps are followed, the results will be a beautifully prepared cake. Sometimes, however, totally out of your control, someone slams the door, and the cake falls. What happened?

The message we often get is that, if one makes the right choices, faithfully invests time in his children, limits negative peer pressure, correctly measures education options, and uses only the best resources, the result will be a perfect child: well mannered, perfectly groomed, with a Ph.D. You do not hear much about parents who encounter a "cake falling" experience. Do you suppose they were less faithful or diligent? Perhaps, they did not measure the ingredients correctly. May we assume they put the ingredients in the wrong order, or forgot to sift?

No. The ingredients were right. The process was right. The players were right. The outcome seems wrong.

Some parents are granted the unique teaching tool commonly known as a Prodigal Son. No matter how godly the parent, no matter how much time and effort a parent puts into a child, there is the possibility he might not turn out right. Homeschooling is not an insurance policy that guarantees he will.

We have the liberty to realize that we cannot be perfect parents or perfect people. We read in Scripture the Parable of the Prodigal Son (Luke 15:11–32). Certainly, this example is given to us to demonstrate our relationship with our Father who continues to love us in spite of our imperfections.

As we read the parable, we see only pieces of a bigger puzzle. Some of the pieces are left to the imagination, with the hues and form missing. We know nothing of the father's parenting skills. We do not know *how long* the younger son wallowed in his sin and selfishness. We do not know *how long* the father watched the road for a glimpse of his wayward son. We cannot know *how long* or *how deeply* the father agonized and despaired. We do know that he watched the road, and that he eventually felt the joy of his son's physical and spiritual return.

God, in His sovereignty, used this teaching tool to shape and mold that father. Certainly, that father learned the compassion, grace, mercy, faithfulness, and sufficiency of our Heavenly Father during his son's absence. Surely, there were days when he was tempted to "throw in the towel," but instead, he relied on His Word in Proverbs 22:6: "Train up a child in the way he should go; and when he is old, he will not depart from it" (KJV). Do you suppose he asked the question, "How old is old?" Did he wonder, "When will he stop departing?"

How do we handle these things? When one has done his best, it can be terribly discouraging to encounter these trials. How do we minister to fellow homeschoolers in these trials? If you are still young in parenthood, pray. Pray for these fellow sojourners; pray for wisdom for yourself as you rear your own children; pray for protection for your children from the snares of the world. If you have brought your children to maturity, be an encouragement to others. Perhaps, you have escaped the trials—Rejoice! Perhaps, you have encountered a similar experience. You can pray *for* them and *with* them. Be careful not to be as Job's friends, passing judgment on actions and efforts. Be cautious not to judge or compare parenting skills. Remind them that their faithfulness and love reflect the love of the Father. Encourage them to keep loving their Prodigal Son and that, even in their pain and heartache, God's grace is sufficient (2 Cor. 12:9). Remind them that children make their own choices. Encourage them to keep watching the road!

If your homeschool journey is like ours, sometimes the cake will be a little lopsided, or the icing a bit too thin. Sometimes, it will burn and you will miss the fragrant aroma. Sometimes, a cake might even fall. Rest assured, though, that if the Lord has called your heart to homeschool, He will be sufficient to carry you through each experience, be it bitter or sweet. Be obedient to the calling. Be confident.

The ingredients are right. The process is right. The outcome will be right...in His time.

Homeschooling Pieces Our Hearts Together

——— *Theresa Osborne* ———

Theresa and Chris Osborne were both raised in the sunshine state of Florida and were married there in 1979. A year later their only child, Josh, was born. Chris began pastoring a fellowship in St. Petersburg, Florida. Since the Osbornes have always done everything together, including ministry, homeschooling was a natural choice for them. Chris and Theresa set up a homeschool support group at their fellowship. Between pastoring, running a coffeehouse, short-term missions, and traveling for drama and worship seminars, life was never dull for the Osborne family. This active lifestyle continues today as they travel nationwide for the homeschool movement as JCT Products (JCT stands for Josh, Chris, and Theresa). Chris has the privilege of speaking to homeschool families through seminars and workshops as Josh and Theresa minister encouragement to new homeschool moms and dads.

Chris pastored River of Life Christian Fellowship for fifteen years, was director/playwright for River of Life Drama Co., was Christian Action Council President for five years, and is a graphic designer. Theresa has an A.A. in preschool education, coordinated the River of Life education ministry, was a member of River of Life Drama Co., and has been a homeschool mom for twelve years.

The Osborne family has authored Internet Yellow Pages for Educational Web Sites, Unleashing the Power of Your Computer, Computer and Internet for Kids, *and co-authored* Click and Learn *software. Their business, originally JCT Shirts, has now expanded to become JCT Products, enabling them to equip the homeschool family with quality computer and Internet resources. They also design and make their own original homeschool T-shirts, caps, totes, and bumper stickers.*

"Is today some sort of holiday? Why aren't you in school?" the inquisitive cashier asked my young son.

My thoughts raced; *Oh no, not THAT question again.* "We homeschool our son," I meekly answered.

"Homeschool? Is that LEGAL?"

"Yes, ma'am, and, yes, it's perfectly legal," I replied, as we shuffled through the line.

When confronted about my activities with my son during "school hours," I always dreaded any kind of conflict in reference to homeschooling. I was not afraid of doing it, just tired of having to explain it. It seemed that when asked, we kind of whispered the word…"homeschool." That was pretty typical for us in the early 1980s, when homeschooling was not so well known. My, look how far homeschooling has come. Why, even "Dear Abby" has letters praising homeschooling! Homeschool conventions that once had limited curriculum selections now have so many choices it is mind-boggling. Not to mention the countless speakers and workshops that cover every topic under the sun. It is exciting to see how quickly homeschooling has spread.

Looking back at that first year, I'm surprised my son learned anything at all. I was so intent on "recreating school" and doing everything "by the book." I made sure he had his desk, marker board, and every book possibly required, while I was equipped with every teacher's manual known to man.

Thus outfitted, onward we would plod. I remember an instance when he was bawling over something he did not understand, and I became completely disconcerted. What was wrong with me? After all, I had a degree in preschool education. If this was only kindergarten, I could hardly wait for the "stressful" years to come! What I failed to remember was one of the main reasons for our homeschooling: unity. We wanted to be close to each other, working, learning, and having fun together as a family, but my "school marm" approach seemed to be frustrating all of us.

As time went on, I began to realize the need to lighten up. I did not trash all the books or become reckless. Instead, a realization began to unfold that Josh was God's gift to Chris and me. What was needed was a teaching style that he could grasp and understand. Instead of basing my lessons on a teacher's manual, I began to rely on what I knew of Josh and how he learned. This way, it would make things easier for him to comprehend and less stressful for me. Reflecting back, I can see where this was the turning point in our personal homeschooling experience. In fact, Josh wrote this in his sixth grade yearbook, "What I liked best about my teacher was that she knows how to explain my school so it is easy to understand." Sounds like we were on the right track.

As time moved on, we saw how we could make our homeschooling experience unique. As I continued to teach Josh the academics, my husband began to show him the basics of graphic design. Our physical education consisted of sports with our support group and scuba diving lessons with dad. With our homeschool support group, we visited nursing homes, went on numerous field trips, started a drama group, and even took a trip to England. Deciding that it would be good for Josh to learn about enterprise, we started a small, family T-shirt business. Little did we know that this homeschool project was about to take on a life of its own! Realizing that there were not many homeschooling T-shirts available, we decided to design one that would capture the essence of homeschooling. Chris and Josh's homeschool research project about famous homeschooled people turned into a shirt entitled, "I am homeschooled and so were..." It shows a collage of famous homeschooled people with a list of their names underneath. The shirt was a big hit with the support group, so we came up with a few more designs. We were on a roll! Our computer became an invaluable resource to us for creating all these designs. Josh found a niche for his creative side through graphic design. That one shirt has led us on a remarkable odyssey as we have traveled nationwide to homeschool conventions.

As parents, we began to realize that our homeschooling experience has not only been for Josh's benefit; Chris and I have also relearned some old things along with the new. It has given us the blessing of working together in business, as well as learning together academically.

While our secular society persists in trying to tear families apart, homeschooling is bringing them together. We are encouraged by what we have witnessed in the homeschool movement: the participation of fathers, the steadfast commitment of mothers, and the development of character in their children. Of all the decisions we have made, besides to the Lord and our marriage, home education was the best thing we have ever done.

We are now fast approaching the twelfth grade. Gratefully, we can see how our involvement with homeschooling has made it possible for us to always be together. The unity that was originally lacking now continues in a way we never thought possible. One of my favorite shirt designs says, "Homeschooling Pieces Our Hearts Together." How true that has become. Let that be the theme for your family—the rewards are countless.

For all of those just starting out, here are some tidbits that we wish we had known that first year. We hope they encourage you in your journey of homeschooling:

1. Pray! Start your school day together in prayer. It is very unifying and gets your focus where it belongs.
2. Be yourself! Do not try to copy someone else's way of teaching.
3. Be confident! Children can sense whether you are insecure, but God has made you unique. He is there for you.
4. Be flexible! Adjust your schooling to the lifestyle of your family. My

husband pastored a church, so our household did not always flow with a regular schedule. If we got in a little late the night before, we would just start a little later the next day.

5. Be creative and have fun! Every minute of every day holds so much learning.

Look for it, grasp it, and enjoy it.

The Family Culture

———— *Diana McAlister* ————

As a married woman and mother of four daughters, Diana McAlister gives praise to the One who over-ruled her intent to never marry or have children. She says, "If I had started sooner, I would have had a dozen of them." Twenty-one years of marriage have brought untold joy to this former political activist, and homeschooling has redirected her crusading heart.

Public classroom teaching experiences taught Diana how much she actually did not know about learning and teaching. Her first teaching assignment in a K–6 one-room school was a great instructor. Completing a Master's degree confirmed for Diana that public schools are less inter-ested in people actually learning important concepts than in teaching hoop-jumping and delayed gratification.

In 1981, Diana co-founded Family Academy, a unique blend of homeschool and private education. Her joy has been orienting other certified teachers to help homeschooling families succeed, establishing a reputation of educational excellence in her profession, and providing a microcosm within which families can strengthen their bonds and further the Kingdom of God. Family Academy is an approved, accredited private school offering a homeschool extension program in which curric-ula is tailored to individual homeschool students.

Co-author of Homeschooling the High Schooler, frequent convention speaker and teacher, and currently serving as Chairperson of Family Academy, Diana's intent is to support excellence and to continue in a significant role leading homeschoolers into government-free instruction for their children.

I wish I had known, early on, that families are not just politi-cians' "building blocks." We are not blocks at all. We are not square, we do not stack, and our substance seems to be more like a colloid suspension: ooey-gooey until struck, then solid as a brick. Life is not waiting to be lived outside the block-like exterior that politicians describe. The richness of culture found inside a family is central to life; family has its own culture that flourishes inside relational boundaries. The microcosm of a family nurtures resilience and personal identity in its members, which, in turn, provides a sum greater than the total of its parts.

Families have delights, problems, and an inherent desire to survive. We are designed by our Creator to be so. As families strive together for self-preservation, being together constantly in the cauldron of close family life keeps us simmering. The heat in a cauldron makes molecules bounce off each other faster, causing water to boil. A rolling boil turns liquid into gas. Life in a family is like that: after the rolling boil of homeschooling, life is a gas! Is there a better analogy for a busy homeschooling family?

What is amazing in homeschooling is that members of a family cannot remain anonymous, or detached, for long. "The world is too much with us," says the poet. Siblings are very present to each other. The laws of nature apply, and the siblings bounce off each other in increasingly creative ways. Family bonds, like the chemical bonds holding molecules together, strengthen our spaghetti-like children—fragile outside the cauldron of family, but made flexible by the time spent in the boiling pot.

My family comes with its own culture, complete with rituals and traditions that enrich, and with unspoken assumptions and expectations that cripple. I grew up in a family of storytellers, and, as time has passed, the stories have been embellished with aspects that still regale us at family gatherings. My dad, at 81, can still handily take in a good-natured guest with his UFO story or his grasshopper-for-fishing-bait story. We all have to hide our faces when he is spinning his web, for we have watched the light of realization dawn on many an unsuspecting face. Coming home or going home, my mother always hugs us at the door—delighted squeals, floured apron, and all. With each new arrival, all ongoing events temporarily cease until greetings are given all around.

However, my sister does not think embellished stories are honest. She thinks some of us tend to believe them, forgetting the tamer true version. But, she cannot tell us that very well. In point of fact, not one of us communicates deeper feelings easily. When one of us does take courage into our hands and admits how we really feel about something, someone else is likely to say, "No, you don't really think that," and proceed to tell us how we do feel. My mom does not like conflict, and we have all learned to "don't go there" when faced with the possibility of feeling vulnerable. We are afraid of being real with one another.

One of the most endearing aspects of Louis L'Amour's *Sackett* series is the commitment to the family that its members hold: if one is tackled, "you'll have to whip us all." And that is my family: when one calls, we all show, and we face whatever is coming, protecting one another's back. Whose heart does not rise to the knowledge that somebody, somehow, will come along to check the progress or fate of a family member?

The rituals, traditions, and unspoken views live on in my daughters, my husband, and myself. Mac and I have tried to teach our four girls how to communicate. We have inside jokes and signals. Mac can do his unique squeak over the top of background music at the grocery store, or in a crowded lobby, and we all know where to gather. My children can read my face and know when I'm cheating at cards, and I can sense when "things are not right." However, since Hebrews 13:16 (KJV) describes communication as a sacrifice, we each face the notion that, though clarity may prove difficult, communication must be attempted. My third-born has had to practice a specific format: "When you do ____, I feel ____. I want you to ____." Each of us has had to give her the wording more than once. Sometimes, we have to fill in the blanks with our own offenses against her in order for her to learn. She is 13 now, and becoming better at accomplishing the struggle to gather herself together to be understood. Why is it so hard for her? Could it be that she has inherited it?

Surely, some of our dysfunction comes from generational sin and some comes from the sins generated in the present. Sin and corruption are the elephants sitting in the living rooms of our nation, and only a few families want to talk about them. Blessedly, in homeschooling, elephants in living rooms don't leave much room for families to get around, so the great, gray beasts are more often discussed and herded out of the house through Jesus Christ's forgiveness. Love, shared by family members, heals. I have found expressions of self-sacrificial love displayed in homeschooling families more immediately and more wholly than anywhere else.

I am mindful of the mother versus alligator story in which the child's only visible scars are not on his sock-covered foot where the teeth laid hold, but on the back of his hand where the mom dug in with her fingernails to win the tug-of-war. Those love scars are the evidence of one mom who just would not give up her child—not to an alligator. For homeschooling mothers, alligators take many shapes. We are no more likely to give up our own children to schools, institutions, or the enemy of our souls, than Alligator Mom was.

The "love that won't quit" is found in every homeschooling mother who unceasingly searches for alternatives to Ritalin for her child's activity level. It is found in the father calling a child into account, and following through with appropriate discipline and training. This love is seen in the sibling who recognizes her hurtful behavior and decides to do something about it, not only by apologizing, but by declaring at the next family meeting that she is purposing to earn her sibling's respect.

Families, with all their warts, emerge from trouble when the going gets tough because of bonds that exist nowhere else. Families can be very dysfunctional and still survive. The idiosyncrasies found in homeschooling families are no fewer than in other families. In fact, they can be more clearly seen because, without the uniformity of that rock-tumbler-type polishing which conventional schooling exerts, the sharp edges are more exposed and, therefore, more visible. Some of the jagged points are loved off and worn down by the family, though the wearing off often leaves its own kind of love scars from intrafamily lacerations and abrasions. Sometimes, the ragged dysfunctions do not get fully eroded, but are accepted as part of the scenic beauty of that personality.

The beautiful part about family cultures is that families who are not afraid of love scars can face and rise above the reality of their dysfunction. They can face the "dissonant music," reassign the soprano voice if needed, add a different harmony, give a bucket to the singer-of-his-own-song who is yet seeking the tune, and still make a joyful noise. We need to apply the old line from medieval times, "every village has its idiot." The care this one received was given because, "after all, he belongs here. He's one of us." Family members know each other's secrets. Love scars become identifiers. They become integral to the recognition of other members and create an intimacy unknown to outsiders. If I had known this confidence early on, I would not have been so scared to be different. I would not have had a moment's embarrassment about our failures, and I would not have needed to protect an invisible image of a non-existent perfection.

I used to be offended at the post-modernists' declaration that all families are dysfunctional. Perhaps I was in denial, not able to face myself. But, today, I know that homeschooling brings dysfunction into focus, much like the magnifying lens did when we used it to start fires in the back yard. After we focus, we know where to direct the love. Then the flame of healing can burn. May we all allow love to do its healing work in our families.

Learning to Adapt

——— *Carol Munroe* ———

Mark and Carol Munroe have been married eighteen years this May (Wow!). Mark works with computers, testing software. They and their five children, ages 16, 14, 12, 10 and 4 years, live in Auckland, New Zealand. They have always homeschooled.

For more than twelve years the Munroes have run a home business, called Christian Education Services, which supplies homeschoolers and Christian schools with educational materials like KONOS, Modern Curriculum Press Phonics, Common Sense Press, Ruth Beechick, Raymond Moore, A Beka, Diana Waring, Greenleaf Press, Saxon, Backyard Scientist, etc. Carol has spoken at seminars on "How to Teach Reading" and "How to Choose Curriculum Materials." She has written a little booklet called "Negotiating the Curriculum Maze" to help New Zealand homeschoolers who are just starting out. The booklet was written to give general principles in choosing curricula and to encourage people to get started with confidence.

The Monroes' goal is to serve home educators by helping to make good materials available that homeschoolers might not get otherwise.

I wish I had understood that children and mothers are different, that what works for one may not work for another, and that God would use my children to train me as much as I would be training them.

I remember reading some homeschooling magazines when we first started, where they had interviews with such wonderful families. The children seemed to be so clever, so neatly dressed, and the mother was so organized, with her house so clean and tidy. She got up at 6:00 A.M. and persevered until the twilight

218

hours. They seemed so perfect, and we were so, well, ordinary. My house looked at times as though a train had gone through it, and I wondered how I would ever meet those standards. My children are not perfect. They sometimes fight each other. Sometimes, I wonder whether they will even visit each other when they grow up!

As a homeschooling mother, I have always struggled with organization, and my energy levels are sometimes low. If I manage to attend our support group meeting, by 9:00 P.M. my eyes are drooping and my mind is slowing, and I sneak out the door feeling guilty, but I know that if I do not get home to sleep, my children will suffer from my short temper. So, I have learned, with difficulty, not to compare myself with other people. I have learned that I cannot do everything: attend support groups, lobby politically for the homeschooling cause, run the business, have two teenage boarders, and continue to teach the children. I have found that, occasionally, I need to say, "No." I need time on my own in order to survive, and now I take that time with no feeling of guilt.

Here is one way that I slip in the kind of special time needed. On Wednesday night for the past three years, I have run our eldest to the local chess club where he can match his skill with others of like mind. I deliberately chose not to attend our church Bible study, which would have meant twenty minutes more on the road and the consciousness of having to leave at a certain time. Instead, I stayed at the club rooms, in the peace and quiet, and quilted or embroidered—I emphasize, in peace and quiet.

Sometimes, if I was bothered, I would pray while my needle was busy, but, alas, most of the time my mind would wander, or just be a blank. I needed that time. No interruptions, no demands, just quiet. Those hours were a respite, and I relished them.

If we had had only two children, I would have always thought that homeschooling was a breeze. As it is, I have also learned to adjust to different personalities in my children, and enjoy them. Our two eldest, David and Andrea, are strong visual learners—they love textbooks and reading, and seem to remember and retain what they learn. They are easy for me to teach. David is very mathematical and seems to be able to make a computer do anything. Andrea loves language, tackles the cryptic crossword with delight, and soaks up books like a sponge.

Then, along came Amy. Learning new concepts is a struggle, and retaining them even harder. It took three years for her to learn her multiplication tables, using many different kinds of methods. Sometimes in the afternoon, I find her working long after the others have finished because she is "behind," or so she thinks. Yet, she has a longing to serve and love God. Her room is tidy, her stuffed toys in a neat little semicircle at the bottom of her (made) bed. She sees opportunities to serve, and will take on a task unasked, just because it needs to be done. But, she struggles. Daddy saw her sitting at the top of the stairs the other day with tears in her eyes: "I have a few moments of happiness followed by hours of depression!!" I remember William Cowper and Martin Luther, who struggled with bouts of depression all their lives, and, yet, left such a wealth behind them for the Church to enjoy.

I thought I had matured greatly in patience and appreciation of differences in personalities, and then along came Jonathan. Jonathan is, well...PHYSI-CAL. If you are standing at the kitchen sink, and Jona is in the same room, he will probably be on your feet. Once, I went to give him a cuddle and kiss good night, and, as I was bending down, he sat up (suddenly, of course), and collected my jaw with his head. I approached him again with more caution and success and went out of the room with my eyes still smarting, a little voice calling out, "Sorry, Mum!," and thankfulness that at least my tongue had not been between my teeth.

The insurance company suffered, too. Previously a good investment risk, the Munroe family lost their no-claim bonus permanently with the advent of Jonathan. He managed to do one thousand dollars' worth of damage when he knocked Dad's razor off the shelf and cracked the basin. The whole unit, as well as the top, had to be replaced because they could not find a modern top to replace the old one. How could a child do such damage in such a short time? He has managed to shatter a sliding glass door, break light fittings and ornaments, and if he walks by a desk with papers on the edge, they will be knocked off. You never dare let him come close to you when you are holding a hot cup of tea.

As well as being physically intrusive, he is VERBAL. When you try to teach him something—he knows already! When he was 6, the family rechristened him "Iknowbut," because that was his response to everything I tried to teach him or ask him to do. I found it very wearing, and I had to learn, relearn, and am still learning how to deal with this kind of child. I remember once sitting at the kitchen table after insisting that Jonathan complete his maths, which he was capable of doing within five minutes if he set his mind to it. After an hour and a half, I thought, "Why would any woman, of clear and sound mind, choose to put herself through this?" Followed by another, equally disturbing thought, "Am I insane?"

I have threatened at times, I admit, to send Jonathan to school to "sort him out." At the bottom line, though, I could not do it. How could I expose such an eager, impressionable young mind to everything in the state school when he still lacks the discernment—and will—to choose between right and wrong? Another factor is that I have feelings for the unsuspecting teacher. How could I do that to another human being?

It took a while, but I finally realized that the "read, talk, and write it" approach, which had worked so well with the older children and which suited my personality, did not work with Amy and Jona. We needed greater variety and unit studies with more hands-on activities so that our homeschooling became more enjoyable, less painful, for everybody.

We need to remember that God made our families as units in themselves. We all do need each other. Our personalities conflict, rub against each other, and, in so doing we learn to appreciate, accept, and love. God's plan has been so much better, deeper, and richer than mine was when we started homeschooling. None of us knows where our children will be using their gifts, or in what capacity, but the training, principles, and skills they have learned and are learning at home, will stand by them for all their lives.

Do the children still fight at times? Yes, they do. Are they improving? I think so. Can we see growth in their spirituality and character, as well as in their intellectual development? Yes, though, on a bad day it seems like three steps forward, two steps back, but, yes, it is there! Would we change our homeschooling choice if we lived our life over again? Not a chance! Not even a skerrick of a chance. Mind you, I'm writing this during the holidays!

Homeschooling with Principles, Not Formulas

———— *Diana Waring* ————

Bill and Diana Waring have been joyously married since 1979 and are the grateful parents of three of the best children in the world. Isaac (17), Michael (15), and Melody (13) have been homeschooled since birth. The Warings reside in South Dakota summer and winter, and on the homeschool convention trail during spring and fall.

Diana studied music, drama, and French in college, with a B.A. in French. These interests have found a fulfilling outlet in homeschooling her children, as together they have performed a family storytelling concert, "Yankee Doodle Tells a Tale," from coast to coast. She loves ethnic cooking, meeting internationals, reading, and crocheting lace. Along with being a wife and mom, Diana has been a South Dakota Touring Artist, a featured speaker at dozens of homeschool conventions, a popular radio show guest, and a regular homeschool columnist at Best of the Christian Web.

The Warings have a family homeschool business, Diana Waring—History Alive!, which produces books, tapes, videos, and history curriculum for the homeschool market. Some of these titles include Beyond Survival: A Guide to Abundant Life Homeschooling; Ancient Civilizations and the Bible; Romans, Reformers, Revolutionaries; What in the World's Going On Here? A Judeo/Christian Primer of World History; The Hilarious Homeschool; The Beyond Survival Homeschooling Class on Video. *Their mission statement is "to encourage, equip, and educate families in an entertaining way."*

✎━━▶ I remember reading of a young man who inherited his grandfather's home and acreage, including an incredibly productive garden plot. To this young man, gardening in his grandfather's plot was simply a matter of planting seeds and watering occasionally. His plants thrived with almost no tending.

The Young Man's Formula: Soil + seeds + water + sunlight = a great harvest.

What a shock it was to him when, on moving to a different location, he planted a new garden and had completely different results! Even though he planted and watered in exactly the same way, this garden was anything but a thriving Eden. The plants were sickly, covered with bugs, and nearly qualified as a disaster area!

Hmmm. The Young Man's Formula did not work in this garden.

This young man then began to ask a lot of questions of experienced gardeners. He discovered, to his amazement, that he needed to carefully analyze the soil, and then go through a process of enrichment to bring it to a healthy state for growing vegetables. Over the course of many years, his grandfather had done this in the first garden, and the grandson had reaped the fruit of that labor.

The Experienced Man's Principle: Analyze your soil, build it up over time, plant seeds, add sunlight, water, and a careful, daily watch over the plants. This will help ensure a good harvest.

This young man's experience with gardens reminded me of what we have experienced in homeschooling. I started off with a "formula" for the perfect homeschool and ended up, instead, with a "principle" for healthy children.

When I first began homeschooling, I was convinced that all that was needed was the perfect curriculum, the right schedule, the proper field trips—and everything would turn out just right. It was important to me to find out what everyone else was using for curriculum, how they structured their days, and which field trips they recommended. That is why my greeting to newcomers at any homeschool meeting was always, "Hi! My name is Diana. What curriculum do you use?"

The Young Homeschool Mother's Formula: The right curriculum + the right schedule + the right field trips = The Perfect Homeschool!

Our first year of homeschooling, we purchased a phonics program that had been highly recommended. It was *very* expensive, and *very* unusable for us. Scratch year one. Later, we purchased a "Cadillac" curriculum (mind you, we could only afford the "Volkswagen" curriculum) because it, too, had been highly recommended. Unfortunately, within a month we recognized that using this curriculum was a disaster for both Isaac and me. Scratch year two. The following year we purchased a cheaper set of textbooks, hoping that better pictures and brighter colors might hold our interest. It too was a failure. Scratch year three.

As to schedules, I hadn't yet figured out how to get laundry off the table and dinner on the table, much less go on educational field trips!

Hmmm. The Young Homeschool Mother's Formula did not work in this homeschool.

The big question for me was: Am I a failure?—a wash-out as a homeschool mom? Or, were there principles that we did not yet understand that would help us learn how to successfully homeschool?

We began asking lots of questions, reading every book we could find on homeschooling, and attending homeschooling seminars and conventions. I discovered to my amazement that I had been using a *formula* of homeschooling without understanding the *principles* for real, live, uniquely individual children. I also learned that putting principles into action requires patience and time—just like the grandfather had given in the first garden.

Here are two of the principles and applications I learned over time:

1. Children are children. They will eventually become adults, but right now they are children.

When our children were young, one of the most puzzling comments my husband used to make was, "Diana, don't forget that they are just children!"

"Huh? Children? I *know* they are children. I just can't understand why they do such *childish* things!"

You see, in my inexperience, I thought that if I simply told my children all of the right things to do, the best ways to behave, and the proper attitudes to have, then everything would flow along as smooth as a chocolate silk pie. I had anticipated, in my parental naiveté, that these precious children should think like me, act like me, talk like me, and process things like me—or, at least, be more mature.

I just could not understand why my children would not *want* to make their beds first thing in the morning, so that they could enjoy that satisfied feeling all day… It was always a police sergeant routine to discover just who had and who had not brushed their teeth at night when I couldn't imagine going to bed with icky, unwashed teeth… And why they would leave a gloppy, sticky knife poking out of the peanut butter jar was beyond me.

Why was it that on Sunday morning my children couldn't just get up and into their church clothes? Why did they think there was time to sit and read a favorite book before getting ready? Why weren't they concerned about being on time like I was?

While I was busy with all of my adult "jobs," cooking, cleaning, laundry, talking on the phone, etc., why were my children wandering around looking at things like butterflies and tadpoles? Didn't they share my sense of responsibility in getting important things done?

In a word, no. No, they did not understand my haste, nor my pressure, nor my responsibilities. You see, they were children. First Corinthians 13:11 states: "When I was a child, I spoke as a child, I understood as a child, I thought as a child; but when I became a man, I put away childish things" (NKJV).

What does that mean? It means that we must understand that our children need to be carefully and patiently taught little by little, precept upon precept, line by line. As they grow older, they will handle more responsibility and reason in increasing maturity. But it is a matter of time and careful nurturing—just like the soil in the young man's second garden.

2. Children need quality time—quantities and quantities of it. The kind of time children need is the kind only parents can provide.

As homeschoolers, we had no trouble coming up with a great quantity of time together. And, in comparison to many non-homeschooling families, it was quality time. But what I did not realize for a long time was that my children needed me to share my very being with them—my life, my experiences, my hobbies, my passions, my desires. It was like creating a meal out of what I had in my own cupboard rather than running out to a restaurant for someone else's cooking.

What makes you unique? What background do you have? What do you love doing? What skills, hobbies, and passions do you have which you can share with your children? What's in your own cupboard? The one thing that no one else can give our children is us.

I remember Bill saying to me, "Diana, our kids need to be on the receiving end of your talents and abilities. You need to give them your best." For instance, instead of using my gourmet cooking skills to wow the neighbors, I needed to prepare some fancy dinners for my children, and teach them how to cook French food. Instead of pouring creative yearnings into church plays, I needed to nurture my children so they could produce their own historic puppet shows. Instead of singing just with adults, I needed to sing with my children and teach them how to harmonize. Instead of always being responsible and sober-minded with my children, I needed to laugh with them daily.

Over time, Michael became my chef d'extraordinaire, cooking meals we could hardly pronounce. Isaac discovered that he dearly loves the "roar of the grease paint and the smell of the crowd." Melody developed such a love for music that she studies voice, piano, and violin, practicing up to three hours per day. And our family thinks it is so much fun to entertain audiences and make them laugh that we go touring together across the country performing storytelling concerts.

As we began giving ourselves to our children—knowing and being known—and as we allowed our children to mature at their own pace, a marvelous thing occurred: homeschool became a place of wonder, of discovery, and of excitement.

A perfect homeschool? No.

A good place to learn and grow? Yes.

An unchanging formula? Never.

Principles used in growing healthy, productive children? Absolutely!

The Experienced Homeschool Mother's Principle: Analyze your children and their needs, build them up over time, plant seeds of curiosity, add your heart, good books, and time, carefully watching over their lives. This will help ensure a good homeschool.

Index of Contributors

Karen Andreola
Charlotte Mason Research & Supply Company
P.O. Box 1142
Rockland, ME 04841
www.charlottemason.com

To further the ideals and practical teaching methods of Charlotte Mason to a new generation of parents through quality books, lectures, and a supply catalog.

Valerie Bendt
Bendt Family Ministries
333 Rio Vista Court
Tampa, FL 33604
(813) 238-3721
Valbendt@aol.com
Valerie's books can be viewed at her publisher's web site (Common Sense Press) at: www.cspress.com

Bendt Family Ministries strives to encourage parents with materials and seminars that nurture lifelong learning.

Michael and Susan Card
Michael Card Music
P.O. Box 586
Franklin, TN 37065
Phone: (615) 790-7675
Fax: (615) 791-0594
cardmusci@aol.com
michaelcard.com

To provide biblical teachings through music and books; to encourage fellow believers to study the Bible on their own. A bi-annual newsletter is available.

Clay and Sally Clarkson
Whole Heart Ministries
P.O. Box 67
Walnut Springs, TX 76690
Phone: (254) 797-2142
Fax: (254) 797-2148
emailbox@wholeheart.org.
www.wholeheart.org.

"Building hearts at home for him." Encouraging, equipping, and enabling Christian parents through quality books and resources for home discipleship, home education, and family enrichment.

Fred and Sarah Cooper
Sing 'n Learn
2626 Club Meadow
Garland, TX 75043-1102
Phone: (972) 278-1973
Fax: (972) 840-3187
fcooper@flash.net
www.singnlearn.com

Sing 'n Learn is a curriculum business specializing in programs that utilize the power and enjoyment of music as a tool in teaching basic subjects.

Ranell Curl
Custom Curriculum Company
76504 Poplar Street
Oakridge, Oregon 97463-9452
(541) 782-2571
ccco@efn.org

We publish three resource guides for historical unit studies, market thousands of books, and offer unit study consultations to individual families.

Jill Darling
Faith Christian Fellowship
27 Beach Rd.
Apalachin, NY 13732
(607) 625-2853

The C.H.U.R.C.H. vision: striving to build a glorious church without spot or wrinkle (Eph. 5:27): **C**hange, **H**onor, **U**nity, **R**econciliation, **C**ompassion, and **H**oliness

Lynnette Delacruz
#30 Cattle Pound Road
Washington, Maine 04574
(207) 845-2777
romdelyn@webtv.net
Creative Memories Consultant

Reestablishing the tradition of photo-historian storyteller and the importance of photo preservation and journaling for future generations through hands-on workshops, photosafe products, and training consultants.

Bob and Tina Farewell
Lifetime Books and Gifts
3900 Chalet Suzanne Lane
Lake Wales, FL 33853-7763
Phone: (941) 676-6311
Orders: (800) 377-0390
Fax: (941) 676-2732
lifetime@gate.net
www.lifetimeonline.com

Lifetime Books and Gifts, a home educating family's business, with *The Always Incomplete Resource Guide*, emphasizes "living books" to create or enhance your Learning Lifestyle.

Bonnie Ferguson
Ferg N' Us Services
P.O. Box 578
Richlandtown, PA 18955
Phone: (610) 282-0401
Fax: (610) 282-0402

Ferg N' Us Services provides selected homeschool resource materials for their customers. They publish *The Homeschooler's Journal* and *The Homeschooler's High School Journal*.

Vicky Goodchild
HIS Publishing Company
1732 NE 3rd Avenue
Fort Lauderdale, FL 33305
Phone: (954) 764-4567
Fax: (954) 768-9313
e-mail address: (hopefully soon)

A home-based publishing company meeting the needs of the homeschool community through the development of resources, and through counseling and speaking at homeschool conventions.

Margie Gray
Cadron Creek Christian Curriculum
4329 Pinos Altos Rd.
Silver City, NM 88061
Phone: (505) 534-1496
Fax: (505) 534-1499
marigold@wnmc.net
Cadron Creek.com

Cadron Creek Christian Curriculum provides academic material to assist parents in training their children in godliness while challenging students scholastically through literature unit studies.

Ed and Kathy Green
Homeschoolers of Maine (HOME) / The Heart of HOME Bookstore
337 Hatchet Mountain Road
Hope, Maine 04847
Phone: (207) 763-4251
Fax: (207) 763-4352
homeschl@midcoast.com
http://members.aol.com/spikefoss/index.html

HOME is a Christian ministry dedicated to promoting home education in the state of Maine.

Sharon R. Grimes
Heir-Raising Tales
RR 3 Box 206
Moravia, NY 13118

Sharon is available to speak at home-school conventions; she has many practical sessions that have resulted from years of experience.

Jody Gutierrez
Sun E Slash Farm & Ranchito de Chihuahuito
Route 1 Box 32A
Lemitar, NM 87823
(505) 835-2299

We grow alfalfa hay and red chili peppers, and raise pedigree Chihuahuas.

Miriam Heppner
Heppner & Heppner Construction
P.O. Box 7
Warroad, MN 56763-0007
Phone: (218) 386-1994
        (800) 257-1994
Fax: (218) 386-1994
family@means.net
Watch for upcoming web site

Joining with Christ's work of building homes and families. Specializing in non-consumable, age and subject integrated materials. Providing the tools needed for a no-nonsense education.

Wade and Jessica Hulcy
KONOS, Inc.
P.O. Box 250
Anna, TX 75409
Phone: (972) 924-2712
Fax: (972) 924-2733
wade@konos.com
Jessica@konos.com
www.konos.com

KONOS is a family owned corporation which writes, publishes, and sells unit-based, hands-on homeschool curricula for kindergarten through high school.

Sharon Jeffus
Visual Manna
P.O. Box 553
Salem, MO 65560
Phone: (573) 729-2100

Fax: (573) 729-2100
arthis@rollanet.org
www.visualmanna.nu

Visual Manna publishes art curriculum, provides high quality supplies, presents support group workshops, hosts a fine arts camp at Branson, Missouri, and encourages young Christian artists.

Steve and Jane Lambert
Five in a Row Publishing
14901 Pineview Dr.
Grandview, MO 64030-4509
Phone: (816) 331-5769
Fax: (816) 322-8150
Lamberts@sprynet.com
www.fiveinarow.com

Five in a Row Publishing creates, publishes, and distributes literature-based unit studies intended to help children ages 2–12 discover the joy of learning.

Camilla Leedahl
Hearthside Productions
15470 County Road 2
Leonard, ND 58052
(701) 645-2578
Hrthside@aol.com

Hearthside Productions publishes *The Home School Support Group* and produces audio tapes from Camilla's workshops and seminars on topics of interest to Christian home educators.

Diana McAlister
Family Academy
23420 Jordan Road
Arlington, WA 98223
Phone: (360) 435-9423
Fax: (360) 435-7632
dianamca@juno.com

Family Academy, the homeschool extension of an approved, accredited private school, achieves enriched schooling by uniting teachers and families pursuing academics and biblical home-centered learning.

Stacy Mhyre
T.E.A.C.H. (Tutoring & Educational Assessments for Children at Home)
3018 Aldergrove Rd.
Ferndale, WA 98248
Phone: (360) 384-4721
Fax: (360) 384-4721 (call ahead first)
smhyre@aol.com and smhyre@juno.com

T.E.A.C.H. is a service for homeschoolers, providing private tutoring services and non-test educational assessments in lieu of standardized testing.

Beverly Miller
Grace Books
1420 Auburn Way South
Auburn, WA 98002
Phone: (253) 833-7959
Fax: (253) 833-9231
bmiller@gracebooks.com

Grace Books is a Christian bookstore committed to providing outstanding service. All profits are given to local ministries to use wisely as God's money.

Mark and Carol Munroe
Christian Education Services
55 Richards Avenue
Forrest Hill, Auckland 10 New Zealand
cesbooks@intouch.co.nz

CES helps homeschoolers have a successful and enjoyable experience by providing quality curriculum materials as well as practical information on methods of homeschooling.

Chris and Theresa Osborne
JCT Products (formerly JCT Shirts)
2813- 59th Avenue N
St. Petersburg, FL 33714
Phone: (813) 528-0327
Fax: (813) 528-1695
jct@gte.net
www http//jct.homes-cool.com

JCT, family owned and operated, has been serving the homeschool community since 1993 with quality T-shirts, caps, totes, and computer and Internet resources.

David and Shirley Quine
The Cornerstone Curriculum Project
2006 Flat Creek Place
Richardson, Texas 75080
Phone: (972) 235-5149
Fax: (972) 235-0236
dquine@cornerstonecurriculum.com
www.cornerstonecurriculum.com

The Cornerstone Curriculum Project designs and develops educational materials to equip parents to build their children's lives upon the biblical world view.

John Rush
New Song Missions
Box 2578
Murphys, CA 95247
(800) 748-SONG
NewSongINF@aol.com
http://members.aol.com/NewSongINF

New Song serves the church with special inspirational speaking on contemporary issues, missions, and Christian world view, and through mission, church, and school planting.

The Man with the Bird on His Head, the story of John's encounter with the Pacific cargo cult, can be ordered from YWAM Publishing at (800) 922-2143.

Robin Scarlata
Heart of Wisdom Publishing
P.O. Box 1198
Springfield, TN 37172
Phone or fax: (615) 382-5500
(800) BOOKLOG (orders only)
RRScarlata@AOL.com
www.heartofwisdom.com

H.O.W. Publishing publishes several titles by Robin Scarlata. Their web site features 100-plus pages of excerpts, articles, and samples focusing on homeschooling and Judaic/Christian studies.

Frank and Debbie Schaner
Home Training Tools
2827 Buffalo Horn Drive
Laurel, MT 59044

Phone: (800) 860-6272
Fax: (888) 860-2344
homett@mcn.net
www.HomeTrainingTools.com

Home Training Tools helps families, through science, develop an understanding and a love for God's creation. They provide a great variety of affordable, educational science products.

Joy Schroeder
408 S. 6th
Bozeman, MT 59715
ucfdick@aol.com

University Christian Fellowship at Montana State University, Bozeman is a campus ministry affiliated with the Assemblies of God Chi Alpha Campus Ministries. Information: ucfdick@aol.com

Gail Schultz
Hillside Academy
1804 Melody Lane
Burnsville, MN 55337
(612) 895-0220

Lessons from History: 1400's–1700's; Lessons from History: 1800's; and *Lessons from History: 1900's.* Helping you organize your literature-based history studies.

Carol Severson
JMD Computer Tech
27855 2030N Avenue
Malden, IL 61337
(815) 643-2157
jmdcomp@theramp.net

JMD sells quality educational software and custom built computers. You can contact JMD for information on their computer ministry or for a computer/software catalog.

Holly Sheen
The Education Association of Christian Homeschoolers (TEACH)
25 Field Stone Run
Farmington, CT 06032
Phone: (860) 677-4538

Fax: (860) 677-4677
raysheen@tiac.net
www.tiac.net/users/raysheen/teach

Statewide Christian homeschooling organization.

Carol A. Singleton
Maple Ridge Books
RR #6, Markdale, Ontario, Canada
N0C1H0
(519) 986-2686

Maple Ridge Books is a mail-order supplier of excellent books and educational materials for children and adults in Canada.

Madelaine L. Smith
700 Narnia Lane NW
Olympia, WA 98502-2592
(360) 866-8878
GSmith1054@aol.com

Successfully homeschooling children from kindergarten through high school.

Janice Southerland
Children's Inductive Bible Studies
P.O. Box 720567
Oklahoma City, OK 73172-0567
(405) 728-0290
cibsokc@flash.net or cibsokc@juno.com
www.flash.net/~cibsokc

Equipping students to dig out and know the truth of God's Word firsthand through Knowledge, Understanding, and Wisdom—the basic inductive Bible study tools.

Debbie Strayer
Family Educational Services, Inc.
703 Willow Brook Court
Lutz, Florida 33549
Phone: (813) 949-8171
Fax: (813) 948-0025
74152,366@compuserve.com

Family Educational Services seeks to encourage homeschoolers in their God-given calling, knowing that it is by His grace that all things are accomplished.

Candy Summers
There's No Place Like Home, Inc.
P.O. Box 613
Fredericktown, MO 63645
(314) 521-8487
jhengst@freewwweb.com

Information on Candy's publications
and ministry is available by writing to
the above mailing address.

Monte and Karey Swan
*Singing Springs Prod./Hearth & Home
Publ./KONOS Representatives*
7072 Singing Springs
Evergreen, Colorado 80439
Phone: (303) 670-0673
Fax: (303) 674-3431
monte@magmachem.com OR
karey@hearthnhome.com
www.hearthnhome.com

As keynote speakers, workshop presen-
ters, counselors, authors, and singers,
the Swans focus their message on the
heart of the child and the vision of fam-
ily-oriented homeschooling.

Katherine von Duyke
KONOS Helps!
429 Lewisville Rd. / P.O. Box 274
New London, PA 19360-0274
(610) 255-0199
vonduyke@Chesco.com
www.Chesco.com/~vonduyke/
KonosHelps.htm

To help parents teach their children in
a Hebrew model, keeping learning relational, wisdom-based, and a delight to
parent and child.

Debbie Ward
Homeschooling Today *magazine*
Editorial Office
P.O. Box 9596
Birmingham, AL 35220
Phone: (205) 520-1145
Fax: (205) 520-1143
76132.1411@compuserve.com
www.homeschooltoday.com

Homeschooling Today magazine, published bi-monthly, offers helps and curriculum for parents of children from
preschool to high school. Subscriptions:
P.O. Box 1608, Ft. Collins, CO 80522

Diana Waring
Diana Waring—History Alive!
122 W. Grant
Spearfish, SD 57783
Phone or Fax: (605) 642-7583
diana@dianawaring.com
www.dianawaring.com

Homeschooling, history, and humor for
homeschooling families through books,
tapes, videos, and history curriculum.
Our focus is on building relationships in
the family while homeschooling.

Barbara West
HEART for Germany
Unit 30400 Box 1584 APO AE 09128
Perm. add.: c/o Shirley Irvin, 1610 S.
Kearney St., Denver, CO 80224-2133
Phone: 011-49-711-810-6999
Batman270@iname.com

H.E.A.R.T. (Home Educators Are Real
Teachers) for Germany links European
homeschoolers together.

Cindy Wiggers
Geography Matters
P.O. Box 15855
Evansville, IN 47716
Phone: (800) 426-4650
Fax: (812) 473-4102.
geomatters@earthlink.net
www.geomatters.com

Serving homeschoolers through teaching innovative workshops and publishing affordable geography supplies,
including laminated and paper mark-it
maps, outlines, timelines and custom
maps for curricula.